FASHION • DIY • KNITTING • S

GARDENING • PAINTING • HOLIDAYS

EMBROIDERY • COOKERY • HEALTH

The PEBBLE MILL AT ONE *Book*

• BEAUTY • TRAVEL • PETS • SUPERTIPS •

FOREWORD

Each week, more than eleven million people take at least one lunchbreak in the company of the 'Pebble Mill at One' team. Over thirteen years it's become something of a national habit to sit back and enjoy the easy-going mixture of topicality, conversation and music brought 'live' from the famous foyer at the BBC's Birmingham studios.

The show gets an enormous response from viewers – the biggest of any regular television programme – and the thousands of letters which arrive in the Pebble Mill office each week stress that the items which encourage people to take up hobbies, activities or pursuits are by far the most popular.

Practical home advice from cookery to gardening, embroidery to health and fitness: viewers seem to want more and more.

Last season, more than 200,000 people wrote in asking for the fact sheets which accompanied the various projects of the moment. These were hastily produced and became a nightmare for the girls in the Pebble Mill duplicating room. But they provided an invaluable written back-up to the many items which attempted to convey detail and expertise in a few minutes of 'live' television time.

So for this 1985-6 season, the team has produced this companion to the series. It is a compilation of original and exciting chapters by our Pebble Mill 'experts' packed with advice, recipes, patterns and tips.

We hope this guide will enhance your enjoyment of your 'Pebble Mill at One' lunchtimes, and finally overcome that frustration when not able to find a pen or pencil at the crucial moment when a tantalising recipe is being read out.

CONTENTS

SEEING STARS

I t may mean a two hour run up the M1 from the Metropolis, but the stars invariably make a point of appearing on 'Pebble Mill at One' while on a visit to Britain. The reason? They like its comfortable relaxed style and the freshness of appearing on 'live' television after years in the arid world of pre-recording. Here presenter Paul Coia recollects some recent encounters with lunchtime guests.

Pebble Mill viewers sat down for their usual relaxing 45 minutes and saw Sebastian Coe running like a clockwork soldier with his legs tied together. "Poor soul," they thought, "The training is obviously getting to him." As Coe ran to be interviewed by me in the Pebble Mill garden, it became apparent something was wrong – because Coe was Coia and Coia was Coe. Since people always say we look alike we had decided to change the roles for a few minutes.

As far as I can see Sebastian Coe and I only look alike from the ankles down, so I was surprised at how many people were fooled.

That's one gratifying aspect of our programme. When stars arrive, no matter how big they may be, they're always willing to join in the fun. Who for instance, will forget the late Matt Monro and the lovely Lorraine Chase singing 'Jingle Bells' with us in OCTOBER? Who apart from music lovers that is?

Lorraine is as natural as she appears on T.V. I remember my enquiry as to where she was going before our interview being answered with "Sorry love, I've got to go to the tinkle house."

Yes, even the stars get nervous. I remember our opening music had started when we were told our first guest, Su Pollard, was still in the shower. She'd forgotten the time, and caused all sorts of panic as we 'busked' the show till she was dressed.

Comedians like Frankie Howerd and Rowan Atkinson are among the most meticulous of our guests. I've acted as straight men to them both at the Mill, and was surprised at how carefully they check everything, then double check. Obviously comedy is no laughing matter!

Yet Cannon and Ball have the perfect answer to cocky interviewers. After a recent show when, mysteriously, our microphones started breaking down, I was panicking. Should I carry out the rest of the interview in semaphore? Would Tommy and Bobby forgive us?

I need have had no fears. Casually, Bobby Ball directed the cameras towards my socks, and the audience fell about. I'd forgotten to change them before the show. While luminous blue socks look quite fashionable with jeans during rehearsals, they do not match a dark grey suit! Thanks Bobby! I'm still recovering from the embarrassment.

Mind you, some star guests have appreciated my wardrobe. One of my sweatshirts now resides in Connie Francis' closet as she made me promise to send it to her after I'd finished with it. Eileen Atkins wanted to know where she could buy one of my jumpers, and Engelbert Humperdink asked if he could pinch my leather jacket. I think I'm in the wrong business.

Clothing can cause embarrassment to star guests on T.V. too. Ask singer Gene Pitney. With seconds to go before our live chat, he spilled a glass of water over his trousers, "I must go and change," he said "You can't, there's no time," I replied. As we started the interview Gene looked

down and everyone laughed. It seemed to viewers that he'd had a very different accident, so an explanation was in order.

Gene, though, remains unspoiled and natural. A couple of his countrymen have caused all sorts of problems because they insist on being seen "from my good side only." Yet they all pile into the Mill. Everyone from Jack Jones to Tony Bennett, Andy Williams and Vic Damone. All with their own fiercely loyal fan clubs who take over for the day.

SEEING STARS

At the other end of the musical spectrum we've welcomed the Thompson Twins and Bob Geldof. I won't forget Gary Glitter dressing up a Pebble Mill studio audience in pink and red punk rock wigs and asking them to wave his fan club scarves.

And when Bucks Fizz arrived for the show, they played a prank on their poor record company executive. He'd been working hard to get their records played on radio and T.V. and they fully appreciated what he'd done. They told him, though, they were very unhappy and would make a formal complaint. He asked me what I thought, but I was in on it too, so I told him they were correct. He then anxiously phoned their manager who bawled him out. It was sweet revenge for us all because he had caught us all out with pranks in the past. Eventually, the group told him they were only kidding and strangely, he's never played a practical joke on any of us since.

Meeting the stars on Pebble Mill is always an education. Did you know for instance that Pat Phoenix's secret passion is science fiction? Or that the thing Engelbert Humperdinck most misses about Britain is a good old-fashioned pint of beer? Or that Toyah was asked to pose for a 'girlie' magazine and sent back a picture with her rude answer painted on her bust?

Although you know that Bob Hope loves golf, did you know that he nearly cost us a fortune?

Viewers will remember us looking at antique golf clubs and balls on the show and demonstrating them on a synthetic golf 'green'. Bob came over and asked to try a club. Instead of picking up a modern ball, he used a very brittle original, which was over 100 years old. He not only hit it, the ball actually went into the hole and dropped three feet onto our stone floor. My heart jumped so much it was returned by a passing American Shuttle.

Thankfully the ball remained intact and we didn't tell Bob what he'd done. But you can see how things can so easily go wrong.

Mind you, they will always go wrong if the guest of the day is being difficult. Unfortunately Raquel Welch had decided she didn't like British men a lot. "All you men over here are just sexist," she told me. "You all have the chance to do good interviews and you throw it away with the same old questions." I wasn't even doing the interview, but had wandered over to say hello. Eventually Ms Welch decided to leave early.

So the next time you see your favourite star on our programme, remember they're just like us. They all have their foibles, their likes and dislikes. And, fortunately, amongst their likes they list a visit to 'Pebble Mill at One.'

The Pebble Mill Garden

Friday is gardening day and Peter Seabrook is there to give expert advice from the Pebble Mill garden.

This year sees an exciting new development in 'off-the-peg' gardening which Peter is devising in conjunction with the National Garden Festival at Stoke-on-Trent. And the idea to which Pebble Mill viewers are being introduced is nothing short of a revolution in garden planning.

But first Peter takes us to the 'Dig This' garden: that tiny patch at the back of Pebble Mill whose fame, it seems, has spread out of all proportion to its size.

"You're taller than I thought" is the most common introduction I receive from Pebble Mill viewers – and they seem to be everywhere. Sign in at an hotel in Boston, USA or Boston, Lincolnshire – walk the street in Berlin or Bruges, study roses in southern Germany and France, shop in Singapore or Toronto;

wherever we go you can be sure there will be a regular 'Pebble Mill at One' fan close at hand.

That height thing is no surprise, really: when the camera lense is circular and the TV screen rectangular, it must squash us all down a bit and plump us out at the sides! Seeing things on the two dimensional, flat screen is deceiving and the first comment from members of our audience visiting the 'Dig This' garden is "how much smaller it is than it looks on the screen".

If you really want to get some idea of the scale, then measure out a 10' x 12' rectangle on your lawn and you can see the exact size of the vegetable plot that was the start of it all more than ten years ago. To help you get your bearings, we have illustrated the garden as it was in the summer of 1985. Close to the veg plot is a similar sized fruit plot and two beds of roses – pink 'Silver Jubilee' produce marvellous blooms year after year, and the dwarf flame-red 'Sunblaze' flowers right through the summer, even to Christmas in some seasons. Then there is the lawn, with surrounding border flowers, evergreen camellias and dwarf conifers under the silver birch, stretching to the Pebble Mill office.

Unlike most gardening programmes, we start in autumn when most growing seasons are coming to an end and work through to early summer, stopping when the new season is just under way. This makes much more sense that might at first be thought, with good gardens coming from careful autumn, winter and spring preparations.

The 1985/86 season has quite as many garden surprises as previous years. One major interest is the month by month preparation at the Stoke-on-Trent National Garden Festival up to the opening on 1st May, 1986 and the Opening Ceremony by Her Majesty the Queen. There's some fun when the TV gardening presenters bring their carefully-tended white plastic urns to Birmingham for judging. We are out and about with our cameras both at home and abroad, bringing you news of gardening and growing, ordinary and extraordinary.

As well as reporting on events like giant sunflowers growing on North Sea oil rigs, care is always taken to include the week by week advice given to gardeners, both experienced and beginners. Special attention is being focused this year on: soil improvement from composting; cropping greenhouses and keeping them filled through the winter even if they are unheated; weed control the easy way, with weedkillers and by mulching; pruning fruits and shrubs; and, of course, answering the steady stream of queries from what we have come to call the 'Pebble Mill family.'

1. 'Pebble Mill At One' office.
2. Rose bed.
3. 10' x 12' vegetable plot.
4. Herb garden.
5. Raised conifer bed.
6. Greenhouse.

THE RAISED CONIFER BED

Evergreen conifers provide attractive foliage all year round and, by carefully selecting the slower growing kinds, they can form a good garden feature both in borders and raised beds. We have converted the raised pool, which had sprung a leak and was proving costly to replace, into an evergreen feature.

The base was dug up first to give free drainage and the area within the low walls filled with good soil. For the immediate future, the selected conifers were left in their pots and the pots plunged in the soil. This means we can rearrange them as they grow and even turn the foliage varieties by half a circle every now and then, so that all sides face the sun and give an even, good colour all the way round each specimen.

Some will eventually outgrow the available space and after one or two repottings and several years' valuable service, will have to be planted in another bed somewhere else in the garden.

While we used quite large specimens in 3.5 to 7.5 litre pots to give instant effect, the price could be much reduced by starting off with younger plants. They will take a couple or three years to fill out and completely cover the ground but the spaces between can be temporarily filled with heathers and/or alpine plants.

We plan to introduce small groups of flowering plants among the conifers to add extra colour and seasonal interest. For example, pots of dwarf hardy cyclamen and colchicums in the autumn, species of crocus in late winter, dwarf narcissus in spring and lilies in summer.

The list and plan, designed by Adrian Bloom, shows what we began with, and this provides a starting point. You can adapt this by replacing some with your own favourite plants, but try to contrast foliage colours and keep the more upright types towards the centre of an island bed and towards the centre back of borders viewed from one side.

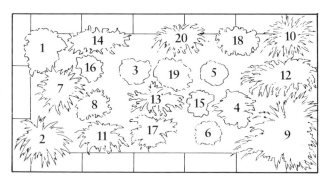

Our bed size 6′ x 12′
1. Abies lasiocarpa 'Compacta'
2. Cedrus deodora 'Golden Horizon'
3. Taxus baccata 'Standishii'
4. Chamaecyparis lawsoniana 'Pigmaea Argentea'
5. Juniperus communis 'Compressa'
6. Chamaecyparis lawsoniana 'Green globe'
7. Chamaecyparis obtusa 'Nana Gracilis'
8. Chamaecyparis pisifera 'Gold Spangle'
9. Juniperus communis 'Green Carpet'
10. Juniperus horizontalis 'Blue Chip' (Blue Moon)
11. Juniperus squamata 'Blue Star'
12. Juniperus x media 'Gold Sovereign'
13. Picea abies 'Will's Zwerg'
14. Picea abies 'Little Gem'
15. Picea pungens 'Globosa'
16. Pinus sylvestris 'Fastigiata'
17. Pinus mugo 'Ophir'
18. Thuja occidentalis 'Danica'
19. Thuja orientalis 'Aurea Nana'
20. Tsuga canadensis 'Jeddeloh'

Most garden centres offer a range of these plants and an extensive list of varieties is available by mail order from Bressingham Gardens, Bressingham, Diss, Norfolk IP22 2AB.

Be sure to keep all evergreens in pots well watered; even in rainy weather the conifer foliage shelters the compost and keeps it dry. Where the peaty compost these plants are grown in does get dry, they need to be stood in a pail of water for half an hour or so to thoroughly re-wet them.

GREENHOUSES

It's lovely to get out of the wind, the wet, and the cold into a greenhouse and for this reason alone they are a boon to gardeners. Don't think, however, they are the answer to every gardening problem. Once plants are brought indoors they become dependent on you for water, fresh air, and temperature control.

Many of us have to go to work during the day and so are not available to open windows at midday when the sun is at its hottest. There are weekends and holidays when the greenhouse and all the plants it contains have to be left unattended. These are the practical problems we are tackling in the two Pebble Mill greenhouses from September round to May.

The first approach must be one of gaining experience, learning just what liberties can be taken. Think of the greenhouse first as a giant cloche giving protection to extend the seasons. Tender young vegetables sown in late summer mature under cover right into the winter. Roses and chrysanthemums flower indoors when the frost, gales and rain have battered all outdoor blooms.

Then spring can be brought forward by a month or two with some overhead protection for hardy plants. Once this experience is gained, the more sophisticated year-round growing of tender plants can be undertaken, introducing heat to the greenhouse in winter.

Ventilation on hot sunny days is essential for virtually all plants except some cacti. For this reason, an automatic vent opener is essential for all glasshouses. The latest designs are very efficient and give long, reliable service. On a cheaper polythene-clad greenhouse, from April to September, it is wise to remove the top panel from the door and replace with open mesh for ventilation.

Growing crops in the border soil again increases the margin for error and, well watered, it will retain sufficient moisture for several days for most crops. Plants in containers will survive up to a week between water during cool weather when growth rates are slow. But as the temperatures increase with longer days and stronger sunshine, automatic watering systems will need to be introduced.

Where the plants are grown in the border soil, disease can build up if the same kinds are grown year after year, Unfortunately, a lot of the popular summer fruiting crops – tomatoes, aubergines, peppers, cucumbers, melons, courgettes–can succumb to the same root-borne disease, so at first signs of poor growth, it is advisable to switch to growbags.

The growbag has revolutionised our approach to

Late November and spray chrysanthemums in flower in pots and growbags in the Pebble Mill polythene house.

Cauliflower 'Purple Cape' sown in early summer, grown in growbags outside all summer and brought under cover early winter provides useful tasty vegetables in February.

greenhouse growing, not only for tomatoes and the like, but also to get the best production from a greenhouse. For example, in summer and early autumn when the greenhouse is full of tomatoes and cucumber, growbags can be used outside for some chrysanthemums, self-blanching celery, anemones, kohl rabi and even 'Purple Cape' cauliflower. Then, when the tomatoes are finished, the other crops in growbags can be lifted in. When those crops are finished, another crop, like strawberries in growbags, can be lifted in in February, for May cropping before the next lot of summer tomatoes.

Chrysanthemums have proved very succesful when the October/November flowering varieties are rooted from cuttings in June/July, grown in pots or growbags and lifted under cover in September. Another very successful plant has been the 'Column Stock'. It is rather like 10-week stocks, but produces one single tall stem for cutting. Sown in greenhouses in the warm, in February, transplanted into smaller pots – selecting the yellow-leaved doubles and rejecting the dark green single-flowering plants – and then planted into the greenhouse soil in late March/early April, they produce super-fragrant blooms in May/June.

11

COMPOSTING

Composting plant debris is one of the best ways the ordinary garden owner can help with the conservation and improvement of the environment in which we live. It is, of course, the natural way to improve all soils, compost providing lots of plant food and a better structured soil which is easier to cultivate as well as helping the roots to grow faster.

Not only do we improve our own gardens and provide the right conditions to encourage earthworms and other soil-improving creatures, but also we avoid adding to the vast quantities of refuse dumped around our towns. All plant remains, alive or dead, will eventually decay and provide sustenance for other living things in the process. Most hardy woody pieces, however, take a long time to rot down and are therefore best left out.

Lawn mowings, falling leaves in autumn and the waste vegetable trimmings from the kitchen are the prime sources of compost material. If the plant remnants are a bit green they will rot down quicker if they are crushed or chopped up before being mixed into the heap.

You only need leave a barrow load of lawn mowings for a few hours, with all the blades of grass chopped and bruised and it will soon get to a high temperature in the centre. Where the material is soft and sappy, like lawn mowings, it will settle down very quickly and become so soggy that all the air is excluded. This provides a very unpleasant form of decomposition – so mix the lawn mowings with some coarser leaves and stems from other plants to keep the compost open and allow the air to flow right through it. Putting some soil in among the plant debris also helps the process.

Compost will rot faster in the summer when temperatures are high. The process can be speeded up from late autumn to early spring by lining a compost container with a heat-conserving insulator like polystyrene sheets. While the compost needs moisture to rot down, it is as well to cover the heap top in winter to retain heat and prevent it from getting excessively wet.

By far the easiest way to compost is with two heaps or bins discreetly hidden behind evergreens or sheds. Use one to accumulate all the plant debris. When it is full, empty out, shaking and mixing different types of material (and wetting if it is dry) as you transfer into the second.

The heap will then heat rapidly, so long as the weather is not too cold and sink down very fast to convert to usable compost.

Most people dislike unsightly compost heaps. One way of avoiding this is to cover a heap of partially rotted down compost with soil. It is taking the old idea of planting a marrow on top of the compost heap one stage further. Incidentally, if you grow a trailing variety of marrow or pumpkin on the heap, the leaves quickly cover it.

A neat rectangular heap of compost covered with soil actually increases the cropping area in a small garden (see illustration). Just take care the heap does not dry out in hot summer weather.

Once it's well rotted, brown and crumbly like peat, garden compost can be used to dig into the soil, to mulch around flowering plants, fruits and vegetables and to sieve for use in plant containers. Get all you can and over the years your garden will improve beyond all recognition.

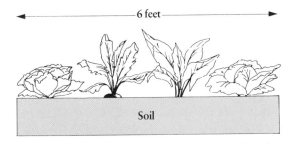

Grow six rows of vegetables like lettuce, beetroot, etc. where there was only space for four!

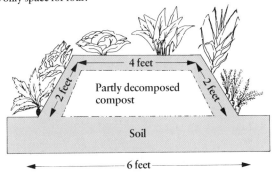

PRUNING

A few rules to remember when pruning:–
1. The harder you cut strong healthy plants, the more they are likely to grow. Tie over strong growth into a curve, pulling the tip down: this checks the growth and encourages flowering and fruiting.
2. Always use sharp secateurs and saws.

3. Before you make the main cut from above, cut the underside of a branch part way. This will prevent the bark from tearing off on the underside as the branch falls.

4. Do not prune in hard frost, because frozen wood is brittle and splits.

5. If in doubt, don't.

PRUNING

TIME OF YEAR	PLANTS	WHAT TO DO	REASON
EARLY SPRING	Late summer flowering shrubs like hardy fuschia; most roses; buddleia, caryopteris and large flowering clematis	Cut back old flowered branches and all dead wood	The best flowers grow on the current year's new growth
LATE SPRING	Early spring flowering shrubs like flowering currant, forsythia, kerria, winter heathers	Cut off old wood which has flowered earlier in the year	Next year's flowers are produced on the new wood which grows after flowering
EARLY SUMMER	Camellias and rhododendrons when old and overgrown	Prune out old unwanted branches which have become bare at the base	New growth will grow below the cuts. If the plant has finished flowering it can be pruned earlier
MID SUMMER	Summer flowering shrubs, rambler and some shrub roses	Just prune out some of the older branches to encourage new growth	Shrubs get overcrowded over the years and flower quantity is reduced
LATE SUMMER	Loganberry, tayberry, raspberry, blackcurrant	Prune out all the old wood which has carried fruit	The best fruit comes on the new growth made the previous summer
	Evergreen hedges, including leyland cypress	Cut back with shears to required shape. Do NOT cut leylands back into leafless wood	Pruned at this time, some new growth will come to cover the cuts
EARLY WINTER	Grapes (and birch if necessary)	Cut vine shoots from the main stem back to a few inches (On birch, just cut to desired size)	Prune after leaf fall, because, if pruned around early spring, the sap bleeds from the wound
WINTER	Deciduous plants, including apples, pears, gooseberries and white currants	Shorten the new growth made in the year on the tips of each branch by half. Thin out dense, intertwined branches	It encourages better growth along the branch and more fruit. Free air movement reduces the chance of disease

WHITE PLASTIC URN COMPETITION

The friendly competition between TV gardening presenters has now become something of an annual event. First, there was the giant onion growing, then the BBC dahlia and now, in autumn 1985, there is the white plastic urn!

There are millions of these cheap plant containers in use throughout Britain; the aim is to make them look more attractive all the year round. The only rule is that a standard container must be used. It will be interesting to see what varieties of plants the gardeners from England, Scotland and Wales come up with.

QUICK GUIDE TO SELECTING WEEDKILLER'S

IMPORTANT: ALWAYS FOLLOW THE MANUFACTURERS INSTRUCTIONS TO THE LETTER, TAKE TIME TO READ THEM CAREFULLY

WHAT TO KILL	THE CHEMICAL	BRAND NAMES	WHERE TO APPLY	COMMENTS
All plants for a season and more.	(a) aminotriazole and (b) simazine	Super Weedex (Murphy)	Paths, drives, bases of fences and walls, along the edges of buildings over paved areas.	Best applied when the soil or surface is moist.
	(a) + (b) and MCPA	Path Weedkiller (Fisons)		
	(a) + (b) and paraquat/ diquat	Pathclear (ICI)		
	(a) + (b) and ammonium thiocyanate	Totalweed (May and Baker)		
All plants, even those with persistent roots. But leave the soil untainted ready for other plants.	glyphosate	Tumbleweed (Murphy)	Any soil where you want a completely clean start.	Apply by sprayer, in calm weather, for greatest area cover. Allow 3 weeks to see the effect.
		Tumbleweed Gel (Murphy)	To paint selectively on leaves.	
Everything down to soil level very quickly. Leaves soil ready for growing other plants immediately after use.	paraquat/diquat	Weedol (ICI)	Between rows of vegetables, among flowers and other plants. Can be used on suckers from trees and shrubs.	Apply through a 'dribble bar' attachment to the can to avoid drift onto adjacent garden plants. In autumn and winter the knockdown of plants is slower but the weed control effects last longer.
Everything except grass.	(a) 2.4-D and (b) dicamba	Lawn Spot Weedkiller (Fison) Weed Gun (ICI)	Lawns and areas where only grass is required.	Apply when grass and weeds are growing strongly. Cut lawn and leave for 3 days before applying and then leave for several days before cutting again.
	(c) dichlorprop and (a)	Lawn Weedkiller (Murphy)		
	(d) mecoprop and (a) and (c)	Lawn Weedkiller (Boots)		
	(e) fenoprop and (a)	New 4-50 Lawn Weedspray (Synchemicals)		Most of these are also available mixed with lawn fertiliser.
	(a) (d) and (e)	Supertox (May and Baker)		
	(f) MCPA + (b)	Turf Weedkiller (Fison)		
Just perennial grasses, especially twitch/ couch among garden plants. Leaves soil unaffected.	alloxydim sodium	Weed Out (May and Baker)	Over any plants other than grass where grass is not wanted.	Apply when twitch is growing strongly. Allow 3 weeks for effect to show.
Grasses, including couch, where soil doesn't need to be planted for several weeks.	dalapon (glyphosate can also be used)	Couch and grass killer (Synchemicals)	On land where grasses are weeds.	
Weeds under shrubs and roses.	dichlobenil	Casoran – G4 (Synchemicals)	Sprinkle granules selectively under shrubs and roses.	Can also be used as a total weedkiller on paths.
Weeds in roses, certain shrubs, fruit trees and bushes.	simazine	Weedex (Murphy)	Water on moist soil in dormant season.	Keep clean soil weed free for a season.
Annual seedling weeds among ornamental plants, strawberries and certain vegetables.	propachlor	Covershield (Murphy)	Sprinkle on recently sown or planted soil to prevent weed seedlings growing.	Very useful when you don't know what the sown plant seedlings look like. It gives them a clean start for a couple of months.
Brambles, nettles and brushwood.	2.4-D mecoprop and dicamba.	New formula SBK Brushwood Killer (Synchemicals)	Areas of rough, strong shrubbery weed growth.	Apply to fast growing young growth for the best effect. Grasses left unharmed.

NOTE: it is worth keeping a special watering can or sprayer clearly marked for weedkillers. If you only have one can or sprayer, wash out thoroughly with water and a little detergent before using for other purposes. Avoid weedkiller spray drifting in the wind onto adjacent garden plants: the calm weather usually occurs early morning and in the evening.

PEBBLE MILL STREET

Garden Festivals are commonplace in Europe and the basic idea of reclaiming derelict land laid waste over the years by industry, inner city building and mining has much to recommend it. Where once there was desolation, these festivals provide great entertainment, inspiration and leave in their wake open space, arenas, sports facilities, gardens and green parkland.

Other European countries, and especially Germany, have considerable experience in this field over the past thirty years, but in 1984 Britain held its first International Garden Festival at Liverpool. A really ghastly site of old oil storage tanks, town rubbish and old dockland was converted into an exciting garden festival and leisure park in just two years.

Each country can only host an International Garden Festival once in 10 years, so the festival at Stoke-on-Trent, opening for six months on 1st May, 1986, will be a national one; our first National Garden Festival. Released from the strictures of international rules, Stoke NGF will have more of the things we have come to expect from a major garden show.

Greenhouse 2000 will house a summer-long programme of exhibits before the local parks department takes over this growers' dream for the next century. There will be cable-car and electric train rides round the 160-acre site. Brilliant bedding plant displays, rose terraces, a maze, palm house and a continuous programme of flower shows are but a part of all the Festival has to offer.

One feature which attracted most of the $3\frac{1}{3}$ million people visiting the Liverpool '84 Festival was the street of 'ideal homes' and their surrounding gardens. The Pebble Mill Street at Stoke NGF will have even more of these, with two terraces of fifteen houses and three detached houses. They are sited adjacent to the new marina and the pub built to serve the festival.

The front gardens of these terraced houses, like so many in Britain, are tiny and demand skilful design to make them useful and attractive. 'Pebble Mill at One' accepted the challenge of organising more than twelve gardens to furnish the street.

First we went to the Horticultural Trades Association – the trade body that administers the Garden Gift Token scheme among other things – and got tremendous support. Their members, spread throughout Britain, were eager to participate and in the end we had to hold a competition to select the best eleven from over 60 nursery and landscape companies' designs. One plot has been left vacant for a 'Pebble Mill at One' viewers' garden planning competition.

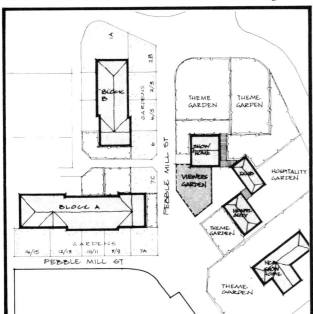

The chosen designs were selected to give the greatest variety and provide home owners with a good, basic plan they could take either as it stands or adapt to their specific requirements. Now we have a series of 'fitted garden' plans that can be installed in much the same way as we have fitted kitchens. High land prices and the dense house buildings they encourage make it even more important to use wisely what garden we have. The correct layout and the best trees and plants can provide a much more enjoyable home environment.

Several of our garden designers speak specifically about the small plot becoming an outdoor room and it is good advice to consider the house and garden as one. The less enthusiastic gardener can be well served by having the garden fitted out from the beginning with the cost built into the mortgage. A professionally landscaped garden often proves cheaper in the long run and certainly gives excellent value for money.

Some people may think fitted gardens of this kind would become boring and lack originality; but, in practice, each home owner quickly stamps his personality onto a garden. Just walk down our street in May, July or September and you will quickly see what variety small gardens contain. All the spring and summer bedding can be different each year in every garden, the underplanting of evergreens and ground cover with spring and summer flowering bulbs of different kinds brings change and you seldom see plant containers, another feature of our gardens, growing the same things.

The gardens at the back of the two terraces and those around the detached houses will also be well worth a visit. They include themes as varied as a Wild Garden, a Garden for Birds sponsored by RSPB, a Fuschia Garden featuring all the different ways of growing fuschias and of furnishing fences and pergolas. But it is the Pebble Mill Street of Front Gardens which is proving the greatest conversation piece. Streets throughout Britain are likely, in future, to be all the more attractive as a result.

And here is a chance too for one of our Pebble Mill viewers to make a mark among our gardens at the Stoke-on-Trent National Garden Festival.

Here's how to enter:

PEBBLE MILL VIEWERS' GARDEN – COMPETITION

Illustrated here is the plot adjoining the Brittania Building Society House Show House, which is similar in size to so many gardens. Imagine you're about to move in and then plan a garden, with the emphasis on a wide range of plants to provide all-year-round colour and interest. It should suit a family with people of all ages and should not require too much hard work

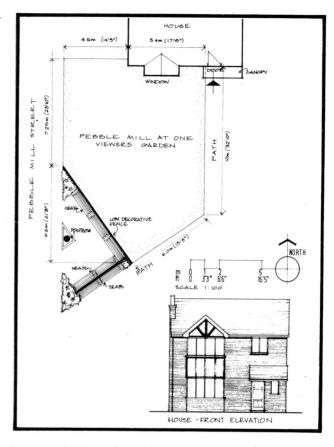

to maintain. We would expect it to have herbaceous plants, conifers and somewhere for tub and container-grown plants.

The winning entry will be professionally drawn, built and planted by Blooms of Bressingham at Stoke-on-Trent. The winning designer will be invited to be present on the day the Queen opens the Festival and will receive a package of plants and planting materials to improve his own garden.

THE RULES
1. The competition is open to all amateur gardeners (professional gardeners, landscapers, nurserymen, BBC employees and their close relatives are not eligible for entry) but is restricted to one entry per household.
2. All entries must be to the dimensions set out in the illustration.
3. The maximum size of the entry is 24" x 18".

4. We are sorry that we cannot return plans, so make a copy.
5. The decision of the judges (Adrian Bloom of Bressingham Gardens, Mark Kershaw of 'Pebble Mill at One' and Joe Samworth of Stoke NGF) is final.
6. All entries should be sent to: Pebble Mill Garden Competition, Bressingham Gardens, Bressingham, Diss, Norfolk, 1B22 2AB.
7. No correspondence can be entered into.
8. The closing date is the 31st January, 1986.

GOOD LUCK!

No doubt many of you will already have some colourful and original ideas of your own but, if you do need some inspiration, we have reproduced the original plans from the winning companies, with notes from the designers on their objectives.

Further details of the recommended plants and likely costs are available from the addresses given with each one.

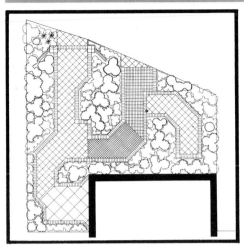

1A PEBBLE MILL STREET
THE SUBURBAN GARDEN

This garden was designed as a carefully proportioned extension of the architectural elevation of the houses in Pebble Mill Street, providing access to front doors and easy to care for planting. Small paving units were used to provide a more intimate scale in the small space, so that the two neighbouring gardens were co-ordinated, yet each had a slightly different character. The paving design incorporated 45° angles instead of right angle corners, reflecting the design of the doors and porches and enclosing several planting beds, filled with perennial, shrub and conifer planting.

Subsequently, the plan was adjusted to suit a different garden plot in the Pebble Mill Street so the geometric layout and circulation pattern now form a self-contained garden. The planting scheme has been adapted to cope with being in the shade of a north-facing wall, using mostly evergreen shrubs, bamboos and various groundcover plants. Hostas and ferns play an important part in the new scheme.

Paving consists of clay pavers and small 300mm square pre-cast paving slabs, to provide paths of various widths without drastic changes in scale or character. Pale, neutral tones will help to add a little extra light to this shady garden, filled with lush foliage in deep beds of solid planting.

Barralets of Ealing, Landscape Dept.,
Pitshanger Lane,
Ealing W5 1RH
Tel: 01-997 0576/7

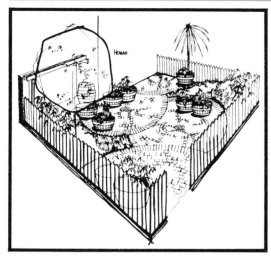

THE EASY, FRUITFUL GARDEN

This garden is designed to provide informal access to the house, instead of the often-seen regimented front garden. It provides an integrated sitting area to take advantage of the aspect over the adjacent marina frontage.

The materials selected for the construction of the garden have been employed to produce a geometric effect and as a vehicle for this type of paving. In addition, the form of construction is a simple and inexpensive surface level construction, capable of execution by a reasonably competent do-it-yourself person. The paving, in particular, whilst producing a geometric effect, is simple to lay on a light sub-base and is sufficiently flexible in concept to accommodate level changes without disrupting the overall effect.

Planted areas surrounding the paving are graded to create space and height and require the minimum amount of maintenance. The garden is created to be enjoyed and not to be endured in terms of maintenance commitments. Within one of the plant containers located on the paving, a herb garden is provided and, in another, soft fruit. In this way, the garden will also be productive as well as practical.

Bernhard's Rugby Landscapes Limited,
Bilton Road,
Rugby, Warwickshire CV22 7DT
Tel: Rugby 811500

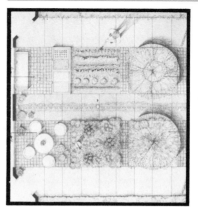

THE GARDEN AS A SHELL

The designers have taken up the challenge and have provided two separate gardens which can be left unaltered when the Festival ends.

The gardens of terraced houses rarely have any sort of unity, but this could be achieved if the developer provided a strong, simple 'shell' which the individual occupants could then develop to their own tastes, rather as a room can be decorated. Assistance could be given to the owner or tenant by the provision of alternative schemes, showing revisions as the needs of the family change, together with suggestions on the choice of plants, methods of constructing pools, sandpits etc.

The designers have suggested just such a 'shell', using a combination of man-made slabs and natural granite setts for the paving, laid so simply that any competent handy-man could 'do-it-himself'. The planting of the two gardens shows how the 'shell' could then be used in two different ways.

One of the gardens is treated ornamentally; a seating area surrounded with hardy shrubs and plants, which provide colour of flowers and foliage to tone in with the warm brown of the brick-work, as well as offering scent and interest for the summer months. The other plot is for the gardener who is anxious to grow as much food as possible, with fruit trees, soft fruit trained on the fences, vegetables, herbs and even a lemon tree in a pot which, of course, must be taken indoors in the winter. A relaxing box-seat doubles as a store for garden tools.

Notcutts Nurseries Ltd.,
Woodbridge,
Suffolk IP12 4AF
Woodbridge 3344

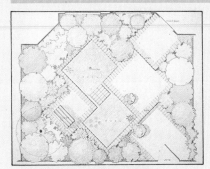

4 and 5 PEBBLE MILL STREET

THE WATER GARDEN

Most front gardens are no more than a piece of land separating the house from the street or road –a barrier to keep out prying eyes, dirt and noise.

This is obviously a function of such a garden, but the potential is there to use the land as an extra room; a show piece to set off or improve the appearance of the house to visitors and passers-by; a live picture to be viewed from the front window, and a pleasing area to walk through every day of the year.

A recurring problem when designing front gardens is the provision of a pathway from the gate to the front door. Here, Guy Farthing of Waterer's Landscape Ltd. avoided the artistic limitations of a conventional straight path by integrating the walking area into the total garden design.

The design is created out of a number of overlapping rectangles of paving, water and planting, forming an ever-changing patchwork. The rectangles are set at an angle to the fence lines to break down the formal right angles of the plot.

The use of water introduces an extra dimension to the garden and forms a focus to the whole space – always fascinating with its reflections on moving water, pond life and dragon-flies. I would like to think of gardens as external rooms and the planting is designed to be the 'walls' – ever changing in colour and form throughout the year and from year to year. Like all rooms, it should have furniture and be lived in. The bench, as well as acting as a focal point, gives the owners the chance to sit and admire their garden, as well as a chance to chat to passers-by and neighbours.

Stapeley Water Gardens Ltd., 92 London Road, Stapeley, Nantwich, Cheshire CW5 7LH
Tel: Nantwich 623868

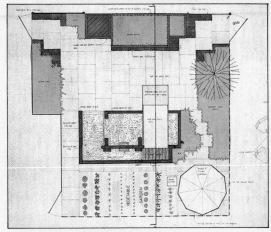

6, PEBBLE MILL STREET

A GARDEN FOR PLAY

We designed this garden very much with the young family in mind, who we considered would be the likely occupants of this type of property.

The centrepiece of the design is a play structure which was conceived to stimulate the young child up to the age of 6, both mentally and physically, with a raised monkey ladder, a swing, a ladder to a raised platform which leads to a wide slide, falling into a pre-cast plastic sand-pit, which can be converted into a paddling pool. Hideaways are created under the slide and platform and the whole of the surface treatment under the active pieces of equipment is forest bark, which has excellent impact-absorbing qualities.

Generally, it was considered desirable to eliminate lawn in such a small area and to provide plenty of flat paving to facilitate tricycling, roller-skating, etc.

A vegetable garden and greenhouse are provided and the general planting was designed to screen the garden from the footpath and to provide scent and colour for the patio area during the summer months.

Wood has been used throughout to harmonize with the play structure, with wooden setts edging the paving, raised wooden planters and a wooden seat.

Watkins Roses Limited, Landscape Division, Kenilworth Road, Hampton-in-Arden, Solihull, West Midlands B92 0LP
Tel: 06755 2866

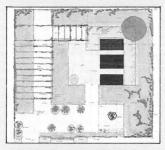

7C, PEBBLE MILL STREET

BLANC DE BIERGES (OR OUTDOOR ROOM) GARDEN

Jardinerie has designed an easy-to-build, attractive, outdoor room. Given our wet weather, all the walking and sitting spaces are quick drying, hard surfaces. We have chosen a concrete base paving and walling system called 'Blanc de Bierges'. This system originated in Belgium but is now available in this country.

All the plants in the garden have been planted in raised beds. Many plants not only look better raised up nearer eye level, but it is also a lot easier to keep the beds weeded or pop in bedding plants, bulbs, etc. Indeed, tending the plants becomes a pleasure. Plenty of space has been left in front of the house for a range of attractive individual containers and a window box for colourful summer bedding. Again, planting in containers makes sense in a small garden where space is at a premium.

Even in a small garden, space should, if possible, be found for a water feature. A fountain enlivens a garden, and waterside plants are among the most beautiful garden plants (and of course a pool does allow fish to be kept). Equally important in a small garden is the need to find space for climbing plants. We have designed simple-to-build timber pergolas to enclose visually parts of the garden and provide a framework for climbing plants. An important consideration in a small garden is that climbing plants are not taking up much valuable ground room. The effect of the planting – by the poolside, in the raised beds and the climbing plants on the pergolas – will be to clothe the garden in foliage for most of the year. Flowers, bulbs and bedding plants will provide the welcome seasonal contrasts.

It is a garden essentially for living in; and because it is so easy to look after, it will be a joy and not a chore to live with.

Jardinerie, Forest Road,
Cotebrook, Tarporley, Cheshire CW6 2EE
Tel: 082921 433

7A, PEBBLE MILL STREET

A RELAXING GARDEN

The house has no rear garden of any size and in view of the fact that the front garden faces due south, it was decided to treat this front garden as a sitting-out area.

The aim of the design is to create a garden which offers a variety of interest and a reasonable degree of seclusion – especially in the summer months when the home owner can enjoy what is effectively an additional 'outdoor room'.

The brick paved area with its climber-clad pergola gives an ideal place for barbecues – and the wooden bench seat is a restful point from which to enjoy colour, fragrance and the sound of water trickling gently over weathered stones into the pool.

The use of permanent shrub and ground cover planting, along with the gravel and paved surface ensures that the garden is easy to maintain. Coarse grade washed shingle (19mm) is used for the gravel as this is less inviting to the germination of weed seedlings. The planting has not been designed to be a 'blaze of colour' but to have carefully chosen flowering plants appearing in specific parts of the garden throughout the summer. The ornamental plant containers give scope for annual summer planting and spring bulbs. Even in winter, however, evergreens, selected shrubs, and the garden's permanent landscape features will provide a pleasant outlook, blending colour, texture and form.

Hillier Landscapes, Hillier Nurseries (Winchester) Ltd.,
Ampfield House, Ampfield,
Romsey, Hants SO5 9PA
Tel: Romsey 68733

8/9 PEBBLE MILL STREET

A COOL SUMMER GARDEN

A garden that is different –

A garden that gives summer pleasure for the Festival –

A garden to show what could be done with the traditional confined space of a terraced row –

These were our aims when we set out to design for Pebble Mill Street. We limited the colour scheme to avoid visual indigestion and chose a theme of cool blues, whites and creams to complement the waterside setting.

We avoided square lines in a small square garden, creating curves and circles emphasised by the outlining of pale Marley Classico setts with terracotta bricks. We felt any grass would be impractical in such a small space and relied rather on a choice of sitting areas, either in the sun or shaded by a tree, with cool, limey-yellow foliage.

We included terracotta pots, so eventually the changes can be rung with summer bedding and spring bulbs.

We tried to create a garden that can remain after the crowds have gone and that will be enjoyed by future residents.

Perryhill Nurseries,
Hartfield,
Sussex TN7 4JP
Tel: Hartfield 377

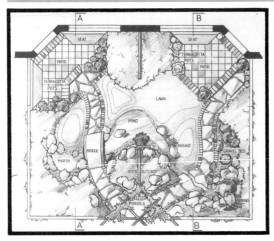

10 and 11 PEBBLE MILL STREET

EVERYONE'S YEAR ROUND GARDEN

Siddeley Landscapes design scheme integrates the two small gardens into one communal space, providing numerous areas of interest for both the active gardener and the passive garden user.

Its function, therefore, is to be used and viewed throughout the year.

The entrance to the garden is through a shared gateway beneath a timber pergola. Each path winds through the garden over the water feature up to private patio areas screened from each other by a decorative timber screen and planting.

From the patios, the lawn slopes down gently to the water feature, the character of which changes from its source – a terracotta pot amongst the rocks and gravel – passing through a pond and terminating in a small marsh area. The planting will be both functional and decorative.

Near to the dwellings, the plants will be colourful and scented and, away from the house, the plant material will have fine textures and subtle colours, giving an illusion of increased length to the garden.

The Olive Tree Trading Company Ltd.,
Twickenham Trading Estate,
Rugby Road,
Twickenham,
Middlesex TW1 1DG
Tel: 01-892 8031.
(containers)

W. Crowder and Sons Ltd.,
Horncastle,
Lincs LN9 5LZ
Tel: Horncastle 6363.
(landscaping and plants)

THE BUDGET GARDEN

The aim of this design is to provide a professionally landscaped garden within the reach of everyone owning a property with a small piece of land.

The objective of the design is to produce an attractive garden, containing features throughout the year which will give enjoyment to the occupier both in the construction and its appeal thereafter.

Based on the aims and objectives, Mr. Trevor Jacques has developed a unique landscape package to be marketed as a Budget Garden on the 'fitted garden' package deal lines, an 'all in the box' garden. It has been designed for construction by the DIY gardener for a relatively small cash outlay.

The purchased box will contain a plan on a 'planting by numbers' basis, instructions for preparing the ground, plants, seeds, grass seed and HTA gift tokens to be used for the purchase of heavy materials such as peats and fertilisers, together with a list of outlets where these can be exchanged within the home locality of the purchaser.

Ned Yates Walk Round
Nurseries and Garden Store,
Moor Lane,
Wilmslow,
Cheshire SK9 6DN
Tel: Wilmslow 522128.

THE EXTRA ROOM GARDEN

This garden, too, has been designed as an extra room for the very small terraced house. The various elements specifically encourage house-holders to adapt them and introduce the gardener's own tastes and interests.

Standing alongside a main footpath and pub, there may be a need for privacy; therefore the boundary fence is substantial, with windows that can be left open or closed by using climbing plants or screens. A welcoming entrance to the garden is important and ours makes use of colour stained timber, lighting and a flowering tree, all to make a guest feel at ease.

The pergola provides a sheltered sitting area and a place for pot plants with barbecue facilities; the pool changes to a sand pit, herb garden, or site for small greenhouse, according to taste.

On the paths, small paving bricks are used to relate to the small garden; a dark grey colour has been chosen as a neutral shade which will not clash with the house bricks, or compete with the colour and interest in the planting.

The plants which hold the various elements of the scheme together provide an evergreen framework with the use of flowering shrubs, climbers and herbaceous material to give all year round effect. White and blue flowers are used at the end of the garden with yellow and reds against the house.

E. R. Johnson (Nurseries) Ltd.,
The Nurseries,
Whixley,
York YO5 8AQ
Tel: Green Hammerton 30234.

'Mastermind' interrogator Magnus Magnusson is the newest member of the Pebble Mill presenting team. He is a prolific broadcaster and author and is no stranger to 'live' television. He presented the much-loved 'Tonight' programme with Cliff Michelmore in the early days of magazine programming.

In his first assignment for Pebble Mill, Magnus travels home to Iceland and he reflects here on how his career and his native roots have always been closely interwoven.

For me, Iceland means one thing above all else. It means home. Home in a very special sense: not where I live, but where I belong.

That must sound a little odd, coming from someone who has lived for 55 years – nearly all my life in fact – not in Iceland but in Scotland. I left Iceland in the summer of 1930 at the tender age of nine months (I had little choice in the matter), because my father was appointed European export manager of the Icelandic Co-op; and for all Icelanders, Europe began at Edinburgh, because that's where the weekly steamer from Iceland made its first port of call.

So I was brought up in Edinburgh with my brother and two sisters, in a home that was always intensely and devotedly Icelandic. My parents always spoke Icelandic to each other and to us children; we learned to speak Icelandic first, and English second. Our house became a sort of home-from-home for all visiting Icelanders, especially after Dad was appointed honorary Consul-General for Scotland.

Every Thursday we used to go to Leith to meet the Icelandic ship, for Dad always had business to transact. All winter, Icelanders who were students at Edinburgh University used to come to our house at weekends for sing-songs and a good feed.

invented). During the war we wore funny warm clothes that fond aunts in Iceland had sent us, and it made us look, and feel, rather alien – so of course we were cast in the role of German spies in the playground games. It taught you to stand up for yourself, at least – and, perversely perhaps, it increased our pride in being Icelandic. At the age of eighteen, when we had to choose which nationality to adopt – Icelandic or British – there was simply no question: we were Icelandic.

And to this day, I still carry an Icelandic passport. It's a funny little blue thing, not nearly as posh as a British one, and it causes much amusement and confusion when my travels take

MY ICELAND

And every evening, at bedtime, mother would tell us stories from the Icelandic Sagas – marvellous yarns of heroes and heroines from Iceland's history, and tales about trolls and the Hidden People, the elves who lived in fairy mounds and rocks. We had all the other legends too, of course, like other children – Robin Hood and Dick Whittington and Santa Claus and Snow White and the rest of them; but the Icelandic stories, the stories from home, gave an extra dimension to the imagination. At Christmas we had a British Christmas Day, with Santa and turkeys; but we also had an Icelandic Christmas Eve with its goblins and elves, and counted ourselves doubly lucky.

School was a little difficult to adjust to at first, because we were so Icelandic (we would be called an ethnic minority nowadays, I suppose, but this was before sociologists had been

me to exotic places far afield. But I find it makes very little difference. I don't believe it is possible to change one's nationality – it's like to trying to deny your identity. I am a citizen of Britain, a Scot by adoption; but nothing can ever alter the plain fact that I am a national of Iceland.

So that's how I grew up, with my actual home in Scotland and doing all the 'right' British things – public school in Edinburgh, then on to Oxford and into journalism; but my real home, my heart-home, you might say, was always in Iceland, where I had aunties and uncles and cousins the way other people have mice.

During the summer holidays, I often went to Iceland –but not on holiday. Icelandic children are all expected to work during the summer, so I was sent to a farm, and developed a life-long love for the countryside and natural history. I also worked on a herring boat off the north coast of Iceland: back-breaking work but a pay-bonanza at the end of it with which to buy my books for my studies at Oxford. I have loved the sea and ships ever since.

At Oxford I read English literature (naturally); and after that it seemed equally natural to study for a post-graduate degree in Old Norse, the language and literature of the Icelandic Sagas. I half intended to look for a career as a University lecturer, I suppose; but there weren't many jobs going in Old Norse, so I sort of drifted into journalism as a reporter on the 'Scottish Daily Express.'

There wasn't much call for news stories from Iceland in those days, until the first so-called Cod War between Iceland and the trawler-owners of Hull and Grimsby in the late '50s. I was sent to cover it for the 'Express', but not very successfully: the Icelandic sources didn't trust me because I worked on a

British newspaper, and the British sources didn't trust me because I was Icelandic. So I got the worst of both worlds, for a change. Anyway, my heart wasn't really in it. I let myself get too involved emotionally (which is unforgivable in a journalist) and kept calling the Icelandic vessels 'fishery protection ships' instead of 'gunboats' and the British naval ships 'frigates' instead of 'fishery protection vessels'! It all depends on your point of view, how you use your words, doesn't it? When is a 'freedom fighter' a 'guerrilla' or a 'terrorist'?

I didn't want to lose my Icelandic studies entirely, so I spent my spare time translating my beloved Sagas with a friend of mine at Edinburgh University – Herman Palsson, now a professor there. The act of translation is a marvellous discipline. It teaches you to weigh words very carefully, to study nuances of meaning, to understand their derivation and style and sound, to analyse the structure of sentences. To translate a great work is like making a tapestry: you have to know the back of it as well as the front, you have to know how it was made in order to try to gain the same effect. It also has a very humbling effect: no translation is ever good enough. It was very good for my English though, and also for my Icelandic – especially when I translated a few of the great novels of Iceland's Nobel Prize-winner, Halldor Laxness.

It was the Sagas, too, that led to my abiding interest in archaeology and history. The Sagas are historical novels about the Viking Age, and I wanted to know if any material evidence

had been unearthed that would throw additional light on them as historical sources – buried buildings, ancient graves, that sort of thing. For instance, two of the Icelandic Sagas describe the discovery and attempted colonisation of North America by Vikings from Iceland and Greenland around the year 1000 (some 500 years before Christopher Columbus); when I was translating them, I had to study the archaeological records in America – especially the remarkable discovery and excavation of a pure Viking settlement on Newfoundland, which proved the accuracy of the Sagas beyond any doubt.

So when a new televison series on history and archaeology called 'Chronicle' was started in 1966, I found myself a founder-member of the team; and the first programme we made was about the Viking discovery of America…

So as you can see, Iceland – or the idea of Iceland – was always there or thereabouts as an influence on my life and career, however indirectly. And when everyone else wanted to go south each summer for the sunny beaches of warmer climes for their holidays, I always headed north for Iceland. I used to spend my holidays as a tourist guide, taking a coachload of Saga pilgrims round the actual sites where the Sagas had taken place, helping to bring them to life by readings on the spot where some great drama had taken place, some awesome tragedy had been enacted. It was a wonderful experience – for myself, at any rate. I can't speak for my 'victims'; one coach-load actually produced a Saga of their own, which they merrily called 'The Saga of Magnus Tourist – Killer!'

You can imagine, then, what an enormous pleasure it gave me when my very first assignment for 'Pebble Mill at One', as the new boy on the team of presenters, was to go to my homeland with a film crew for a little series of programmes about Iceland – my Iceland.

It was an intensely personal pilgrimage in many ways. I went to the places that had the closest intimate associations for me – the house where I was born, and the farms where my parents came from, up in the north of Iceland. I went to the very heart and core of Iceland's history – the great natural arena of lava called Thingvellir, where Europe's oldest Parliament was founded in the year 930: what a Saga that was, and still is – every stick and stone there has a story to tell.

We visited many of the exciting areas where Iceland's tremendous reserves of geothermal energy (underground hot water) are being harnessed, not just for natural central heating and electricity generation, but also for health spas. I spent an afternoon on horseback, riding a splendid Icelandic pony – these large ponies are the pure-bred descendants of the Viking horses brought to Iceland from Scandinavia in the Settlement days, and Icelanders are passionately fond of them to this day. We saw rare books being printed and bound – for Iceland, as befits the land of the Sagas, is the most literate country in the world, and publishes more books per head of population than anywhere else (which explains why such a tiny population of only 250,000 people managed to produce a Nobel Prize-winner).

We saw something of the modern industries that keep Iceland's economy ticking over nicely. But above all, we talked to today's Icelanders about the people who inhabit Iceland today, because I tend to be hopelessly biased and see Iceland through violently rose-tinted spectacles, and we wanted a more objective view.

But to be honest, I find it impossible to be objective about Iceland. To me, it's spectacularly beautiful, endlessly fascinating. To me, it's simply home.

T·R·A·V·E·L

Jill Crawshaw is three-times winner of the Travel Writer of the Year Award. She's also 'Pebble Mill at One's holidays expert, advising on the best deals and campaigning for ever-higher standards for the British tourist abroad.

But this year Jill turns her attentions to the home market, looking at just how varied and competitive holidays in Britain can be.

As a travel broadcaster and journalist, I've had some unforgettable experiences: gazed on the Taj Mahal and the Pyramids, swum from Copacabana beach, sailed off the Barrier Reef and trekked through the Himalayan foothills; rediscovered 'lost' cities in the deserts of Jordan and the Andes of Peru.

Breathtaking stuff . . . which makes me appreciate the amazing diversity of the world we live in, but which also makes me appreciate more and more the qualities and diversities of Britain – the great sweep of East Anglian skies, the sturdy villages of Yorkshire, the rainbow colours of the Scottish moors and the modest grandeur of the Welsh hills. I'm mellowed by the colour of Cotswold stone, thrilled by the historical richness of this country and reassured by the basic 'niceness' of most of our people – all perfect ingredients for perfect holidays.

So it is only right that holidays at home are booming as never before, bringing in billions of pounds from foreign holiday makers, saving many millions more from those of us who've decided to 'Go British.' Our tourist industry is a vast employer and by 1995 is expected to be the largest – so tourism matters to all of us.

There is of course our weather; as I write this, the sun is shining, the lilac is in full bloom. But, as Byron declared: "Summer comes somewhere between the end of July and beginning of August", and as holidaymakers we've at last learned to live with it. Now you can have theatre breaks in London in November, a wine-making weekend in January, or a week learning just about anything from hang-gliding to yoga, at any time of the year.

And if the concept of service with a smile and much of our hotel accommodation have still a long way to go, both in quality and value for money, the self catering sector, which includes log cabins in the forests, or cottages in Cornwall, has improved immeasurably, to provide really economic holidays in the most unexpected and magic places.

The packaging of many of these holidays has become more slick and convenient too – previously it was almost easier to book a trip to Greece, Spain or even Hong Kong. Now, thanks in large part to the excellent publications and marketing of local tourist boards, plus local inventiveness, there are more British holidays to pick off the shelf than ever before. Not everything in the garden is perfect of course, and I'll continue to press for inspection of properties offered to the holidaymaker if they're to gain a genuine seal of approval. But we are getting there.

Here, and in the series of programmes on 'Pebble Mill at One', I'm highlighting the real value-for-money holidays – farmhouses, where they serve up the best English breakfast outside the USA; the activity and special interest holidays that offer a chance to try something new, perhaps develop a hobby for life. New ideas for children to get out and about for a challenge in safety; weekends to explore bits of Britain you may never have known existed.

There's never been a better time to discover Britain.

CHILDREN'S SPECIAL

Parents who have to embark on that annual survival course called 'living peacefully with your child during the long summer holidays' will no doubt be delighted that there are an increasing number of summer camps for kids, if their own courage, stamina or inventiveness fails.

Summer camps have been very much part of the American way of life and 70% of French and German children regularly take these holidays. In Britain, we've started late, but are catching up fast.

There are two basic types: The <u>Day Camps</u> centred around cities with coach pick-ups near your home, using the facilities of school and colleges in the area; and <u>Residential Camps</u> which lie further afield, some abroad. Accommodation is in tents, hostels or dormitories, some at centres which offer a wide range of activities, others specialising in such subjects as computers, football or language study.

I've visited many of these summer camps and certainly the scene I witnessed at a day camp, taking place in a public school in the summer holidays, would have allayed parents' worries about the safety of their offspring. The offspring themselves would also be assured that these day camps were not merely manifestations of the Parents' Liberation Movement and that they were not being fobbed off on just another version of school.

A small but very earnest group of children were making and filming their own cartoon in one corner of the spacious grounds, while another little gang was absolutely intent on capsizing their canoes in the swimming pool – which I learnt was all part of the course.

A team of five year olds were wielding rackets almost as big as themselves, displaying enthusiasm, if not expertise, at badminton; and through the open window of a nearby hall, you could hear the clicks and squeaks of computers.

When the time came to finish each activity, monitors personally escorted their groups to the next activity.

"It is our firm policy never to let a child wander off on his own," explained the organiser. "We pick the monitors carefully; they are mainly sports students from teacher training colleges, sometimes staff at the school itself. We instil in them an absolute standard of safety."

My own son Toby, now ten, already a veteran of day camps, tried a residential camp last summer for his first ever week away from home, with definite views about what he wanted: sport and adventure and sleeping in a tent.

So, off he went to Boreatton Park near Shrewsbury, slightly apprehensive as the coach left London, but supplied with three stamped addressed postcards and instructions on how to reverse the telephone charges if he was homesick.

The first postcard arrived on the third morning: "Things are brill and I got mud in my ears." That was the sum total of our contact for a week.

He arrived back exhausted, himself and his gear filthy apart from his flannel which was pristine. His mumbled reminiscences were, in truth, fairly brief . . . "amazing shooting, the abseiling was the scariest thing I've ever done – it was my favourite . . . monitors were just like the boys . . . soggy sandwiches every day.

"Next year I'd like to do abseiling and BMX bikes . . ."

Yes, clearly it had been just 'brill'!

■ **Safety** In residential centres, do they hold fire drills?
■ **Extras** What is included in the price? How much pocket money is advisable?
■ **Accommodation and Food** Are there drying rooms? Remember the children seem to care more about food than facilities.
■ **Contact** Can the children phone you (or you them) without their having to make an issue of it?
■ **Experience** How long has the company been in business and would they be prepared to put you in contact with parents who have used their company?

ADDRESSES
PGL Young Adventure, 2-5 Market Place, Ross-on-Wye.
Dolphin Adventure Holidays, Grosvenor Hall, Bolnore Road, Haywards Heath, West Sussex.
Camp Beaumont, 9 West Street, Godmanchester, Cambs.
Colony Childrens Holidays, (same address as Dolphin).
Soccer World, 10 Fir Tree Road, Banstead, Surrey.
Millfield Village of Education, Street, Somerset.
Ardmore Adventure, 23 Ramillies Place, London W1.

CHECK LIST

Perhaps it is a typically British quirk that if you want to go into business running a kennel, there are all sorts of rules and regulations and inspections you first have to go through, but if you're in the children's holiday field, you can just go ahead and open up – there are no legal standards (apart from fire regulations), nor any kind of registration or inspection, though this is at least beginning to be discussed.

So before you book, go through a check-list.

■ **Suitability** Some children prefer to specialise, others will get bored by one activity and would be happier with lots of choice. On the whole the younger the child, the more activities the better.

■ **Medical** Is there a doctor, nurse, or similarly trained person on hand?

■ **Supervision** Get details of the people in charge, their qualifications, age and expertise. In the United States, these are specified – depending on the ages of the children, there should be one organiser for every 5-10 children. And what happens during the children's free time?

FARMHOUSE HOLIDAYS

It's easy to see the appeal of a farmhouse holiday – lots of fresh air, home cooking, mooching about in old clothes and wellies, warm friendly farmhouse kitchens, perhaps above all the factors which I call 'animal appeal.' Farmers' wives have told me that many city children are amazed when they actually face young lambs, or come across eggs which don't come in polyurethane boxes. Yet children are rarely sentimental creatures and they'll gladly play with a lamb during the day and eat a hearty meal of leg of lamb in the evening.

There are now thousands of farms in Britain taking in paying guests and the number is increasing every year. They vary from smallholdings of a few acres to large estates and from the sheep farms of Cumbria and Yorkshire to dairy farms and fruit and arable farms.

The guest house side is usually run by the farmer's wife, most letting out two or three rooms for pin money, though others are expanding into businesses almost as big as the farms themselves with chalets, cottages and caravans. "At least with our paying guests, the Common Market doesn't tell us how many we can have," said one farmer wryly.

Before booking, you should make sure that the farm is really a working farm and not just a rustic guest house with a few chickens in the back. We once spent a few not too happy days in such a place in Ireland, the 'farm' being in a suburban row and the animals consisting of a donkey and a handful of chickens and ducks.

Some farms may not be suitable for holidaymakers with young children since they only provide bed and breakfast and you are more or less expected to be out of the house all day. In general, though, children do love the life, though since farming has become a skilled and mechanical business, the jobs they can do are necessarily limited. The machinery is complicated and dangerous, but on the right farm, they should be able to feed lambs, watch the haymaking and help with poultry.

On most farm holidays, a car is essential as you may be somewhat isolated. Don't expect much in the way of evening entertainment, apart from the local pub.

CHECK LIST
■ The Farm Holiday Bureau at the National Agricultural Centre, Stoneleigh, Kenilworth, Warwickshire CV8 2LZ lists hundreds of farms, the majority working ones with some amazingly low prices – from around £50-£60 for a week's bed and breakfast, £75-£90 with evening meal. National and Regional Tourist Boards also publish guides and lists.
■ If you have a dog, you must find out whether farms will take them. Those with livestock often won't.

ACTIVITY HOLIDAYS

"Three hundred and eighteen different courses and eighty-three different activities for families, adults and unaccompanied young people" splashes the cover of one brochure (with not a bikinied model to be seen), and inside the choice ranges from archery to fencing, judo, tennis and trampolining – to name just a few.

"The new brochure is twice the size and offers action at one hundred and sixty hotels, including ballooning, water sports, carriage driving, shooting, racing and jousting " – a release from a hotel group.

The traditional British seaside holidays may be having a thin time, despite the British holiday boom, but our activity holidays appear to be alive, thriving and jumping, from Land's End to John O'Groats.

And what, just a few years ago, was more or less confined to a few activities such as walking, riding and cycling has blossomed into sophisticated and often highly technical sports and hobbies that can be tasted over a weekend or sampled in a week.

Even the traditional YHA has introduced parachuting and cave and mine exploration alongside its better known pony-trekking, walking, sailing and climbing holidays.

In the English Tourist Board's 'Activity and Hobby Holidays' book, some of the largest sections are for air sports such as ballooning and hang-gliding.

Certainly as a nation we are getting more and more interested in health and fitness and moving away from 'do-nothing holidays' – inevitably so, with working hours getting shorter. And there's no doubt that some of the newer sports attract the least hearty people who wouldn't be seen dead donning a pair of walking shoes, but are ready to put on a wet suit.

Every new trend brings its own problems: there can be little risk in a ramble across the countryside, but some of the newer activities require a sophistication of equipment, instruction and safety procedures which can, at times, be sadly lacking.

I was first alerted to this by an appalling incident I witnessed in the Seychelles some years ago. A woman had inexplicably allowed her seven year old son to go parascending from the beach, but being too light, he had floated into the trees on the water's edge.

He appeared safe enough until rescue could arrive, but the boatman who had been towing him, confused by the noise and lack of language communication, and totally untrained in the sport, revved up his engine and, in the hope of getting the child airborne again, hauled him out at full revs.

I shall never forget the sound as the child hit the ground, nor the sight of his injuries.

Since that occasion, I've seen rusty diving equipment, riding schools either without hard hats or hats that were completely the wrong size, and gliding schools abroad that would gladly have taken me on without having any common language in which to teach this potentially dangerous sport.

Admittedly, most of these weaknesses I've seen were abroad, but we are not completely in the clear here, either. Air sports, riding and watersports in the English Tourist Board guide, are approved and recognized by the relevant governing bodies, but that doesn't stop any cowboy from jumping on the bandwaggon and producing his own brochure.

"The golden rule", says our Sports Council, "is to check whether the sports or activities have instructors trained and tested by the governing body of the sport. Ask the firm. Check with us. Many of these sports also have their own safety officers who recommend and inspect."

Safety apart, you must also consider how seriously you want to go into the many activities now on offer. Do you want to learn as a serious pursuit, or just have a bit of fun and a change? Obviously some courses, like the Sports Council's own at their sailing centre in Cowes, mountaineering in Wales or watersports near Nottingham, are for the dedicated enthusiasts.

Generally, the longer the holiday, the more serious the intent.

Many of these centres offer little in the way of extra-curricular evening entertainment beyond slide shows and video, leaving it up to the guests to make their own entertainment. This, a good proportion being singles, they seem to do quite successfully.

There is growth, too, in the family activity market.

"We tried it tentatively a few years ago", I was told at the Millfield Village of Education, "and now it's a third of our market.

There's no doubt that such holidays can take the tension out of togetherness."

This certainly seemed true with a family I met at Millfield. The wife was doing gymnastics and jewellery making, while the husband was tackling cricket and golf. Their two little sons were engaged in trampolining, nature study, judo and swimming, yet all had enough breath and enthusiasm left to hold discussions in the evenings about the day's activities.

This year for the first time, Millfield have introduced a Club 55 for the older holidaymakers who want to combine a programme of activities with tours and excursions around the lovely coast, lanes and by-ways of the West Country.

Another organisation, PGL, perhaps better known for their centres for unaccompanied children, have introduced holidays where parents can try canoeing, hill-walking, pony trekking, wind surfing and sailing, secure in the knowledge that their four to six year olds are enjoying play schemes back at the centre. Or they offer self-catering at Stirling University for the whole family who can then try different pursuits.

It's impossible to generalise about cost. The more technical and sophisticated the activity, the more expensive it is likely to be. And with some sports such as parachuting, flying and hang-gliding, you may have to go back several weekends to get the right weather, having the indoor or theoretical instructions one weekend, and the real thing another time.

Other sports and activities you can perhaps learn, or at least sample more quickly. Indeed, one organisation aims to give you a scare-a-day in the Peak District, trying out potholing, climbing, orienteering, pony trekking and sailing. And those taking part are not all potential Daley Thompsons either.

They are looking for a challenge and, over the wine and good food that thankfully accompany this particular 'holiday' (I do believe that if you're going to torture the body, you should also pamper it), they display their bruises with pride.

CHECK LIST

■ If tackling very strenuous activity, find out first how fit you need to be and, if necessary, be prepared to exercise before you go. If in doubt, consult your doctor.

■ Make sure of what is included in the advertised price. Do you have to pay extra for tuition, equipment hire, entrance fees and so on? And, irritatingly, check whether VAT is included in the price – some brochures do include this, others leave it out to be able to shout about a low 'from' price. Remember that 15% is quite a whack on your bill.

■ On potentially dangerous activities, you may find that normal holiday insurance gives you no protection, and you will need to take out (and pay for) extra insurance.

■ How expert are the courses and the other participants? It's no fun being a novice amongst experts – or vice versa.

■ The English, Scottish and Welsh Tourist Boards each publish booklets (there may be a charge) on Activity and Special Interest holidays in their region.

SELF CATERING

In our family, there's Toby and Dominic. They're two small boys, blonde and bouncy and with their individual whims. When they were very young, these were centred around the table. Their love of nature extended to trying to eat flowers, plastic, paper or real. They collected around them an armoury of knives, forks and spoons and then tackled their rice pudding with their fingers. We could just about put up with all this – in fact, we didn't have much choice. But it was the sort of thing that turned head waiters pale and trembling in hotel dining rooms, while keeping other guests spellbound in horrified fascination. And it did nothing for our own peace of mind and relaxation.

We also claim that Toby is intelligent and has an inquiring mind. These attributes manifested themselves in his love of exploration and discovery – along dangerous balconies, in other guests' hotel rooms and, on one never-to-be forgotten occasion, into the depths of the linen cupboard.

It was after the linen cupboard incident that we decided that 'self-catering' holidays might be the solution for a few years.

There were other reasons as well, of course. Like Oscar.

No, Oscar wasn't another delinquent offspring, but a blue roan spaniel with a pedigree that read like a Who's Who of the Dog World. He was very affectionate and firmly believed that he was a person, not a dog, and saw no reason why he should be left out of any holidays. He sat on the suitcases and peered at us with those melting brown eyes. So if we could, we took him too.

And we took luggage . . .

Every year, I issue good and true advice to my readers about how to pack neatly, what to take and how to save space. I tell them to take only half of what they think they'll need, and even that will be too much.

My advice is, of course, absolutely right – it's only that I couldn't quite follow it myself.

So we set off in the car like there was no tomorrow. How could we survive possible floods without the extra pair of wellies? But what if the sun shone non-stop, and there was no pool nearby? Surely, Toby's paddling pool wouldn't take up much space?

My husband has his dreams about fishing – a sport for which he shows neither talent nor patience, as one weekend on the Thames proved when he caught one tiddler, a mop, almost a swan, plus a cold. So in went the fishing rods.

And what would Oscar sleep on? Along came his basket, plus drinking and feeding bowls as well as bottles of water in case he got thirsty en route.

All very necessary, but try getting it all into a hotel room on a fortnight's holiday. Hopefully a cottage, villa, chalet or apartment would accommodate our little load.

Nearly everyone I meet who has tried self-catering holidays sings their praises.

And the biggest plus-point is almost invariably 'freedom.'

Freedom to go out for the day, coming back when you please. Freedom to snatch an extra forty winks in bed without the rigid timetable of a hotel dining room. Freedom to brew up or have a drink when you feel like one without having to worry about catching the waiter's eye, about service charges, licensing hours or VAT. To wear a bikini or jeans with holes in the knees without incurring the visible displeasure of some stony-eyed hotel receptionist.

"Will I be exchanging one kitchen for another?" many may well ask. And if so, how much of a holiday is it really going to be?

In practice, I haven't found this much of a drawback, nor have friends and readers with whom I've discussed this. I don't think that at home my husband knows where the sheets are kept, but he'll quite happily make beds when we are on holiday.

Even children, who are masters at disappearing at the slightest chance of housework at home, can often be persuaded to wield a tea towel when away. It all becomes an adventure.

I myself, who hate housework of any description, get a doll's house mentality and enthusiasm about a strange kitchen, provided it is well-equipped. We've stayed in or inspected places all over the world and the worst thing I've found in common about all of them is their name, 'self-catering.' Would that some enterprising travel firm could come up with some more evocative title!

How can 'self-catering' describe those white-washed thatched cottages in the West of Ireland with their pine furniture, straw crosses and stable doors? Here the kindly villagers arrived with 'a couple of old sods' of peat for the fire and delicious soda bread for our breakfast.

Or the modern, but traditionally built, little timber chalet on the Pembroke Coast, when we enjoyed some magnificent walks along the Welsh coastal footpaths, with the wind and spray in our hair and the sea birds defying the crashing waves.

While staying in the converted granary of an old farm in North Devon, we learnt about mushrooms from generous locals. Where to find them, which to eat, and we picked them for some never-to-be forgotten breakfasts.

And we learned to love the badger as, one night, with a farmer to guide us, we watched them coming out for their nightly stroll.

We had a dream holiday in a little Norfolk cottage – with pheasants, rabbits and hares, herons and kingfishers as our only neighbours. They were good company.

In the evening, as daylight gave way to dusk, we sat outside and through field glasses watched the wild geese fly in 'V' formation, all the birds hurrying towards we knew not where, to find shelter for the night.

An Englishman's home is his castle – or so the saying goes. Perhaps that is one of the reasons why we take to the holiday home so readily – because it becomes a home from home in a way even the most comfortable hotel room never can.

There are already personal things around the place and you add your own: Big Teddy and Little Teddy can be found chairs to sit on between meals and the vase on the dining room table has wild flowers you yourself picked on a walk.

Quickly you stamp your identity on the place. You begin to feel part of the community – as long as you are prepared to talk and to listen.

"Four gallons of four star," my husband asked the petrol pump attendant.

"You like marrows?" came the reply, in the form of a question.

They discuss the virtues of marrows as a vegetable. Although the petrol was eventually delivered and paid for, so were two huge marrows. They were not paid for. They were delicious and never forgotten.

CHECK LIST

You can find self-catering properties through big agencies, from Tourist Board publications, or private lets (usually single properties) advertised in newspapers, but as this is often quite unregulated, it's a good idea to make your own check-list.

■ Ask for a photo and written description – the number of rooms, who sleeps where?

■ Where is the property in relation to the shops, services, main road, the sea and other necessities?

■ How is the house heated, who pays for it, and how?

■ Is there a phone and how are calls metered? Also television?

■ What children's hazards are there – unfenced gardens, difficult stairs, ponds and so on?

■ Is there a washing machine, or a launderette at least, nearby?

■ Can they give you someone's name as a reference, who has stayed there?

■ If you have a dog, will they allow you to bring it?

■ Above all, to whom can you turn if something goes wrong?

Nobody lets their cottage, flats, home or even caravan for fun; they do so for money. I get complaints from people who write and tell me that the place they rented was 'sparsely' furnished and that the fittings were not new. In many cases, I find that, on checking, the price they paid was so low they were lucky to get a roof over their heads. So remember, in the main, you'll get what you pay for.

The easiest places to assess before you go there are the large complexes, the holiday villages and the purpose-built developments. The hardest are the private homes.

One reader wrote and told me of her experiences in a holiday flat advertised for nine people. To fit everyone in, three children had to sleep in what was a single room (two in a large single bed and one on a camp bed), while two adults had to share a put-you-up in the living room which doubled as a kitchen. Another complained – I've heard this often – that the room her son had to use had all the personal possessions of the owner – posters, photographs and even clothes, so that, as she said, "We felt like intruders!!"

SOMETHING DIFFERENT

FORESTRY CABINS

The Forestry Commission, 231 Corstorphine Road, Edinburgh. Timber log cabins and a few stone cottages in villages, as well as some really isolated places. They are largely in the West Country, Wales, Scotland and the North. You need to book early.

LANDMARK TRUST Shottesbrooke, Nr. Maidenhead, Berkshire. A charity with some really interesting properties – castles, mills, all carefully restored and preserved. Again, book early.

NATIONAL TRUST PROPERTIES, 42 Queen Anne's Gate, London SW1. These may be farm cottages on country estates, follies, even in one case part of a forge, all tastefully furnished. Not cheap, but of a high standard and interesting. Need I say it? Book early.

WEEKEND BREAKS

Highlifes and Hushways, Superbreaks and Stardusts, Breathers and Breakaways, Camelots and Crestrests – they may sound like packets you put on the breakfast table every morning, but they represent some of the most forward-looking ideas in British holidays, marketed with all the competitiveness of the sunshine cereal manufacturers.

In the dozen or so years since their introduction, they've proved one of our biggest success stories. "Let's Go," the weekenders' Bible, now lists some 15,000 hotels at prices around £45-£55 per person for two nights half board. Last year the group alone brought out 450 different breaks at 172 hotels in 160 locations, while one enthusiastic lady we interviewed on 'Pebble Mill at One' has enjoyed no less than 100 breaks from another consortium in the last four years.

Many of the best deals are in the off-season when the tourists go home – in country inns or seaside hotels – and offer a great opportunity to explore undiscovered parts of Britain really cheaply.

And not everyone wants to wake up with the birds. London is one of the biggest weekend holiday magnets, when holidaymakers can fill beds vacated by businessmen during the week. Some weekend holiday firms throw in theatre tickets or offer discounts on shopping excursions or transport. Other industrial cities like Bradford, Nottingham, Manchester, Bristol and Liverpool have built a thriving tourist business based around their industrial heritage of railways, mills, canals or mines.

While the countryside or cities form the bread and butter of the market, there's a big increase in the special interest sports weekends, too, and the plain gimmicky theme which is just a thinly disguised excuse to get away for a couple of days at short notice. Or, as one group hypes its breaks: "from the crazy to the creative, exhausting to exhilarating," with themes such as Shark Fishing and Parachuting, to a Real Ale break in Dorset and a Hangover Break in Cumbria where ". . . you can extend your knowledge of the largest range of malts south of the border." The recovery hangover pack comes as part of the package.

Before you decide whether to go into hangovers or hang-gliding, you need to sort out your own needs – are they fun, comfort, or a chance to take up a hobby or activity more seriously.

The weekenders I met at the Earnley Concourse in Chichester had no doubt where their priorities lay. "If we'd just wanted fun, we'd have booked a trip to Majorca," they reprimanded me when I tentatively asked if all that hammering and chiselling and chipping and sawing they were doing to make window frames wasn't all too much like hard work. Last winter, Earnley's weekend cost about £50-£60 for two days with all meals and included Basic Wok Cookery, Making the Most of Your Greenhouse, Self-Defence for Women (why not for men, I ask?) or if you are not certain how to replace a ball valve or unblock a drain, how about a weekend Plumbing?

Serious they may be, but the surroundings are not too spartan, with lovely grounds and such distractions as swimming pools, table tennis, squash and billiards.

Undoubtedly the prize for the most boring-looking brochure of the year usually goes to the National Institute of Adult Education's 'Residential Short Courses.' Yet, inside its cover, it contains details of weekend breaks where you can study just about everything from Astronomy, Fungi and Yoga to "Winkles" and "Who Wrote Shakespeare." They act as a clearing house for various organisations with the courses taking place in colleges and hostels, from as low as £25 a weekend, but generally averaging about £40-£60.

If you are looking for something more epicurean, a browse through the Prestige Group winter breaks brochure would be welcome reading; Christopher Chapman's Castle Hotel in Taunton featured "Fine Wines" (. . . dinner with the great wines of Burgundy . . . gala dinner featuring Château Petrus 1964) at around £270. At the other end of the budget scale, even the holiday centres are getting in on the act. Warners, for example, offered Nostalgia, Edwardian and Cockney Weekends as well as BMX challenge, fireworks and other sporting activities all around £32-£35 in their chalet centres. Pontins went one better in 1985 with a whole new Hobby and Leisure brochure containing dozens of different weekends (and weeks) based around 'Electronic Organ' or 'Beauty Know-How,' 'Netball,' 'Wine-making,' 'Learn to Swim,' or 'Aerobics.'

In the middle price range, there's lots of choice, attractive locations and good rail discounts from Camelot Mini Holidays and Superbreaks in different locations all over Britain.

One of Trust House Forte's popular offerings has been a 'School for Detectives' break based on 1920's style plots and dress, where during the weekend "a web of suspicion and intrigue develops and students who become involved could face the prospect of poisonings, shootings and even the odd kidnapping or two." All this for £90 for 2 nights with all meals.

More relaxing, perhaps, was a 'Weekend Unwinder' at the Bell Hotel in Mildenhall with "brandy and radox" on arrival. I quite fancied that one myself, though not as much as the luxury weekend in Leamington Spa which included a £50 shopping voucher, another voucher for £50 worth of wine, a hot air balloon ride and a Sunday lunch of caviar, steak and Dom Perignon (the price, ssh . . . £299)!

Among the most eccentric weekends, two that seem to figure most are four poster beds and ghost hunting – apparitions, though, are rarely guaranteed!

CHECK LIST
■Some firms offer full board, and include VAT and service in the package deal. Make sure you know what exactly is included.
■Single holidaymakers and families with children benefit particularly from reading the small print. Children (under 16, for instance) can travel and stay free with some firms providing they share their parents' room.
■Take that simple "Bed and Breakfast." With some, it means a simple continental breakfast. Others serve the full English variety. On a frosty winter weekend with a nip in the morning air, you may be glad you settled for eggs and bacon . . .
■A number of offers include rail travel from your home town, usually a real bargain.
■"Let's Go" is published by the English Tourist Board every autumn. The Welsh and Scottish Tourist Board also issue wide-ranging publications.

An important element of our Travel series is to reflect the interests of disabled viewers.

Anne Davies is an author and broadcaster and since becoming wheelchair-bound through multiple sclerosis has taken a special and personal interest in holidays for the disabled.

TRAVEL FOR THE DISABLED
ANNE DAVIES

Finding a suitable place for a holiday if you are disabled can be quite a problem, but not so difficult now as it was a few years ago. So much depends on the type and extent of your disability and age. Careful planning is essential.

Let's start with the youngsters. There's the Calvent Trust in Cumbria and the Kielder Adventure Centre in Northumberland, which both provide accommodation suitable for all disabled people and give everyone the opportunity to 'have a go' at all sorts of activities such as canoeing, rock climbing and swimming. The Churchtown Farm Field Centre in Cornwall is similar and has accommodation for up to 60 people. They will assist with mobility problems and personal care, too, if needed. The Netley Waterside House near Southampton is a purpose-built holiday hotel for several disabled people and they run special weeks for children and young people, with lots of fun and activities.

Many national organisations have their own 'hotel-type' accommodation, as well as self-catering 'mobile' homes. I've visited the Multiple Sclerosis Society's Holiday Home at Exmouth and the Winged Fellowship Trust's Jubilee Lodge at Chigwell. Each has its own adapted mini-bus for outings and entertainment several nights during the week. The John Groom's Association owns two hotels, each with adapted bathrooms and showers. One is at Minehead, the other at Llandudno. A less expensive way of having a break is to book a self-catering 'mobile' home. These are usually adapted for wheelchair users (and that includes a special W.C. and shower). They sleep up to 6 people and there's plenty of room, as some are 46' in length. Most sites have a shop and restaurant, some have swimming pools.

If you wish to find out more on these holidays I suggest you look at the R.A.D.A.R. Holidays Book. It costs £2 and is excellent value, as it covers the whole of the U.K. as well as giving hints on travel abroad.

Some of you may prefer to travel independently, staying in ordinary hotels; but this is where you have to be very careful, checking every detail when you book. But more and more hotels are providing special facilities – even a few three star hotels. I visited a particularly pleasant hotel in Paignton which had two such rooms and glorious views across the bay from the lounge and garden. However, in such places, a car would be essential, not only to get down the steep road to the beach, but to explore the many sights and delights of the nearby villages and towns such as Cockington and Exeter.

Travelling by car is not so exhausting as it used to be. Most of the service stations have snack-bars and, what is even more important, special toilet facilities for the wheelchair user. If you like touring I suggest you get a copy of the AA Guide for Disabled Travellers (free to members).

Something a little more relaxing! What about a leisurely cruise on a narrow boat through the waterways of Britain? Some of the boats have lifts and some enable a disabled person to 'skipper' the boat from a wheelchair. All the details are in the R.A.D.A.R. book.

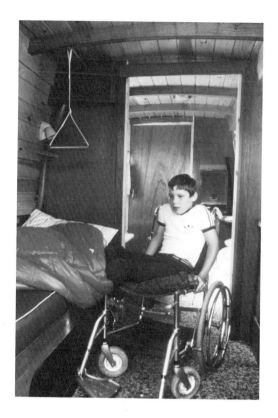

One or two firms have specialised in providing this type of holiday and they ensure arrangements are made at airports, and transfer to hotel at destination. They check resorts and hotels for suitability and give actual measurements of doors, lifts etc.

I've bumped over cobbles in Denmark and Holland; and was amazed at the wonders of Disneyland in Florida.

New this year are five European Holiday Tours with a list of hotels on route. They range from a 290 mile trip around Northern France to something for the real adventurer – a 2,561 mile route from Cherbourg to South of France, to Rome and back via Switzerland, Strasbourg, Luxembourg and Calais.

It is possible to have a wonderful holiday in this country as well as overseas, especially if you take heed of these few points.

CHECK LIST
■ Be honest about the extent of your disability.
■ Plan ahead and book early.
■ Point out the facilities you are looking for when you book the hotel.
■ Know the width of your wheelchair, so you can check width of bathroom door, lift, etc.
■ Take out insurance.
■ Take with you an ample supply of medication.
■ Take with you a sun hat and plentiful supply of suncream and go easy on the sunbathing.
■ Take a pump and spanner if you use a wheelchair.
■ Do not plan on travelling alone unless you are completely confident that you will NOT need any assistance from anyone whilst you are on holiday.
■ Going abroad, check that your passport is valid and ask your doctor about vaccinations.

Bon voyage . . . enjoy yourselves . . .

Another source of information is the Holiday Care Service which provides information and advice on holidays for disabled people as well as for the elderly. They don't make bookings, but they do provide, on request, details of accommodation, inclusive holidays, transport, and other facilities.

Holiday Care Service will also be able to give details of adapted self-catering farm cottages which are suitable for wheelchair users. Some of the cottages are part of a working farm and fresh milk, fruit and vegetables can be purchased on the spot.

Now, just a few words on holidays abroad. I've tried out quite a few myself and have found it is possible to enjoy an ordinary holiday with family and friends – but you must be very careful and be honest about your disability and your capabilities.

ADDRESSES
Holiday Care Service, 2 Old Bank Chambers, Station Road, Horley, Surrey RH6 9HW. Tel: 0293 774535.
R.A.D.A.R. 25 Mortimer Street, London W1N 8AB. Tel: 01-637 5400.
Threshold Travel Wiendal House, 2 Whitworth Street, Manchester.

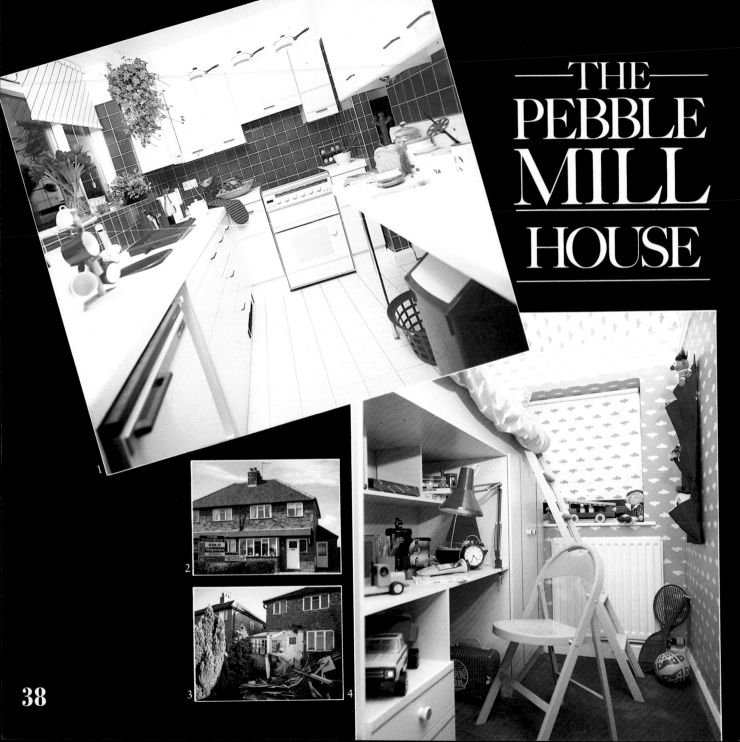

THE PEBBLE MILL HOUSE

1
2
3
4

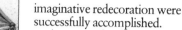

In the space of a few weeks, a rather seedy run-down semi in Solihull was taken in hand by Pebble Mill experts and transformed into a three-bedroomed home to be proud of.

Number 79, Damson Lane was bought for £18,750 – deliberately chosen because it posed just about every structural and decorating problem imaginable. This was so viewers could relate the experience of renovating our semi to any problem they themselves might face.

For £15,000, and with a great deal of imagination and expertise, problems like subsidence, inadequate foundations, the replacing of a lean-to wooden kitchen with a modern extension, and a total

7

6

5

imaginative redecoration were successfully accomplished.

A separate booklet giving details of all the expert advice available, the suppliers of furniture and materials and costs is available by sending a stamped addressed envelope to the Pebble Mill at One office, BBC, Birmingham B5 7QQ.

1. Our super new extension with breakfast bar and utility room – the up-to-date units from 'Be Modern' at all Gas Showrooms.

2. 79, Damson Lane, transformed from a run-down semi to a dream home.

3. The transformation begins – and the lean-to kitchen just has to go.

4. In the smallest bedroom, a desk-bunk unit makes the most out of a very limited space, as does the choice of wallpaper and fabrics.

5/6. By knocking through a wall and installing sliding doors, the sense of space is increased in both the lounge and dining room. Both become lighter with more potential for new design concepts.

7. The main bedroom was given a sumptuous romantic look. One cheap but highly imaginative idea was to use a curtain pole to create a canopy effect.

J an Beaney's first series with 'Pebble Mill at One' was nothing less than sensational ... over 70,000 viewers wrote to us for the fact sheet and diagrams which we frantically devised to meet the demand for more information.

So Jan is back with her highly original approach which has helped elevate embroidery to an art form.

Detail of a curtain: machine embroidery on hot water dissolvable fabric.   June Lovesy

EMBROIDERY

FINDING INSPIRATION

There is one aspect of creative embroidery which seems to daunt people more than any other. They seem to face a total lack of confidence when trying to come up with their own design ideas.

My first and most important tip, is to pick one subject or theme which forces you to look really closely at the world around you.

Gardens are always an exciting source of design ideas whether they are carefully planned and manicured or overrun with weeds. They are just full of marvellous starting points for embroidery projects, giving masses of ideas for colour schemes, textural surfaces and patterns.

The obvious starting points are the flowers, vegetables, shrubs and trees – but walls, fences, broken down sheds, rust and erosion can also be really inspiring.

Even in winter a garden has a lot to offer but with the help of last year's snapshots, gardening books and seed catalogues, you shouldn't feel at all inhibited. You can find exciting colour combinations and designs at any time of the year. There are all sorts of treasures in your own back yard.

CHOOSING A COLOUR SCHEME

Choosing colour schemes can often be confusing and worrying, but it is the first step in any project, and while the actual technique might not present any difficulties, deciding what colours go together can!

To begin, I would like to suggest one way that you can achieve unusual and workable schemes. To start with, make yourself look carefully at everything around you. For instance, take an old stone or brick wall, a piece of corrugated iron, or a flower bed. From a distance it may appear grey or rust colour. Make a mental note of that fact. Then come up very close, select and look at one slab of stone, one brick or a centre of a flower. List the colours and their varying tones …grey, greyish green, a little pink, mauve or a flash of ochre and so on. Sketch or make a diagram and label the coloured areas with the describing words which mean the right colour to you.

The next important step is to note the colour proportions – always the secret of transferring a successful colour combination from its natural surroundings. Make a sketch of a block of stripes, each stripe representing the amount of colour you think you can see. This completes your colour scheme.

After making your diagram, seek out threads and fabric strips to wrap around a piece of card, trying to match the colours and their proportions. This exercise can also be carried out by cutting and tearing

Colour scheme inspired by rusty corrugated iron.

coloured papers from magazines. Your unusual colour scheme could inspire appliqué and patchwork projects, a colour plan for a room or an outfit of clothes. More importantly, you will probably discover a whole range of unexpected colour combinations that you were not aware of.

41

Julia Barton

MACHINE EMBROIDERY

I know that a number of people would love to machine embroider but think it's a technique well beyond them. It really isn't. If you have a swing needle machine you can have a go.

1. Read your manual and set the machine for darning. Thread it up ready for use. A size 80/90 needle would be more sturdy for your experiments.

2. Make sure that all the dials are set to '0'.

3. Remove the foot and following your manual's instructions, lower or cover the feed teeth. This will enable you to move the fabric in any direction rather than just forwards or backwards.

4. Select a narrow round (tambour) frame with an adjustable screw measuring about 7½–8″ in diameter. Preferably bind one of the rings with tape to ensure a tighter grip of the fabric.

5. Stretch your material, such as smooth cotton or calico, very tautly in the frame. Keep the grain of the fabric straight.

6. Put the frame under the needle with the material flat against the machine top (so you machine into the well of the frame).

7. Put down the pressure foot take-up lever which engages the tension. This is really important and it's easy to forget to do this if there is no foot in place. I often suggest that beginners put the darner foot on. I do, even after years of working on the machine!

8. Before you start stitching, always bring the bottom thread up through the fabric.

9. Hold the frame firmly but in a relaxed way and start to machine. Move the frame easily in all directions trying to keep a steady constant speed. Make lots of circular, square and loopy 'doodles' until you feel more relaxed; and don't go too slowly!

An easy first design to suit this method is to do a simple herbaceous border. Using fabric paints, either sponge or brush on the areas of colour and then loosely add the details with the machine thread. Don't try to depict each flower – just define areas, shape and the overall effect.

WATER DISSOLVABLE FABRICS

I would like to show you some super effects that you can get by experimenting with the comparatively new hot and cold water dissolvable fabrics.

Having freed your machine as shown previously, you prepare and work the machine in exactly the same way, but substitute these dissolvable fabrics for the ordinary ones.

There are two factors to remember – machine your design lines several times to make quite a heavy line, and make sure all the shapes connect with each other or your designs will fall to pieces when you dissolve the backing fabric.

Boiling Water Dissolvable Fabric
(Spun Alginate)

1. Machine the motif and cut away excess fabric.

2. Plunge into boiling water. The fabric will dissolve instantly and the embroidery shrinks up into a small shape.

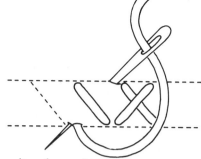

3. Take the embroidery out of the water and rinse in cold water.

4. Stretch out the embroidery to the correct shape, pin out and leave to dry.

As this process has a stiffish finish, it can also be modelled while wet and will keep its shape when dry. The more plunges in the boiling water, the softer the finished result. Most threads react quite well but a few shrink, so always experiment first before undertaking a big project.

Cold Water Dissolvable Fabric

1. Machine as above and cut away the excess fabric. You might find that you need to use a finer needle to prevent tearing the fabric.

2. Place into a bowl of cold water to dissolve the fabric as before.

This is an easier method but the fabric is not so nice to work on initially and it has a soft finish unless metallic yarns have been used. Simple appliqué shapes can be incorporated in both techniques. Each method has its advantages and disadvantages, but I think in time they will replace the machine lace techniques of using varnishing muslin or the acetate/acetone dissolved method.

The uses and applications of these techniques are limitless – staying with the 'garden' theme, how about some textile jewellery based on flowers and leaves, or some pretty summery curtains, or why not try using the delicate designs to brighten up part of last year's wardrobe?

CROSS STITCH

Cross stitch can be a challenging technique and I would like to suggest two possible starting points.

The first involves using iron-on or transfer fabric paints, and painting your design onto smooth, non-absorbent paper. Iron off onto a fabric such as poly-cotton, but through a net mesh fabric. This will leave your design transferred and already squared up: each square representing a cross stitch.

Subtle colours and a less formal design can be achieved with this method without having to count threads – the

tedious factor which puts so many people off.

Much freer cross stitching can also be very enjoyable. We have all been so conditioned to such a static approach to this technique. Correctly stitched and counted cross stitch borders can be delightful but other avenues can be explored, and give a much greater sense of creative achievement.

Detail of brick wall worked in cross stitches.

Janet Galloway

The second starting point could be a moss or lichen covered brick wall or a herbaceous border, and I am suggesting that you look at your design and decide which are the major colour areas (in the case of the wall it would obviously be the stonework and lichens). Block these in using thick thread – this could be carpet thread, fabric strips or ribbons.

Once these are established, use thinner threads (cottons or silks) to add the interesting detail such as other plants and insect life on the wall.

This would build up to lovely coloured and textured areas by encroaching and layering all sizes of cross stitches.

A more abandoned approach is what I'm aiming for!

43

FELT APPLIQUÉ

Felt is easily available, cheap to buy and is easy to use as it doesn't fray. However, it cannot be washed and should be dry cleaned. These factors should be considered when planning any projects.

Often in the past, felt has been used in a boring way, but if several layers of felt are used and areas of the design cut away to expose other colours beneath, more exciting effects can be obtained.

Initially, I suggest that you make a cut paper design. Draw a simple outline shape of a flower that you like. Don't worry about things like perspective but

take note of the general shape and size of the flower and its petals, and draw it like a diagram or make a flat pattern shape of it. Look carefully at the length of stem and the shape and size of the leaves. Once you have done the drawing, cut the shape out of the paper. Use this as a pattern for cutting several more. With a number of identical paper shapes, try arranging them into a pattern. By making the shapes join up or dovetail with each other, new patterns made from the background shapes emerge.

Layer and pin two or three pieces of different coloured felt together, having transferred the design by tacking around the paper shapes on the top fabric. Stab stitch, running stitch or free machine stitch can be worked following the lines of the design. With sharp scissors, carefully cut away the top layer of felt in selected areas to expose another colour beneath. Further cutting of the second layer will reveal the third.

Obviously you can see that the design and colour schemes can be developed into very rich decorative pieces and there are many possible variations on this theme. The completed design could then be used for wall hangings, panels, purses, belts and many other fashion accessories.

Felt sampler by Sheila Gray

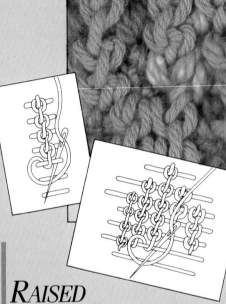

RAISED CHAIN BAND STITCH

As with the last series, I wanted to play around with a particular stitch to show how its applications can be widened simply by using a little imagination. Raised chain band stitch is one of my favourites. So often it is presented in books as a simple line stitch, a type of chain worked over parallel bars. As you can see in the accompanying diagram, straight, bar-like stitches are worked first and then the chain part is worked over them. This is the conventional manner, but by experimenting with varying threads and changing the scale of the stitch, simple but interesting effects can be built up. If you get the chance, do have a practice before the series begins.

A more unusual way of working the stitch is to build up solid areas and levels. To do this you can vary the length and spacing of the bars and then, working with a range of threads, start and end the chain part of the stitch in a random way. To make the surface even more raised, work new bars over the existing stitches and continue completing the chain. This action can be repeated until the desired height is reached. As you can see, this stitch can be quite versatile and can result in purely decorative work as well as embellish various articles, like floor cushions, shoulder bags and clutch bags.

I hope the series gives some fresh ideas and encourages more people to experiment and be more flexible with their embroidery techniques.

As ever my grateful thanks to Jean Littlejohn, my friend and colleague at Windsor, and all our students there who are always willing to give practical help and moral support.

USEFUL ADDRESSES

Send S.A.E. for price lists.

Madeira Threads (UK) Limited,
15 York Road, Knaresborough,
North Yorkshire HG5 0AF
Tel. 0423 868701

Manufacturer and supplier of cotton, metalised and synthetic yarns for machine embroidery, including Super twist, Toledo and Neon.

Silken Strands,
33 Linksway, Gatley, Cheadle,
Cheshire SK8 4LA

Range of machine embroidery threads.

Shades
57 Candlemas Lane, Beaconsfield,
Bucks HP9 1AE

Small quantities of cold water dissolvable fabric, boiling water dissolvable fabrics, machine embroidery threads, square net white polyester (7–12 holes to 1″)

Whaleys (Bradford) Limited
Harris Court, Great Horton, Bradford,
West Yorkshire BD7 4EQ
Tel: 0274 576718/9

Larger quantities of silk, boiling water dissolvable fabric and other fabrics suitable for dyeing. Send for price list and minimum length requirements.

Terry Taylor Associates Limited,
27 Woodland Road, Tunbridge Wells,
Kent TN4 9HW. Tel: 0892 35472

Fabric Paints: Deka silk, permanent, fluorescent and Iron-it-on. Send for details of nearest stockists and price lists.

USEFUL BOOKS

EMBROIDERY: NEW APPROACHES
Jan Beaney
Pelham Books £8.95

STITCHES: NEW APPROACHES
Jan Beaney
Batsford £14.95

'THE NEEDLEWORK SCHOOL'
PRACTICAL STUDY GROUP
Windward £9.95

MACHINE EMBROIDERY
Lacy and See-through technique.
Moyra McNeill
Batsford. November 1985.

Enquire at your nearest College of Further Education for details of recreational and exam classes for embroidery.

The Embroiderers' Guild holds lectures and day schools throughout the country. Information about local branches can be gained by sending S.A.E. to the Embroiderers' Guild, Apartment 41a, Hampton Court Palace, East Moseley, Surrey KT8 9AU

Felt, embroidery, knitting and crochet threads can usually be purchased from department stores or specialist shops.

An up-to-date list of suppliers is printed in EMBROIDERY magazine, published quarterly by The Embroiderers' Guild.

THE HERITAGE TAPESTRY

Marian Foster looks back over one of the most successful, some would claim historic, projects ever mounted by 'Pebble Mill at One'.

The Duchess of Devonshire looked slightly stunned as she inspected the latest priceless acquisition at one of Britain's most beautiful stately homes, Chatsworth House in Derbyshire.

The object which held her admiring attention as it went on exhibition was no antique. It was nevertheless an original. The Pebble Mill Heritage Tapestry was an historic tribute to the modern age by the people of that age, a work of artistry, craftsmanship and historical significance which may, in time to come, rival the celebrated Bayeux and Overlord tapestries of the past. It took up the entire length of her Grace's private dining room, blocking the fireplace and the door. Frankly, Her Grace hadn't realised it would be quite such a size, for Chatsworth was already overflowing.

She wasn't alone in her surprise for we'd all been astounded at the loving detail and beauty of each 6" component square, painstakingly created by thousands of Pebble Mill viewers of all ages, from every part of Britain. Already it was 14 panels long with each 8' x 2' panel containing the colourful efforts of 56 pairs of hands: and the work was only half done at this stage!

Who would have thought that the great British public, men, women and even children, would meet the challenge of sewing a 6" square with such relish? For the man who devised its creation, it was like a dream come true. Kaffe Fassett is a distinguished international knitwear designer, a man with a great love of natural textiles, textures and wonderful subtle tints and colourways. With the help of the British Wool Marketing Board, Kaffe launched an appeal on 'Pebble Mill at One' requesting 6" tapestry squares from viewers on the theme 'Count Your Blessings'.

Any Doubting Thomas's were soon proved wrong as thousands of squares poured out of bulging post bags sent in by old and young. The standard was exceptional and the choice of subject amazingly varied.

Chatsworth House is in the centre of a traditional wool region and the Heritage Tapestry, all sewn in wool, was proud testament and proof that one old skill hasn't been lost.

Many people depicted their own homes, thatched and terraced, treasured pets and favourite hobbies.

A phantom jet, for instance, was sewn not by a teenager but by our oldest sewer, Mrs Westley who is in her eighties, because her grandson was a pilot in the RAF. Mrs Pither, a farmer's wife from Gloucestershire, also had us fooled. Her Gertie the Cow was obvious enough but it was done in a geometric style we thought was deliberate until we discovered it was her first attempt and she didn't know how to do the round bits!

Yet another surprise came from Alf Cross of Longeaton. He did the view from his window – a power station with steaming cooling towers. He's been doing this sort of thing for years; but Morgan Francis, a carpenter by trade, had never held a tapestry needle in his life before. Nevertheless, while recovering from a bad back, he did a funny dark brown thing (a woodwork plane he explained afterwards) and was delighted he'd done so well.

The breathtaking ice dance of Torvill and Dean inspired armchair enthusiasts to show off their own artistry and 'frieze' their favourite champions for posterity and we were pleased to see that another TV show, a certain lunchtime extravaganza, proved popular too. Nice to know we're a blessing even if sometimes it's in disguise.

My own attempt, like many others, recalled Britain's rapidly disappearing seafaring days, and my childhood on the River Tyne, where I spent my holidays aboard the S.S. Cairngowan. My father had been a captain and I'm sure he would have loved to see how his six year old grandson Paul helped me with my effort. He did it at school, he told me.

Cats, dogs, budgies, robins, otters, bluebirds, tortoises and horses, every pet and animal you could think of had its

portrait done that summer – even Gillis. He was Donny MacLeod's pet beagle saved from a life of experimentation. Years later, he still has tattooed identification on his ear, but now he's spoiled rotten and loves every bit of it!

There are cups of tea, rugby, computers and coalmines, swimming and cycling, hamburgers and music, trams and landscapes and, yes, even Pythagoras' Theorem for mathematicians amongst us.

One large wide panel is on permanent display in Pebble Mill itself. A cheerfully embroidered Santa Claus became the central feature of our Pebble Mill Christmas card last year. It was, however, upstaged by a card sent to me by Cynthia Weatherby with greetings and a Christmas scene all hand-sewn.

Our Heritage Tapestry has been exhibited in a dozen towns and cities and attendance figures were doubled at galleries the length of the land. Now, spurred on by our efforts, village and townswomen's groups from the Hebrides to the Midlands are making their own heritage tapestries.

Since our first panels were completed at the Embroiderer's Guild Headquarters at Hampton Court, other groups have helped us out too. Each square has had a border added to make them all exactly the same size; work which cannot be rushed. Seven additional panels have just been added and there's still more to come from Styal Mill in Cheshire where the final work is being sewn together. So a second tapestry is beginning to take shape. It will probably turn out to be as enormous as the first.

When we announced that we were looking for a permanent home for this second masterpiece, we were inundated with requests from stately homes all over the country. Eventually, after much deliberation, we have accepted the kind offer of Harewood House, set in the beautiful Yorkshire countryside.

So, well done all you sewing bees. But if you have any more ideas, don't tell Kaffe.

Moyra Bremner is presenting a new series of her ever-popular 'Supertips from Pebble Mill', having spent a hectic year travelling the length and breadth of the land collecting more time and money-saving ideas. Here she reveals more of her acquisitions.

You've probably noticed that the curious thing about flypaper is that it collects more flies than you actually see buzzing about. Well, tips are rather like that – there are a lot more of them around than you'd think. If you read my first book 'Supertips To Make Life Easy,' you might think it just about exhausted the supply of ways to save time and money. Not a bit of it. As you'll have seen on 'Pebble Mill at One,' there were topics, like gardening and child care, which I didn't have space for. Then, once 'Supertips To Make Life Easy' was published, and people knew I was interested in tips of all kinds, I suddenly became a magnet for everyone's favourite short cuts and money-savers and it became clear that I'd have to write another book to put them in. So 'Supertips 2' was born. And, for me, the fascinating thing was the way the tips turned up in the most unexpected places.

I was signing copies in a bookshop in Liverpool, when the manageress took me aside and said that she and her mother had devised a marvellous way of transferring feathers from an old eiderdown into a pillow, without them flying everywhere. She said they'd cleaned out their vacuum cleaner, attached the empty cushion in place of the hoover bag and simply used the vacuum cleaner nozzle to suck the feathers out of the eiderdown and straight into the pillow. And if you've ever tried to transfer feathers and had them stick all over both you and the room, you'll realise just how much hassle this marvellously practical idea can save.

The next day a girl in a television make-up department showed me how she hung the clips for heated rollers neatly round the edge of a glass. In this way you can easily pick out the size you need with one hand, while holding the roller in place with one hand, while holding the roller in place with the other – easy and effective. Then I was talking to a senior executive from a cosmetics company and she pointed out that make-up pencils often broke when she sharpened them because the centres were soft. She told me they'd last much longer if you always put them in the fridge for a while to harden, before sharpening them. She was right. Two good tips for a 'beauty' chapter.

I dropped into a house which was being done up into flats to see if I could buy a second-hand door and a workman, who said he'd seen me on 'Pebble Mill at One,' called me over to look at the way he put a screw into chipboard without the chipboard breaking. Just a matter of drilling the right-sized hole and gluing in a Rawlplug to hold the screw securely. Obvious really, but I certainly hadn't ever thought of it.

Then a man who'd also seen me, one lunchtime, demonstrating how to saw the bottom off a door, wrote to tell me an excellent solution to the problem of it being left a touch too long, and then dragging at the carpet. He said all you had to do was slide a large sheet of sandpaper under the door, stand on each end of the sandpaper and swing the door to and fro over it. I found it worked like a charm, though I did have to add my own modification; to get the door to clear the carpet completely, you need to gradually raise the sandpaper by sliding sheets of newspaper under it.

It often happens like that: people send me tips which almost work, but need some extra touches to make them really effective. That's why I like to check every tip myself and see just how they work for me. I was horrified to discover that a lot of people imagined I simply wrote down the tips just as they were sent or had a team of researchers checking them for me.

Of course not all tips need to be checked; some are so obviously excellent that I immediately know I'll want to use them. For example, in response to a competition run by 'Woman's Hour,' on Radio 4, a listener wrote in to say that if a garment needed to dry on a hanger the best way to hang it on a washing line was to put it on TWO hangers, with the hooks facing in opposite directions – then it would never fall off the line. The perfect solution to what I, with a very windy garden, had always considered one of washday's most irritating problems.

And it was from another BBC listener that I received a real time-saver for a chapter on surviving one's children. A mother pointed out that when children first transfer from a cot to a proper bed, they don't use the lower half of the bed, so she suggested making up their beds with just one sheet folded in half like an 'apple pie bed,' so it acted as both top and bottom sheet. A tip which halves the time it takes to change the bed and also halves the sheet wash.

Being interested in keeping the number of poisonous chemicals in our environment down to a minimum, I was interviewing some biologists at the University of Southampton about using pheremones to trap destructive tree moths, when I heard that biological controls were now available to gardeners and hastened to get the details for a gardening chapter.

But the road to collecting tips doesn't always go smoothly: unfortunately, some tips are learnt the hard way.

Being organised is something I find necessary, but I can't pretend it comes easily to me. So tips for my chapter on getting organised tended to come from bitter experience. It was only AFTER I'd lost all track of the food in my freezer that an organised friend suggested putting one label on the food and a twin label on the outside of the freezer (which you peel off when you remove the food). It works wonderfully and even my children can now find what they want.

Happily this process of tip-gathering never seems to end, but that does mean I've been given a number of excellent tips since I finished 'Supertips 2.' So maybe the best way to see they aren't wasted is to share some of them with you. For example, a journalist on the 'Daily Mirror' buttonholed me to say she'd found a way to prevent water ruining a book it was split on: her solution was to dab off the worst of it and dry the page rapidly with a hair dryer. And certainly this has worked extremely well on the books I've tried it on and it's prevented the paper crinkling up, though I can't be certain it will work safely on all types of paper.

On a radio phone-in, one woman rang to say that she'd found a way to get fragile cakes unbroken out of the cake tin she'd cooked them in: she used a loose-bottomed tin and cut them from the base with a piece of strong cotton, which she said was far less likely to break them than a knife. And it is. Then another rang to say that, being elderly, she tried to avoid climbing ladders and found a garden hoe an excellent implement for stripping wallpaper at the tops of walls. Of course, you do have to be a bit careful how you wield the hoe or you could end up with holes in your walls, but having an elderly mother who's far too keen on ladder-climbing for my peace of mind, I'm all for a tip which keeps elderly feet firmly on the ground.

It was a man on the same phone-in who pointed out that you could use interlocking children's bricks to plan out decorative brickwork for the home and garden and to calculate the number of bricks you would need. An ingenious idea, though you have to be absolutely sure the proportioning of the

49

miniature bricks matches that of the real ones, or you could be in trouble. And it was a lighting man for a television programme I was on who told me he saved the polystyrene packing from equipment like hi-fi's and microwave ovens, cut it into mats and used these to lie on when he was doing the car repairs. Warm and waterproof, it is indeed ideal for the job.

Hearing this, the presenter of the show chipped in and said her mother had found a new use for microwave ovens – she used them to give new life to her old lipsticks. Apparently she scrapes the left-over ends into the type of plastic box with tiny compartments designed for fishing tackle, then pops the box in the microwave and melts the lipsticks so she has a smooth palette of colours. Not having a microwave, I scraped some lipstick ends into such a box and descended on my local Bejams, asking if I could try to melt them in a microwave. The manager looked around nervously – he was one of those who can smell a journalist a mile off. "Where's the 'Candid Camera,'" he muttered. I reassured him that this was just some research for 'Pebble Mill at One' and nothing to be afraid of, and we all stood round and watched while the lipstick resolutely refused to melt. Not until three minutes were up did the desolate lumps of colour suddenly transform themselves into the smooth palette I'd been told about, but the end result really was worth having. Though I have to admit that the best part about it was the hit or miss element. I'd put several stumps into the same compartment to see if they'd blend together, and they blended beautifully – but it would take a very good eye for colour to predict whether a certain combination of stumps would give you a colour you'd love or loathe.

Of course not everyone who buttonholes me has a useful tip to pass on.

Just as doctors get accosted at parties by people desperate to describe their symptoms in alarming detail, so I get cornered by those whose meringues unfailingly weep and whose children have poured ink over their three-piece suite.

I am also sent tips which leave me scratching my head and wondering what on earth the writer could possibly be meaning. One such letter came from a pharmacist, on smartly headed notepaper. It said "Dear Madam, here is a tip which will be useful to people who are wondering what to do about falling hair. My tip is, put it in a cardboard box." Never let it be said that tip collecting is dull!

TEN TOP TIPS
From Moyra's current 'Pebble Mill at One' series.

1 To avoid getting specks of paint on a pair of glasses, DIY decorators can smooth cling film tightly over the lenses.

2 Avoid the temptation to change an attachment on an electric drill without unplugging the drill by tying the chuck key to the plug end of the cable. The bonus is that you won't lose the chuck key either.

3 An elastic band tied around the telephone and over the rests can prevent blocked incoming calls and accidental dialling while a child is playing with the receiver.

4 To ensure fair share when dividing up children's treats, let one cut and the other choose. Divide and rule!

5 The burnt bit of grilled or roast meat can be scraped off more easily after being covered with a damp cloth or kitchen roll for a minute or two.

6 If you don't have time to clear up a sticky, jammy spill on a hard floor, sprinkle it with talc. It won't be clean but it won't be sticky to walk on either.

7 Buttons will stay on twice as long if you rub the thread through beeswax before sewing. Beeswax blocks can be brought from most hardware stores.

8 If really sharp creases are needed in heavy woollen trousers, rub a candle down the crease line on the wrong side before pressing in the crease.

9 Lawn mower blades will stay in good condition throughout the winter if they are oiled. To do this safely, put the oil on an old fashioned cotton dish mop. It slides in between the blades easily and keeps fingers out of the way.

10 Tie trees to stakes using an old nylon stocking wound in a figure eight. It is cheaper than buying a tree tie and won't rub the bark off as it sways in the wind.

MEDICINE·MATTERS

Pebble Mill's medical man, Dr David Delvin, answers queries on a whole host of health topics, everything from varicose veins to multiple sclerosis.

And as a medical journalist and writer of world-wide acclaim, he is always investigating breakthroughs in surgery and medical practice.

Here he highlights the work being pioneered in two areas of medicine which affect us all.

NEW APPROACHES TO HEART DISEASE
THE SIZE OF THE PROBLEM

Breakthroughs are desperately needed in the field of heart disease. For this is Britain's No. 1 killer!

Rather surprisingly, very few people seem to know this. A recent Gallup poll showed that most of the population were quite unaware that it's heart trouble that is likely to kill most of us.

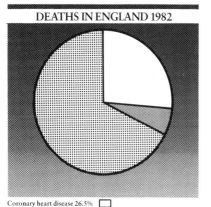

DEATHS IN ENGLAND 1982

Coronary heart disease 26.5% □
Other heart related diseases 6% ▨

The 'Pie diagram' shows just how massive this problem is in Britain today.

Another thing that many people fail to realise is that it's only in Britain and in Western countries that people are affected by this terrifying epidemic of heart disease. In most under-developed countries (for instance, Jamaica – where I worked for some years) heart disease is a great rarity. Recent research has suggested reasons why we should be so very vulnerable to this deadly killer whereas people in other countries aren't. These include the typical Western diet with its high content of saturated fat and the high level of smoking in developed countries.

Sorry to start off on such a gloomy note! But we have to be very clear that this is a frighteningly common disorder. Heart disease now touches nearly every family in the land.

It's alarming to report that in the last few years, post-mortems on young soldiers or even young teenagers killed in road accidents have shown that – thanks to our Western lifestyle – most of them already have the early stages of heart disease in their bodies.
WHAT IS IT?

To understand the advances that have been made in treating heart disease, you first have to understand what heart trouble is.

If you look at figure A, you'll understand the basic nature of the problem. Figure A shows your heart – and, as you can see, there are a number of little tubes running round it.

These tubes are the coronary arteries. They're absolutely vital, because their job is to supply blood (and therefore oxygen and fuel) to the muscular tissue of your heart.

If these coronary arteries become blocked for even a few seconds, you will experience severe pain in your chest.

Fig. A

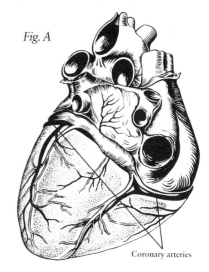

Coronary arteries

51

If the blockage lasts more than a minute or two, part of the heart muscle will die – as you can see from Figure B.

Fig. B

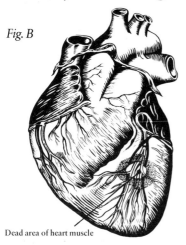

Dead area of heart muscle

And if the damage is bad enough – well then, sadly enough, the owner of the heart will die too.

That kind of blockage produces what's called a heart attack. Its medical name is 'myocardial infarct'. Many people call it a coronary thrombosis – though, as we'll see in a minute, that term is actually incorrect. However, the popular abbreviation 'coronary' has now passed into the language.

WHY DOES THE BLOCKAGE OCCUR?

But why does the blockage of the coronary arteries occur?

Why do so many men (and women) collapse – and often die – with a blocked artery?

Many people think they know the answer to that one. They've heard the phrase 'coronary thrombosis', and they know that 'thrombosis' means 'clot'.

So they assume that these heart attacks occur because a clot (thrombosis) develops inside a coronary artery – and blocks it.

Unfortunately, recent research shows that in most heart attacks, that just isn't true.

Clots <u>can</u> block the coronary arteries. But in many cases, post-mortem examination shows that there just wasn't a clot there.

It now appears that in many coronaries, what has happened is that the artery has just gone into a kind of spasm. As it's only a very narrow tube, just a minute or two of spasm can have really disastrous results.

One final and very important point: it's now clear that <u>any</u> type of blockage of the coronary arteries is much, much more likely *if* your coronary arteries have already been narrowed by the fatty, degenerative disease which (as I've said) affects most British adults to a greater or lesser extent.

At the end of this article, we'll deal with ways of trying to prevent this dangerous and deadly fatty infiltration.

WAYS OF TREATING HEART DISEASE

But first, what modern methods are available in treating heart disease?

Many exciting advances have been made in recent years. They include:

- Heart transplants
- Artificial hearts
- Coronary by-pass operations
- New drugs
- New psychological approaches.

We'll look at these breakthroughs in turn.

HEART TRANSPLANTS

Heart transplants are now giving really good results. When a person's heart is hopelessly damaged by the type of coronary diseases we've been talking about (or sometimes by some other disorder) then it's sometimes the case that a transplant is the only answer.

In fact, while this Pebble Mill book was being prepared, Mr Terence English

(who is one of the world's top transplant surgeons) told me that many more lives could be saved in Britain if only he and his Cambridge team were able to carry out cardiac transplants more regularly.

The chief problem is that not enough people realise what spectacular advances have been made in transplant surgery – so they're reluctant to carry cards making their hearts (and other organs) available in the event of a fatal accident.

Today's cardiac transplant surgery is an incredibly sophisticated (and usually highly successful) operation. But the essentials of the operation are clear from Figure C.

Healthy area of heart: not removed

Diseased area of heart removed

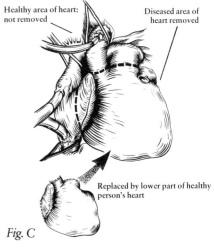

Replaced by lower part of healthy person's heart

Fig. C

As you can see, the basic idea is that the surgeon <u>doesn't</u> remove the whole heart (as most people think).

Instead, he removes the lower ⅔ of the heart – which is the part where coronary artery disease has usually produced its worst ravages.

The topmost part of the heart isn't removed. Fortunately, it's not often affected by coronary disease. But the reason why it's retained is that it's here that the nerves which fire off the heart (and so make it work) actually enter the heart muscle – as do the tubes which bring blood to the heart.

The diseased part of the heart is then replaced by the equivalent area of a healthy person's heart. Fortunately, in the last year or two the problem of <u>rejection</u> of this new tissue has been minimised – thanks to the skilled use of anti-rejection drugs such as azathioprine.

THE ARTIFICIAL HEART

In the last year or so, the Americans have achieved the astonishing success of implanting a small number of artificial hearts into people with severe heart disease.

Basically, these artificial hearts are just pumping devices. They use a hydraulic system (powered by an electrical source outside the body) to drive the person's blood round his circulation.

Unfortunately, the results so far have not been very good. This is mainly because of the truly immense difficulties in safely joining up the plumbing of an artificial heart.

Unlike human tissue, plastic doesn't heal up along joins, so leaks are common. Also, clots tend to form on the surfaces of the synthetic material used for the artificial heart. The results can be disastrous.

So it seems unlikely that the artificial heart will replace heart transplanting – or, indeed, replace the remarkable advance described in the next section.

CORONARY ARTERY BY-PASS

Though few people seem to have heard much about this operation, it has been – or so cardiac surgeons claim – one of the great advances of modern surgery.

What does it involve? Figure D makes it all clear. As you can see, when a section of the coronary artery is dangerously narrow, the surgeon can simply remove it – and then replace it with a short segment of vein, taken from the patient's leg! The life-giving blood can flow through it again.

Fig. D

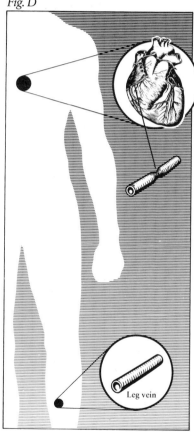

Narrowed coronary artery is removed and replaced by leg vein

Some thousands of patients have now undergone this dramatic life-saving operation. Among them are such famous names as General Al Haig.

OTHER OPERATIONS

Regrettably, other headline-catching operations on the human heart have not been as successful. The much publicised recent cases of animal hearts (e.g. baboon hearts) being transplanted into children have not so far resulted in any lives being saved.

NEW DRUGS – AND NEW WAYS OF GIVING THEM

The last year or two have seen the development of a series of new drugs which are extremely effective in treating many people with heart problems.

Also of interest are new ways of giving drugs to patients with heart disease. Most importantly, a way has been found of giving heart patients a <u>continuous</u> dosage of a drug which helps to keep angina attacks away.

Until now, it's been difficult to achieve continuous dosage, since absorption of drugs by mouth is rather unreliable.

But as you can see from Figure E, a very clever new advance is a method of delivering the drug by impregnating a special sticking plaster with it.

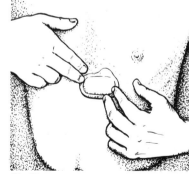

Fig. E

All the patient has to do is to pop the sticking plaster on his/her chest – and the drug will be safely and continuously absorbed through the skin over the next 24 hours.

NEW PSYCHOLOGICAL METHODS

The fact that stress is probably a factor in at least some cases of heart disease has recently led to a re-appraisal of psychological methods of treating heart patients.

In other words, some doctors are beginning to adopt the attitude that if you can help a person to reduce his stress level, there may be less chance of him having a further heart attack.

Meditation and acupuncture are being extensively used in this way. An interesting new development is the use of a relaxation technique called autogenics, which aims to help people conquer their stresses through conscious relaxation of the body.

It's claimed that this technique will reduce a person's high blood pressure, without the need for drugs, and make him or her less liable to attacks of angina.

PREVENTION OF HEART DISEASE

Finally, what about prevention of this killer epidemic of heart disease, which causes so many premature deaths in the UK?

There's much controversy about this, but most doctors are now agreed that these are the really important preventive measures which everyone in this country should take:

■ Avoid smoking – this is believed to be the biggest single avoidable cause of heart trouble.

■ Keep your intake of saturated fats down to a reasonable level. Saturated fats are mostly, though not entirely, <u>animal</u> fats, such as those found in fatty meat, butter, cheese, milk, cream, lard, and eggs. Margarine contains saturated fats too – but it's widely felt that soft margarines may be safer.

■ Take a moderate and sensible amount of exercise.

On other aspects of prevention of coronary heart disease, there's violent dissent – with the manufacturers of certain foods getting exceedingly upset if doctors suggest that the public should cut down on this or that item of diet!

But perhaps the most interesting suggestion to have emerged this year is the new claim that eating fish just once or twice a week could help protect you against the national epidemic of heart disease.

There's no way it's going to be proven for quite a few years. But the evidence is persuasive – so much so that I personally am going to be eating a lot more fish during the next run of 'Pebble Mill at One.'

ADVANCES IN ANTE-NATAL DIAGNOSIS

THE SIZE OF THE PROBLEM

Nearly three-quarters of a million women have babies in the United Kingdom each year. Unfortunately, it has to be admitted that quite a lot of those babies are born with some serious or minor abnormality.

Indeed, every mother's (and father's) secret fear is that 'there might be something wrong with the baby.'

Happily, exciting new techniques have recently been developed which enable doctors to make the diagnosis of abnormalities during pregnancy itself.

Very often, these new techniques make it possible for something to be done about the condition. Indeed, we are now rapidly moving towards a situation when it will be possible for surgeons to operate inside the mother's womb in order to correct defects in the unborn baby!

There is also very real hope that doctors will soon be able to manipulate genes to ensure that babies are not born with appalling genetic handicaps.

ULTRASOUND – THE GREAT NEW REPLACEMENT FOR X-RAY

Until recent years the main way of finding out what was going on within the womb was to X-ray the mother. Unfortunately, X-rays didn't give all that much information about the baby (though they could at least tell you how many babies you were going to have!). Also, there's no doubt that they were dangerous.

So X-raying of pregnant mums has now more or less stopped in Britain. It's been replaced by the remarkable technique of ultrasound.

What is ultrasound? It's a type of soundwave which penetrates solid objects (anything from metal to mums, in fact) and bounces back. From the speed with which it rebounds from the various layers of the object, it's possible to construct a picture of what lies within.

Ultrasound was first used by engineers in order to find out what was going on deep within the layers of certain metal objects. Today it is used by obstetricians to find out exactly what is going on inside an expectant mother's womb.

The type of picture which is produced is shown in figure A. Ultrasound does not let the obstetrician see your baby's face – or whether he's handsome or not! But it does allow the doctor to see the general structure of your baby and whether there are any major physical abnormalities. Also, if the picture is taken at the right angle, it is sometimes possible to tell whether the baby is a girl or boy.

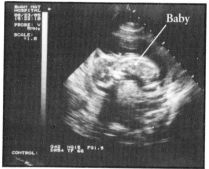

Fig. A

Ultrasound is also very very useful as an aid to some of the diagnosis techniques which we are going to look at in a moment. This is because when a doctor has to put a needle into the mother's womb, it's very helpful to have an ultrasound picture which tells him just exactly where the baby is lying.

ALPHA-FETOPROTEIN – THE CHEMICAL CLUE

One of the great tragedies of obstetrics is the fact that so many babies are born with severe abnormalities of the brain and spinal cord – particularly spina bifida.

This last abnormality is tragically common in certain areas of the British Isles and yet we are uncertain as to its cause.

However, research in Scotland has come up with the surprising finding that expectant mothers whose babies are likely to have spina bifida (and certain other abnormalities), usually have a high blood level of a chemical called alpha-fetoprotein (AFP). So, the mother's blood level of AFP can now be used as a screening test for spina bifida. I <u>must</u> emphasize that not every woman who has a high AFP level is necessarily going to have a child with spina bifida. However, if her blood AFP level is high, she should go on to have a further investigation. This will involve taking some fluid from inside her womb by a process known as amniocentesis (see below) so that this fluid can be tested for AFP.

If the AFP level in the womb fluid is very high, then this is a very strong indication that the baby could have spina bifida.

AMNIOCENTESIS

Amniocentesis just means putting a slim needle through the mother's stomach and into her womb – so as to draw off some of the fluid in the womb for testing.

This is not very painful – at least, so I'm told by mothers who've experienced it! However, it has to be said that there is a very small risk of miscarriage associated with this procedure. So it certainly shouldn't be undertaken lightly. I can't foresee a time when every single pregnant mother will have amniocentesis done.

What is the test done for? Well, as we've seen above, one use for it is to test the levels of AFP in the womb fluid in order to check for spina bifida.

Another important use is in the test for Down's syndrome (formerly known as mongolism). The fluid which has been withdrawn contains a number of living cells. These cells can be 'cultured' in a laboratory to show up their chromosome patterns, patterns which will indicate the likelihood of Down's syndrome or other chromosome abnormalities.

CHORION BIOPSY

One of the most amazing new techniques which has been developed in the last year or so is the diagnostic method called chorion biopsy.

What does this mean? Well, you can see what's involved from figure B.

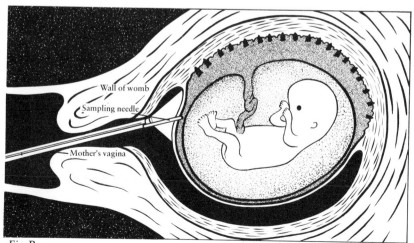

Wall of womb

Sampling needle

Mother's vagina

Fig. B

Chorion biopsy, also known as chorion villus sampling (CVS), is a very clever method of removing a tiny amount of tissue from inside the womb very early in pregnancy. In fact, it can be done much earlier in pregnancy than amniocentesis can – which is a great plus.

As you can see, the technique is done from below, so that there is no need to push a needle through the skin of the mother's abdomen. For this reason, some doctors are claiming that CVS is less likely to cause miscarriage than amniocentesis is – though this hasn't been conclusively proven yet.

What is the point of doing the test? Well, the little pieces of tissue which are removed (which are in fact tiny fragments of the membrane surrounding the sac in which the baby develops) contain many clues to the child's future development.

The cells in the tissue can be used for genetic analysis and for very early diagnosis of congenital abnormalities.

The results take only two to three days compared with about three weeks in the case of amniocentesis.

FETOSCOPY – LOOKING INSIDE THE WOMB

A quite astonishing advance has been the development of fetoscopy, which simply means looking inside the womb. This is done with a special instrument which is shown in figure C.

The exciting thing about fetoscopy is that not only does it let the obstetrician see the baby and the cord and the placenta, but it also gives him or her the possibility of actually <u>treating</u> the baby within the womb as well.

As you can see from figure C, the surgeon pushes a slim instrument through the wall of the mother's abdomen and into the womb. The instrument contains a light source so that he can look down directly into the cavity of the womb. With the type of

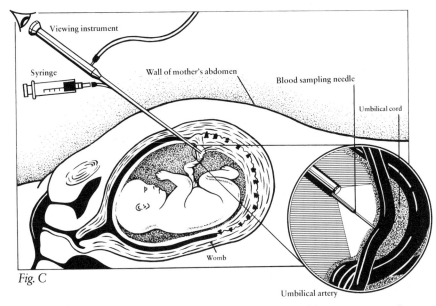

Fig. C

instrument shown in our diagram, it is possible for him to put a sampling needle straight into one of the blood vessels of the umbilical cord (the umbilical artery) and draw off samples of the baby's blood into the syringe which is attached to the instrument.

Naturally, these blood samples can be used for testing for congenital diseases. But the needle can also be used to give the baby a blood transfusion.

It can also be used to give him special nutrients or, if necessary, drugs.

Very soon, doctors hope to be able to use the same technique in order to infuse certain special cells through the needle in an attempt to correct genetic defects.

Furthermore, they intend to try the same method in order to transplant bone marrow directly into the foetus, to treat certain very serious cases of congenital anaemia.

Finally, it is now hoped that a sophisticated development of this

technique will enable surgeons actually to operate inside the womb – to correct structural developments, such as cleft palate or hare lip.

Surgeons are hopeful that it will be possible to use surgery inside the womb to treat more severe and life threatening conditions, such as heart and lung abnormalities and even spina bifida.

Curiously enough, surgery within the womb could be preferable to surgery after the birth of the child because it is believed that the healing process after surgery is probably a great deal better inside the womb. So it is very possible that surgery done during ante-natal life would leave no scars at all.

child care

Penelope Leach would hate to be described as an 'expert' on child care. She takes great pains to stress that all she wants is to share the skills and experience of others. Parents must decide for themselves what is best for their child.

Penelope has been a frequent broadcaster and contributor to newspapers and magazines since her first book 'Baby and Child' was published in 1974. She first appeared on 'Pebble Mill at One' last year and, this season, returns with more help and advice to help parents deal with some of the more common problems they may have to face.

NEW BABIES How to judge whether they are 'OK'

The trouble with taking a brand new baby home from hospital is that he or she is so new that nobody yet knows them – not even you! Once you have had them around for a few weeks you will know how much they usually cry, sleep, suck and look at you; you will know what their dirty nappies usually look like and what sound they make when they are hungry or pleased or frightened. Once you know all that, you will be able to tell whether today's crying is 'too much;' today's sucking is 'too little' or whether today's nappies or sounds are 'peculiar.' You will have baselines for their behaviour when they are 'OK' and that will make it much easier for you to know if something is wrong.

For the moment, though, while you are getting to know them, you need a sort of checklist in your mind that you can run over whenever you feel concerned about your baby. You need to know, for example, that refusing a feed is far more likely to suggest trouble than is refusing to sleep. Unlike older babies or toddlers, brand new ones cannot afford to skip feeds entirely because they must have the liquid in their milk, even when they are not very hungry for the food part of it. And if they will not sleep today, but only cry, you need to know that wakeful days are normal and that lots of crying is only likely to mean anything if your baby doesn't stop when you pick him up.

There are comforting guidelines to help you stay relaxed between the midwife's welcome visits and to help you decide when it really would be sensible to use that telephone number that she – and later your Health Visitor – will have given you.

For the first ten days your Community Midwife will call every day and you will have a telephone number on which you can reach her, or one of her colleagues, in an emergency. Later on, your Health Visitor will also give you a number so that you can call on her when the Midwife has 'signed you off.' Nobody will mind if you scream for help 'unnecessarily' because they know how much anxiety a new baby can cause and they must know that instant reassurance is necessary for you even if there turns out to be nothing wrong with the new baby.

When a small baby – say one who is under 3 months – is unwell, the signs and symptoms you need to watch out for are sometimes very different from the ones you will notice when the baby is older.

We all know that sick babies and children usually run temperatures. Many families use a thermometer or fever-scanner as an important aid to recognising children's illnesses. Very young babies often don't run a fever at all even when they are quite definitely unwell; on the contrary, a baby who is really in trouble may have a very low temperature. He may be very, very quiet, too, unlike an older baby who will probably be fretful if he feels unwell. Since it's especially important to 'play safe' with very young babies, we hope these tips will make it easier for parents to judge when to seek a doctor's advice or reassurance.

Crying and comforting are important topics for anyone who is caring for a baby. Whether you are a parent, a grandparent-in-charge or a childminder, it's very hard to stay loving and patient with a baby who cries a great deal and seems impossible to comfort. Sometimes it gets to feel as if the baby were doing it on purpose: refusing to stop crying just to keep you awake or make you feel bad.

If the baby is crying because he needs something definite, like more food, nothing will stop him except meeting that need by feeding him. But if he is crying because he is generally uncomfortable or vaguely discontented, there are lots of ways

57

of comforting him which are worth a try. No single one of them will work every time for every baby, but having something to try usually helps adults to feel less helpless and sometimes some combination of comforts really does produce the jackpot of peace for everyone.

Here then are some of the tricks (I hope you will see them work on at least some of our miserable babies!) so that you can have them at the back of your mind for the next time you find yourself saying "I don't know what to do; I've tried everything…"

There's wrapping a small baby up, for instance. This modern version of old-fashioned swaddling sometimes provides a baby with a kind of comforting 'holding' which cuts out the disturbing outside world and enables him to relax into sleep. There are lots of different kinds of rocking, from walking with the baby to sitting with him in a rocking chair. Parents who say rocking doesn't help their babies are often rocking too slowly; there is a particular speed which calms most babies and it is just the speed they probably got used to as their mums moved around while they were still inside. Then, of course, there is the sucking. There's a lot to be said for encouraging a breast fed baby to suck for comfort as well as food. Some mothers avoid this in case their nipples get sore but, once breast feeding is properly established, most nipples can stand almost anything. Very 'sucky' babies can sometimes get comfort from their own thumbs or fingers from a very early age, but, if yours is one of the many who finds its own thumb too small for proper suction, dummies are worth thinking about. There are pros and cons, but a more contented baby right now may be more important than the problems you might have in getting off the dummy later.

Development is a process not a race and, once you are sure that your baby is well and reasonably contented (most of the time!) a lot of your concern will probably turn to how well he or she is doing. Parents who want their babies to be especially 'forward' and are depressed whenever a neighbour's baby seems to be growing up faster than their own, let themselves in for a lot of unnecessary anxiety – anxiety which can rub off on the child, too.

While there are standard milestones, like learning to roll over, sit up, crawl, stand, walk and talk, perfectly normal babies do these things at quite different times and going slowly between, say, learning to sit and learning to crawl, does not mean that a baby is 'slow' overall.

Although these milestones are useful to the staff of your clinic, whose job is to pick up the tiny minority of babies who really might have developmental problems, they are by no means the most important signs of your own baby's overall

development. That baby who sits – and sits and sits – while all his little friends crawl away may be doing much more adventurous things with his hands and his toys than they are. A baby cannot learn everything at once. Some concentrate on one kind of activity, some on another. It is only if you consider the whole child, as a real person, that you can really tell how he is doing.

SAFETY

1. Mobile babies will come next because as your baby does start to crawl, stand, cruise and then walk (or preferably before they do any of those things) you really do have to consider their survival in a home made for large, sensible adults.

Safety precautions are not just for your child, they are for you as well. If you have ever been with a parent and mobile baby or toddler in a home which was not 'child-proofed' you will know that the adult simply cannot relax for a moment or do anything but follow the child around. If you have to live like that, day after day, you will soon feel that you are getting nothing done at all. Every home needs at least one area (and it must be the area where you want to spend most of your time) within which a crawler or a toddler is reasonably safe from everything but his own bumps and bangs. 'Child-proofing' most homes is not very difficult and it need not be expensive. There are extremely useful safety-gadgets on the market (dummy electric plugs, for example) but more important than what you buy is the child's eye view you take of 'his' space and the imagination you bring to making it safe for him as well as comfortable for you.

Once your baby can crawl, he will travel about the floor taking a close look, making a grab for, and putting in his mouth, anything he can get hold of. If you get down on your hands and knees and look along floor-level, you may see all kinds of things that he'd better not be able to see…Is that the cat's dish of food? If this is the place the baby is to play, the cat will have to be fed somewhere else from now on. Are those your best records on the bottom shelf? If you do not want the covers chewed, they had better find a higher home.

Babies start the business of learning to walk by pulling themselves up from a sitting to standing position using any convenient piece of furniture. Although tumbles are inevitable at this stage, you do not want your baby to fall over backwards with a coffee table on top of him, so you need to check that all the furniture in 'his' space is solid and firm enough for him to pull up on safely. If you don't want to move a too-flimsy chair or plant-stand altogether, you may be able to wedge it under something else, or re-arrange the rest of the furniture so that the baby cannot get to it. You will also need to think about your comfort habits in relation to his safety. There's no reason why you should not have your beloved open fire provided it has a p<u>roper</u> child-proof guard which is <u>always</u> used. You can have your relaxing drink if you want it, but the alcohol will have to be stored in a locked cupboard or another room. As for your cigarettes and matches, they should be carried on your person and never be left lying around or in the handbag your baby will so much enjoy exploring.

Once children are past the toddler stage, home-safety is usually less of a problem because they are more able to cope and safety habits (like locking up fluids) have become a habit for all of you.

SAFETY

2. Pre-school children out and about raise vital questions about their safety in the streets and in the community. Sexual abuse is every parent's horror. We think that the conventional advice to teach children 'not to talk to strangers' begs some very important questions and we have a rather different line to suggest.

It is a really important lesson that children shouldn't go with strangers the moment they can walk and talk without reporting in to whoever is in charge.

These lessons can start in the park when the child wants to move from the sandpit to swings, and can be carried on to when the child starts school; he must come home from school immediately and report home before he goes out to play. No child has ever come to harm just through talking and since talking politely to adults outside the family – doctors, teachers, nurses, shopkeepers – is something we want to encourage, conventional teaching seems misplaced.

We also think that while the Green Cross Code is admirable in its way, parents can do much more to help their children cope with modern road conditions than just teach that code. There are some basic precautions which really help your under-five to avoid perverted people: for instance, has it ever occurred to you that if children wear a tee-shirt with their name on it, any stranger can address them by name and easily pass as 'a friend of Daddy?'

Just as a baby who cries a great deal can make your life miserable in the early months, so a child who is very shy or aggressive can ruin everything in the toddler and pre-school years.

Helping your child to be sociable is about children and 'outsiders'; other adults and other children. Children vary in their reactions to other children (just as they vary in everything else) but sometimes parents expect too much sociability from children who are too young to get much out of companionship. If a year-old baby is pressured to let go of mum and crawl off with the others at the mother-and-toddler group, he may become afraid and shy. If he is allowed to watch

them from her lap and play with some of the toys at her feet, he is far more likely to wander off of his own accord a few months later. Real sociability – real pleasure in the company of children of his own age – is not likely to begin until the child is mature enough to see the point. 'Taking turns', for example, is just a boring wait until you are clever enough to understand that waiting means you really will get a turn where just pushing means that you probably will not! Being kind to other children also has to wait until a child is capable of 'putting himself in someone else's shoes' and understands that, when he pulls someone's hair it hurts, just as it hurts when his hair is pulled. Trying to teach this too early (perhaps by pulling the child's hair to show him what it's like) simply does not work. It just makes the world seem a more violent and hurtful place; a place where he had better learn to protect himself by violence. Fortunately there are other ways of coping with children who pull hair, bite, spit and push. Most of them unfortunately involve constant vigilance and physical control by an adult. It is no good saying "No" to someone eighteen months old unless you also act "No" by physically controlling the arms that are coming out to scratch.

Children who are very shy with adults can be a pain, too. A shy child may spoil everyone's time when you visit friends because he insists on sitting on your lap and cries if your friends try to speak to him. You may never be able to leave him with anyone outside his immediate family and you may wonder how he is ever going to cope with playleaders or school teachers. 'Stranger anxiety' (in babies <u>and</u> older children) is actually provoked by the insensitive way a lot of adults treat children. Would <u>you</u> like it if a perfect stranger rushed up to you in the street, hugged you and gave you a kiss? Wouldn't you expect to be introduced first? Making the right kind of introductions – always, making sure your child is treated just as 'politely' as you will expect him to treat adults and giving him the chance to be the one to make the advances – builds up a child's confidence and interest in other people. Make the best use of mother-and-toddler groups, playgrounds, even shops, so that by the time your child is ready to attend a playgroup or nursery without you, he finds its adults (as well as the other children) interesting rather than alarming.

USEFUL BOOKS
BABYHOOD by Penelope Leach £5.95 (second edition Penguin 1983)
BABY AND CHILD by Penelope Leach £7.95 (Penguin)
THE PARENTS A –Z by Penelope Leach £6.95 (Penguin)
BOOK OF CHILD CARE by Hugh Jolly £12.95 (George Allen and Unwin)
READER'S DIGEST MOTHERCARE BOOK £7.95

59

Yorkshire's Ashley Jackson returns to 'Pebble Mill at One' for a new series after a gap of seven years during which he has become one of Britain's most acclaimed watercolour painters.

Ashley invites guests from many walks of life to join his 'Pebble Mill at One' masterclasses. They come from show business, sport and politics, but these amateur artists have one thing in common – a deep love of the British landscape.

Here Ashley explains how his own inspiration is derived from his native hills and gives pointers in style and technique to accompany the series.

My Favourite View

A WATER COLOUR PAINTING LESSON
WITH ASHLEY JACKSON.

Painting the moors of my beloved Yorkshire is a privilege; to see her in her 'wild mood' is out of this world.

I've been trying to capture her wild mood for some 27 years. Yorkshire has a character all of its own when the rain sweeps over the moorland. Standing up there, you can see the moving light. Some say that I should experiment – painting subjects other than Yorkshire moorlands and pits – but Yorkshire is such a varied county. If I go up onto the Pennines on different days with the light constantly changing every second, I have to experiment all the time, and I feel that I have not wasted my time devoting myself to the painting of the Pennines for the rest of my life.

I was sitting high above the mill town of Holmfirth early one Saturday morning with an artist friend of mine from London. We were listening to the skylarks and the curlews. I commented that when I hear the skylark, I know that I am in England; more particularly, Yorkshire.

You see, I will only paint the clinging cottages of the Moorland Uplands and the fullness of the open moorland, not at a given time, but when the hairs on the back of my arms stand up rigid, and you get a feeling that no amount of money can buy.

My paintings depict the rain, the mist and the wind. I want to give the feeling that your boots are sodden and your socks squelching, because that is what happens each time I try to capture her wild and romantic beauty.

Anybody can be taught to paint a picture because it is mechanically constructed. I would go as far as saying that one needs to be taught the mechanics. However, the main ingredient of all is 'putting your soul into the picture' which then becomes a 'painting.' I execute most of my works out on location, in the wind and the rain.

I have been asked why do I paint miserable scenes, instead of sunny days? Sunny days to me are like champagne parties: you go to one every day, and it becomes boring.

My favourite view is Upper Knowles Farm, Bradshaw Moor, where all my thoughts come together, and I am at peace with the world. I am using it as a subject here, and to demonstrate my own techniques I'm imagining that you are following step by step as the painting takes shape and colour.

The materials used in this picture are:- 4B pencil, Prussian Blue, Ultramarine Blue, Burnt Sienna, Cadmium Yellow, and Yellow Ochre. Saunders 140lb weight Rough Paper. A large squirrel hair brush. Nos.6 and 8 Sable brushes. A white porcelain or metal dish to mix colour in, and a big jar of water.

Avoid using cake colours (pans) as this will give you weak colour, and you will be painting with coloured water, instead of watercolour. Tubes are preferred.

The finished size of the painting in the illustration is 18½" x 14".

FIG. 1. DRAW YOUR COMPOSITION

Draw in your composition, using a 4B pencil. Do not use a hard pencil such as HB because watercolour paper easily indents, and you will not be able to remove these marks even with a rubber.

Don't go for detail at this stage; simply think of your subjects as silhouettes, and draw the outline shapes. The paper I use is Rag Paper, so called because it is actually made from cotton or linen rags. The surface texture I choose is called 'Rough.' There are three surfaces of Watercolour Paper – 'HP' meaning Hot Pressed, is a smooth finish. 'NOT' is medium (the Americans call the 'NOT' surface Cold Pressed) and finally 'Rough.' I never use anything less than 140lb weight, as this doesn't crinkle as much.

'Saunders' is the paper I am using for this particular study.

This is the time to remember that only through light does one get shape. So, before you put pencil or brush to paper, identify the source of your light, the direction from which it is coming.

I have frozen my light with an arrow in the top left hand corner of Fig. 1, and whatever the light does during the rest of that day, I shall continue to work from this first impression.

Now you are ready for Figure 2.

FIG. 2. SKY AND WASHES

Clip your paper to a board, or tape it down, and then place your board ready to start painting at an angle of no more than 45°. Now we begin. Wet the sky area all over down to the horizon with clean water, using a squirrel hair wash brush. Then mix your sky colour from Ultramarine Blue, Prussian Blue, and Burnt Sienna.

Starting from left to right at the top of the paper, bring the colour down to one third of the sky. For the far distant sky, the third nearest your horizon, add a little touch of Cadmium Yellow. To prevent the blue and yellow from mixing together, drag a moist brush along the surface of the paper, between the two colours. The brush will sap up any colour on the paper, blue or yellow, leaving you with white paper, which will give you the effect of clouds.

This exercise needs to be practised on a trial sheet of paper, before attempting the experiment on your painting paper, but after 10 minutes or so you should begin to get the feel of this particular technique.

Now move down to the foreground – the bottom of your painting – and lay in a light wash of Cadmium Yellow, Prussian Blue and a hint of Burnt Sienna. This wash can be applied right up to the edge of your distant hills. Do not wet this area with clean water, but paint direct onto paper with the wash itself.

With Yellow Ochre and a hint of Cadmium Yellow, you then give the light sides of the buildings a coat of paint. Be patient and wait for the washes to dry in this instance, because you do not want the effect of colours blending together. Now give your roof a coat of Burnt Sienna, Yellow Ochre and Prussian Blue. Use the same colours on your gable ends, and any dark tones you see in Fig. 2, common sense telling you that you need to use more Blue than Burnt Sienna.

By now, the only thing we haven't washed in are the distant hills. This is done with the same mixture used for the sky, with a little more Ultramarine Blue and Burnt Sienna added.

When cutting in round your sheep with your field colour, you should have left the sheep White (paper) and this applies to all the Whites you see; you leave them out in the first instance. Don't think of leaving White, think 'light' instead.

FIG. 3. DETAIL AND SHADE

First a reminder of Fig. 1 and the arrow indicating the direction of the light, which must be painted to all the time.

Mix Prussian Blue and Burnt Sienna and give a second coat of this wash to the foreground and the gable ends of the buildings in the shade.

You will observe this in Fig. 3. Moving on to the field in the middle distance, give this a second wash of Cadmium Yellow, Prussian Blue and Yellow Ochre still cutting round your sheep and the areas of the paths. Now get your sky colour, and wash in the shaded sides of the distant hills. With the same colour, wash your barn, the distant walls, and work forward to your foreground wall. This will give you the coolness you need in the shade.

Now is the time to paint in the detail. Never ever paint detail at the beginning of a picture, because this will make your work very tight and lacking in mood. The detail always goes in just before you sign your name.

The detail colour has more Prussian Blue than Burnt Sienna. It is made up of Prussian Blue, Burnt Sienna and Ultramarine Blue. No Black or White is used at all. Your sheep are tinted in with your dirty wash, and the heads are put in with the detail colour. At this stage add the telegraph poles and fences.

LET NATURE WORK FOR YOU

Experience will soon teach you that nature is always ready to assist those who are willing to receive her messages.

As a rule, nature offers her best colours and tones in the summer between the hours of seven a.m. and eleven a.m. and four p.m. and seven p.m. Those are the magic minutes, when an understanding of the complexities of perspective in colour tone will be that much easier to grasp.

For instance, the grey of a misty summer morning or evening will illustrate tonal value better than any words of mine.

Try to avoid the harsh light of high noon on a hot summer day. In this country, there is no subtlety to be found in this sort of condition. Overseas, where the light is cleaner and dryer, there is a different philosophy to consider. But in this country the rule is simple – don't do it!

On the same theme, one of the commonest mistakes students make when coping with problems of landscape concerns scaling down. They will work hard to scale down the landscape and subject to suit the size of their paper on canvas – carefully encompassing a scene half a mile wide and eight miles deep in a ten by fifteen inch canvas. But they rarely bother to put the same effort into scaling down the colours in the landscape. Thus their painting becomes flat and boring.

THE FINAL FACTOR

You can call it what you will – inspiration, soul, whatever. It is the ingredient within a painting, which has nothing to do with tonal value, colour perspective, eye level lines, composition, or anything else you can explain rationally.

Some paintings are invested with a quality which casts a universal spell. I do not suppose that even those responsible for their creation could begin to tell you how they achieved such feeling.

All I can do is give a little advice which may help you to find something within

Fig. 2

music is important when I am trying to transport myself back to some special place. Tchaikovsky, Chopin and Delius are my companions in those situations. Lowry used to paint to chamber music.

But you must find your own route to inspiration and I wish you good fortune.

I shall leave you to ponder two lines which have always appealed to me.

"It is only with the heart one can see right.

What is essential is invisible to the eye".

yourself.

To start on a mundane, practical note – always carry a sketchbook wherever you go. Everyone with artistic potential will occasionally and unexpectedly be galvanised by some scene upon which they stumble, and lose whatever is being communicated to them because they have no means of recording it there and then.

Whenever that happens to me, I can feel the hairs rising along my arms and I cannot wait to get back with my sketchbook to begin work.

When you are ready to commit colours to paper, I advise you to study the sketch for a while then place it face down on a table. Then try to travel back mentally to the location which moved you and paint from memory. Take an occasional extra look at the sketch if you must, but work as quickly as possible whilst the image is still imprinted on your mind.

There are other useful aids. For me,

Fig. 3

63

Cookery has always been the single most popular ingredient of a 'Pebble Mill' lunchtime and this season we range from the capers of the Cooking Canon to the speed and efficiency of our new 'Microwave Magic' series.

But first, 'New English Cookery' from the Grand Master, Michael Smith. And here Michael explains just how he was inspired to lead the crusade to restore English cuisine to its rightful place in the dining rooms of the land.

—NEW— ENGLISH COOKERY

Had anyone said to me thirty years ago when I returned to this country, hot from the stoves of Switzerland's famous hotel school, that I would be championing the cause of English cookery, I'd have said "Don't be daft!"

At that time I was happy to be one of those early birds

who, after the war in battle-scarred Britain with food rationing still in progress, was to start encouraging housewives and other cooks to make patés and quiches, mousses and marinades, Coq au Vin, Steak au Poivre. Caneton à l'Orange and many other 'foreign' dishes to tempt our deprived palates.

I was also very early on the cookery demonstrating platform when, in 1953, I installed a dozen cinema seats for customers to observe the kitchens of my restaurant, which in those days was a handsome Victorian mansion set in a woodland landscape between industrial Leeds and the satellite dormitory town of handsome Harrogate.

Curious customers who had never heard of the aforementioned dishes and who, for almost ten years had survived on a diet of dried eggs, whale meat, powdered milk, Spam and a weekly ounce of butter, were keen to have the recipes for inclusion in their own post-war repertoire as life gradually returned to normal and entertaining in the home began again.

It is hard to imagine, as I write in 1985, that you could have counted on the fingers of one hand the restaurants of any repute in the Yorkshire of those days.

And before we had time to think, Cordon Bleu cookery had taken hold.

'Mousse Basque au Chocolat' – from the hands of the late Constance Spry and her Cordon Bleu team – 'Galette aux Fraises' and the ubiquitous 'Crème Brûlée', were presented for dessert at every dinner table from Perth to Penzance.

How could we be so treacherous to good old Britain as we hurtled down the path of 'gourmet cooking', ignoring our national dishes which had understandably, because of the war, slipped into oblivion as we all shared our meagre rations in shoulder-to-shoulder necessity! But we did, and I aided and abetted the situation, for wasn't that what I'd been sent abroad to be trained to do at the hands of my masters in Lausanne's Hotel Beau Rivage, with its clutch of deposed royalty as residents? This experience was followed by stints at such glamorous emporia as The Hotel Crillon, handsomely sited on the Place Vendôme in Paris and, for me more interestingly, The Palace in Copenhagen where, in its chic night club, Oscar Peterson tinkled the ivories each night as Europe's demi-monde came back to life and dined out in such places in order to re-establish their lost social scene.

By now you may be asking "How did he make the transition from French cookery to his obsession with English food?"

Well, it began when a deep-rooted sense of history and a love of music drew me to Harewood House, one-time home of the late Princess Royal and now the Yorkshire home of the Earl and Countess of Harewood.

Back in the early 50s, I was present at some recitals given by that famous music duo, Benjamin Britten and Peter Pears. Despite this magnificent 18th century mansion being my local 'stately home', I had never been inside – the boom in stately home visiting hadn't got underway at that time.

Then in 1958, as part of the celebrations for the centenary year of the Leeds Triennial Music Festival – I was asked to mastermind a series of banquets following recitals given by such eminent musicians as Arthur Rubenstein, Tamas Vasary, Nathan Milstein and Hans Hotter. The Princess Royal, being principal Patron of the Festival, hosted these elaborate affairs, designed to draw money from the wealthy to help the Festival. They were truly grand occasions. European royalty joined many of our Royal Family, who all rubbed shoulders with the world of music and the well-heeled commoners in the beautiful state rooms at Harewood.

The keys to the strong rooms were handed to me as there was an unlimited choice of gold, silver, china and ornamentation. With a guiding hand in the early days from Mr Blades, the butler, who had an historical story to tell about almost every piece, every detail from food and flowers to security and cloakroom attendants had to be planned by me. Routes had to be mapped and charted with coloured ribbons to guide my staff – who were not used to the house – from the various service pantries, hidden behind concealed doors in the state rooms, to the nether regions where the kitchens, butteries, store rooms and wine cellars were. Each pantry had its own stone-stepped staircase leading to a veritable maze of corridors at the service level. And there were no lifts! Our feet ached and we lost pounds in weight after each of these occasions.

French food was served, as this was the only food considered suitable for such occasions in those days. But working in Harewood House was, eventually, to bring about a major change in my views on food and, if I were to plan such a function today, the bill of fare would be very English.

Handling the priceless plate and Derby Sèvres dinner service was but a small part of the influence Harewood was to have on me over the years.

The Adams Brothers had imposed their classical mark on its design and Thomas Chippendale himself, born but five short miles away in Otley, carved in wood the simulated swagged taffeta pelmets in their long gallery.

We would put to their original use the handsome inlaid winecoolers, and the 18th century plate carriers.

Preparing the huge silver-gilt candelabra for the head table was a morning's job. The precious metal was washed and polished and tall beeswax candles were fixed in as many as forty branches before being topped with vellum shades on brass candle slides, a crystal candle drip having first been slotted over to catch any wayward wax. Festoons of fresh flowers for the buffet tables were designed to complement the plaster-cast urns, bowls, masks, festoons, rosettes, acanthus, celery, daisy and honeysuckle unbelievably adorning the ceilings; cascades of such exotica as eucomis and freesia, astromaria and gerbera were massed in the priceless Gold Warwick vases (much to Her Royal Highness's horror –she was later to take great interest in my schemes for these occasions).

Paintings by Reynolds and Gainsborough watched us from the walls and the handsome ceilings, painted by Biagio Rebecca and Angelica Kauffman, looked down on my 20th century interpretation of things.

All this did imbue me with a first awareness of English domestic history from the grand angle and, as I considered the ensuing decade, I realized that there was, in fact, a culinary history to match the 'Grace and Flavour' of all this elegant 18th century design.

Then came total revelation. By chance, I attended the first-ever sale of cookery books when Lord Westbury's collection came under the hammer at Sotheby's on 16th February 1965.

Here in these famous London salerooms, alongside such pundits as Elizabeth David and Robert Carrier, who also were bidding against mighty odds from world book dealers, I brought home Mrs Elizabeth Raffald's 'The Experienced English Housekeeper' – the 1776 edition which was later to be the reason for a special visit to New York during their bi-centennial celebrations to choreograph and cook a celebratory banquet for the International Wine and Food Society.

It was also at the Westbury sale that I bought Ann Peckham's 'The Complete English Cook' (1780 edition) and discovered that in those old days in Leeds you could eat 'Soals in Wine'. This was to become my Fillets of Sole in White Wine with an orange, capers, anchovies, and walnut garnish – delicious and totally English based.

Mary Kettleby's 1724 recipe for 'Spinnage Tart' was a revelation for example: it proved that Quiche had found its way to the East Midlands 250 years ago. And so my restoration of English cuisine began in real earnest.

I will be ever grateful to Northamptonshire's Ann Blencowe who in 1694 wrote down her receipt for 'Butter'd Orange'.

I like to feel that my interpretation of her receipt for this dish has brought a deal of pleasure and no little surprise to many people both here in England and abroad and by restoring it to its rightful place in the English repertory has, in some small way, helped unfurl our culinary flag.

Along came another favourite such as 'Marbl'd Veal'

65

MINI SHEPHERD'S PIE

which has gained a new reputation, its progress followed by the cameras at Pebble Mill. It is now a combination of Elizabeth Raffald's 18th century receipt and the stalwart Agnes Marshall's 19th century version, plus the idea of pressing it into 'seams' from Cassell's 'Household Guide' (1876), which uniquely illustrated book was, together with various editions of Mrs Beeton, to be my almost sole source of reference for all the food I did on television's 'The Duchess of Duke Street', and 'Upstairs, Downstairs'.

The American food historian, Lorna Sass, on her frequent trips to Britain while researching for her own books, was to urge me to look further back into our archives as she enthused me with her own writings on medieval cookery in England.

In return for my revealing to her the delights of folk museums, she arranged for my first sighting in the British Museum of that rarest of cookery manuscripts 'A Forme of Cury', compiled by the master cooks of King Richard II in about 1390, from which stemmed, via Lorna, the 'Tart de Bry' served at Malcolm Livingston's restaurant The English House in London.

And so I have spent the past twenty years delving, reading, experimenting, cooking and eating that which matched everything else in refinement in our age of elegance.

But life goes on and life changes – sometimes almost imperceptibly, sometimes suddenly, as in the field of modern science when some new discovery or other is launched into our lives without so much as a by-your-leave, shaking the very foundations we had carefully laid.

Having by now helped to re-establish our culinary heritage, I was indeed taken aback and in no small way shaken when Michael Guerard introduced his Cuisine Minceur theory some ten or twelve years ago.

The notion found an elitist level fairly quickly, but not before other French chefs such as Roger Verge, Paul Bocuse and the Troisgros brothers had taken up the idea, given it a quick face-lift and re-launched it onto the idea-greedy journalistic world as Nouvelle Cuisine, or New Cookery, ridding us of the classic French cookery we had grown to know.

These men based their new thinking in some small part on Guerard's 'think thin' notion, but more so on a simpler combination of flavours, unhampered by strong masking sauces.

An exploratory trip to Japan also led them to present dishes in a simpler, more artistic way. (Some might say that the presentation is so meticulous that there is precious little to eat and, in many cases, they might well have a valid point.)

But what was I to do?

I had only just got people in Britain used to the idea that, for improved results in the kitchen, you do have to use good ingredients: butter, cream, wine, fresh herbs, better cuts of meat and farm-fed poultry. Suddenly the French deliver a body-blow to the western world, leaving us reeling and confused. To a certain extent they are right in their attitude to a healthier and simplified cookery, though there are many who see Nouvelle Cuisine as yet another affectation.

There was only one way to go. Join them at their own game. But in so doing we must retain the national identity so much needed by us British as tourism fast becomes our biggest dollar earner. An English 'Bill of Fare' is a necessity.

This is exactly what I've done in 'New English Cookery' (BBC Publications £5.75). It is the basis of my latest series at Pebble Mill and a sample of the recipes is reprinted here.

You will recognise the name of many of the dishes; you will have been making most of them for many years though there are hundreds of new recipes. They all come in a new guise; lightened, enriched, beautiful – in fact, improved in such a way that they will stand safely alongside their foreign counterparts, leaving us with heads held high in the knowledge that we still have a national identity in our kitchens.

QUEEN'S PUDDING AND CHILLED SEMOLINA PUDDING

MENU 1
CLEAR MUSHROOM BROTH
Serves 4

Mushroom essences and mushroom katsup (or ketchup) have been part of the English culinary scene for centuries, although they have fallen into disuse since the turn of this one with the advent of Oxo and, more recently, the stock cube.

This exquisite new broth is a timely reminder of how excellent and fitting mushrooms are to the English palate. Serve in smallish cups with perhaps a cheese straw or a couple of lightly buttered fingers of brown toast as an accompaniment.

1 oz (25g) unsalted butter
4 oz (110g) onion, peeled and roughly chopped
2 lb (900g) sliced mushrooms (half flat-cap and half button if possible)
2 tbsp salt
½ tsp ground mace or ground coriander
½ tsp milled pepper
¼ pint (150 ml) dry madeira or amontillado sherry
2½ pints (1.4 litres) cold water
Juice of ½ lemon
To Garnish
1 oz (25g) white button mushrooms, finely sliced and quickly browned in ¼ oz sizzling butter
2 or 3 coriander leaves if you can lay your hands on some or
1 oz (25g) wild or brown rice, boiled and rinsed as per instructions on the packet.

Melt the butter in a large pan until foaming. Add the onion, stirring in well, lower the heat and cook, covered, until soft. Add the mushrooms and all the remaining ingredients. Cover with the water, bring to the boil slowly and cook at a good simmer for 1½ hrs. Cool. Strain through a heavy felt jellybag for a clear broth. (A couple of clean white felt squares lining a sieve will do quite well if you don't have a jellybag. These should be washed afterwards in biological powder, rinsed, soaked in cold water overnight, rinsed again and dried.) Discard the mushroom pulp which will have had all the goodness cooked out of it.

To serve, reheat the broth to boiling point. Warm soup cups or tea cups and rinse them with a teaspoon of sherry or madeira. Add 2 or 3 slivers of mushroom or 1 teaspoonful of cooked rice to each cup.

CURRIED LAMB WITH APPLE AND PINEAPPLE
Serves 4

2 lb (900g) fillet of leg of lamb (yields 1¼ lb (550g) when boned and trimmed)
4 tbsp coconut oil
1 small onion, finely chopped
2" (5cm) piece of green ginger, peeled and finely sliced
1 clove of garlic, crushed
2 heaped tsp mild curry powder
2 Cox's apples, peeled and cored
½ small pineapple, peeled and cored
1 oz (25g) butter
Juice of 1 small lemon
Salt, pepper and mace
1 tsp sugar
¼ pint (150ml) cream

Cut the lamb into ½"(1 cm) cubes. Heat the coconut oil until smoking and fry the lamb in batches to seal the meat on all sides, removing it to a plate with a slotted spoon when this is done. Add the onions to the pan and soften them in the residual fats. Return the meat to the pan, add the ginger, and continue cooking over a high heat until tender; the whole operation should take about 8–10 minutes. Work over a good heat so that the meat is frying and not 'stewing'.

Meanwhile, cut the apples into quarters, then eighths; toss the pieces in the lemon juice. Cut the pineapple into pieces the same size. Melt 1 oz (25g) of butter until it is foaming, add the fruit, season with salt, pepper and mace and the small amount of sugar. Add the lemon juice.

Stir the curry powder and garlic into the meat and fry for a further minute, stirring all the time. Stir in the cream and bubble until it has cohered well. Add the apple and pineapple, which should be just cooked but still crisp. Reheat and serve with plain boiled rice.

CHILLED SEMOLINA PUDDINGS
Serves 6–8

A far remove from that schooldays horror, I assure you!
¾ pint (400ml) single cream
½ pint (275ml) double cream
1 oz (25g) semolina
2 tbsp castor sugar (or to taste)
1 tsp finely grated zest of an oily orange
1 tsp gelatine crystals, dissolved in 1 tbsp cold water
4 egg yolks, mixed
8 apricot caps, blanched (or fresh, or tinned, or reconstituted dried ones)
Knob of softened, unsalted butter
Apricot Sauce
¾ lb (350g) fresh or drained tinned apricots, pitted
Sugar, if needed
1 tbsp apricot liqueur or Grand Marnier

In a non-stick pan bring the single cream, sugar and zest slowly to the boil, rain in the semolina, reduce the heat and simmer for 3 – 4 minutes. Remove from the heat and, whilst still hot, mix the softened gelatine and the egg yolks in well. Cool. Whip the double cream just to the ribbon stage and cut into the mixture.

Have ready 8 lightly buttered individual moulds (use coffee cups if you don't have a set of tin ones). Put an apricot cap in the bottom of each, curved side down. Fill with the semolina mixture. Chill.

Purée the apricots for the sauce in a blender or food processor and then rub through a fine-meshed sieve. Add the remaining ingredients and chill.

Turn the semolina puddings out of the moulds by easing the edge with your finger. Dip each tin for a couple of seconds into a basin of boiling water and wipe dry. Turn onto individual plates in a pond of apricot sauce.

MENU 2
SPINACH AND SALMON 'CUSTARD'
Serves 6–8

The vivid green of this most English diet is very eye-catching. Serve it as you would a terrine.

1 lb (450g) young spinach, well washed, de-veined, and patted dry
1½ lb (700g) salmon, skinned and boned
2 large eggs, beaten
¼ pint (150ml) single cream
1 tsp salt
1 level tsp milled pepper
½ tsp ground nutmeg

Preheat the oven to gas mark 4, 350°F (180°C). Butter a lidded terrine or loaf tin and line the base with a piece of buttered paper. Cut half the salmon into ½" (1cm) cubes. Season lightly. Cut the rest up roughly. With the metal blade fitted to the food processor, drop in the eggs and seasoning. Next add the roughly cut pieces of salmon, and purée finely. Feed in all the spinach and blend everything finely. Scrape the mixture into a bowl. Stir in the cream and the cubed salmon. Pour into the prepared mould and cover with a lid.

Fill a deep container with hot water (it should come to within ½" (1cm) of the rim of the terrine). Fold a piece of newspaper into 4 layers, and place in the bottom. Stand the terrine on this and

cook for 1 hr or until the custard is quite set. Cool, then refrigerate overnight. Serve cut into ½" (1cm) slices.

MINI SHEPHERD'S PIES
Serves 4 – 5

1 lb (450g) rump steak or leg fillet of lamb minced twice
1 tbsp plain white flour
1 small onion, skinned and finely chopped
1 tsp olive or soy oil
½ pint (275ml) red wine
½ pint (275ml) beef stock
¼ pint (150ml) tomato juice
Salt and milled white pepper
12 – 16 small potatoes, baked in their jackets
<u>For the Topping</u>
2 parts mashed potato
1 part choux pastry
1 tbsp freshly grated Parmesan cheese

Preheat the oven to gas mark 6, 400°F (200°C). In a heavy-bottomed casserole, heat the tablespoon of oil and fry the onion until golden-brown, stirring to prevent burning. Add the mince in small batches, and continue to fry over a <u>high</u> heat until all is well sealed. Sprinkle over the modicum of flour, stir it in and fry for a minute or so. Season to taste. Add all the liquids, cover with a lid, and over a <u>low</u> heat cook for 30 minutes, stirring from time to time. By now you should have a rich, well-amalgamated mixture. Leave it to cool.

Scoop out all the inside from the baked potatoes, leaving just the thin crisp skins. Reserve enough potato to use in the topping, and keep the rest for another day. You should now have 12 – 16 potato shells: fill each one to the top with the minced meat mixture.

Prepare the topping. Press the reserved potato through a potato ricer and beat well with a little butter and ¼ pint (150ml) hot milk. The mixture

should be fairly firm. Mix with the choux pastry and pipe, spoon or 'fork' the mixture on top of each shell. Sprinkle with a little Parmesan cheese. Bake in the preheated oven until the topping is well puffed up and golden-brown (about 20 minutes). These quantities should give you about 10 – 12 pies, depending on size – allow 2 –3 per serving.

CHOUX PASTRY
Makes 20 – 30 buns

This pastry has endless uses, both sweet and savoury. The choux buns can be made in advance and either frozen or stored in an airtight container.

7½ fl oz (210ml) water and milk, mixed
2½ oz (60g) unsalted butter, cubed
3¾ oz (90g) plain white flour sieved with ¼ tsp salt and ½ tsp castor sugar
3 large eggs, lightly beaten
<u>To Glaze</u>
1 small egg beaten with 1 tbsp milk

Preheat the oven to gas mark 6, 400°F (200°C). Bring the butter, water and milk to the boil in a pan; remove from the heat. Have the flour, salt and sugar sieved onto a paper. Tip this at one fell swoop into the pan, stir in, and beat vigorously with wooden spatula.

Return the pan to a low heat; mix in and gently beat the mixture until it has dried a little and has formed a single ball of paste. Tip this into a bowl. Gradually beat in the beaten eggs: this can be arduous as you have to continue beating until the mixture acquires a silky sheen. The operation can be done in a food processor: if you do, though, be careful not to overwork the paste.

Brush a baking sheet with a little melted butter – heavy-handed buttering of the shell creates crusty bases to the buns. Pipe or spoon the required shapes onto this. Brush each shape very lightly with beaten egg and milk (this is optional). Bake in the preheated oven for 10, 15 or 20 minutes, depending on their size. Frankly, I don't like my choux pastry to be too dry. Experience will tell you when they are cooked to your liking. If you want really crisp buns then open the oven door an inch or two after the first 5 minutes to allow any steam to escape, then close it again.

QUEEN'S PUDDING

Serves 6 – 8

Again all the traditional elements are here: the bread, however, now plays a subservient role!

½ pint (275ml) single cream
½ pint (275ml) rich milk
1 tsp finely grated lemon rind
2 oz (50g) castor sugar
4 small eggs, beaten
1 oz (25g) or 1 tbsp fresh white breadcrumbs, finely grated.

<u>Meringue Topping</u>
2 large egg whites
2 oz (50g) castor sugar

<u>To Garnish</u>
Lemon curd, or redcurrant jelly, or sieved raspberry jam.

Preheat the oven to gas mark 3, 325°F (170°C). Lightly butter 6 ramekins. In a non-stick pan bring the milk, cream, lemon rind and sugar to the boil. Pour over the beaten eggs, whisking well. Stir in the modest amount of breadcrumbs. Ladle the mixture into the ramekins and stand them in a water bath to bake until they are set.

For the meringue topping, whisk the egg whites until stiff and then whisk in the castor sugar. Using a piping-bag fitted with a plain ⅛″ (0.25cm) tube, pipe a collar of this topping round the rim of each ramekin and make a criss-cross pattern across the surface of each. Add a blob of lemon curd, jam or jelly. Return to the oven for a further 5 – 10 minutes for the meringue to set and brown, or stand the puddings under a medium-hot grill.

The puddings can be served cold, but

70

HADDOCK FISH CAKES WITH ENRICHED TARTARE SAUCE

in this case the 'custard' will be firmer, so use only 3 eggs. You can, of course, make one single big pudding. Pipe the meringue in 1" (2.5cm) squares to create a lattice pattern and make a mosaic of colour by decorating with different jams at will.

MENU 3
TOMATO AND PLUM SOUP
Serves 5 – 6

This soup is bright red and tastes very fresh. Serve hot or chilled.

2 oz (50g) onion, skinned, chopped
1 fl oz (25ml) olive oil
1 lb (450g) red plums, stoned
1 lb (450g) tomatoes, deseeded
½ pint (275ml) fresh tomato juice
1 pint (570ml) chicken stock
1 sprig fresh thyme
1 tsp castor sugar
Salt and milled pepper
To Garnish
2 plums, stones and diced
1 level tbsp finely chopped parsley
1 level tbsp finely snipped chives

Soften the onion in the oil without colouring it. Add all the remaining ingredients. Bring to the boil and simmer until the fruit is soft (about 12 – 15 minutes). Cool a little, then blend and rub through a fine sieve.

Reheat or chill. Serve with a spoonful of the mixed garnish.

HADDOCK FISHCAKES WITH ENRICHED TARTARE SAUCE
Serves 5 – 6

All the elements of the traditional fish cake are brought together here, but the ingredients are all raw: the result is a remarkable renaissance for this favourite dish. You can serve them with lemon wedges for breakfast or, accompanied by my new enriched tartare sauce, they will grace the brunch table or act as a dinner-time starter.

1 lb (450g) fresh haddock, filleted, skinned and boned
2 beaten eggs
8 oz (225g) raw potato, peeled and cubed into cold water
2 slices white bread, crustless, cut into small squares
⅛ pint (75ml) single cream
Salt and milled pepper
Clarified butter or soy oil for frying
For The Sauce
½ pint (275ml) home-made mayonnaise
A little lemon juice or water
1 – 2 dashes tabasco
1 hard-boiled egg, shelled and halved
4 – 5 American cocktail gherkins, finely chopped
1 tbsp chives, finely snipped (or parsley or other green herb)
1 oz (25g) prawns, chopped
3 – 4 anchovy fillets, separated and diced

Make a fine purée of all the ingredients in a food processor, adding the cream last of all so that it isn't overworked. For an extra fine texture, rub the mixture through a fine sieve.

The mixture should be softish. Scoop out spoonfuls on to a wetted work surface, dipping the spoon in water each time. Using a wetted knife or palette knife, level and shape the cakes which should be about ½" (1cm) thick.

In a skillet or frying pan heat 2 – 3 tablespoons of clarified butter or soy oil to smoking point. Have ready a jug of cold water and a dessertspoon (for large cakes) or a teaspoon (for small ones).Lift and slide the cakes into the smoking oil in batches of 4 or 5. Turn them after ½min, when a golden crust will have formed. Lower the heat and cook and turn them for 3 – 4 minutes. Drain on kitchen paper towels. Add a little more oil or butter when required.

For added luxury, a large peeled 'crevette', or American shrimp, can be pressed into the mixture and half a clove of crushed garlic plus 2 tablespoons of finely chopped fresh parsley can also be added. The cakes are delicious served cold, sliced and dressed with oil and vinegar or mayonnaise, or with my special tartare sauce. To prepare this, chop the hard-boiled egg white and sieve the yolk onto a saucer. Mix the mayonnaise to the texture of double cream with a little lemon juice or water. Add the tabasco. Stir in the sieved yolk, retaining a spoonful to sprinkle over as a garnish if you like, and mix in the remaining ingredients. Cover with plastic film and chill ready for use.

RUM CUSTARDS
Serves 8

1¼ pints (900ml) milk
¼ pint (150ml) single cream
3 whole eggs
3 extra egg yolks
2 – 3 oz (50 – 75g) castor sugar
½ tsp vanilla essence
2 tbsp Bacardi or other light rum

Whisk the whole eggs and the yolks with the sugar without overworking them. Bring the milk and cream to the boil. Add the vanilla essence and rum. Pour the hot mixture over the eggs, whisking well in. Strain through a fine sieve back into the pan or into a jug. Pour into individual custard pots or ramekins and stand these in a deep ovenproof dish or tin filled two thirds full with hot water. Cook at gas mark 4, 350°F (180°C) for 12 – 15 minutes, until just set. Cool, then chill. Serve decorated with a blob of whipped cream.

The microwave oven is turning out to be the greatest revolution in kitchen technology since the invention of electricity. An estimated million and a half ovens will be sold this year, rivalling video recorders and home computers as the most popular household acquisition.

Beverley Piper is a home economist with her own Microwave Cookery School. She explains how the microwave can be used most effectively and creatively and accompanies her Pebble Mill series with a selection of delicious recipes.

Microwave cooking is a new and exciting method of cookery. The microwave oven is an extremely versatile appliance which can cope with about 75% of all your cooking, and also can defrost food from the freezer and quickly reheat cooked foods.

THE PRINCIPLES OF MICROWAVE COOKERY

Normal electricity comes into the appliance through a 13 amp plug, so the microwave is plugged in wherever there is a normal supply of electricity. This means that the microwave may be moved from room to room if necessary and this may be useful should an elderly relative or sick person require hot drinks or snacks during the day as the microwave may be installed in their bedroom during the day and then moved back into the kitchen later.

Once inside the oven, electricity is converted into microwaves by the heart of the machine – the magnetron. These 'microwaves' are then transferred into the oven cavity where they bounce off the metal sides and penetrate the outer 2-4cm (1"-1½") of the food. They pass through the non metallic containers, on which the food is cooked and cause friction heat as the molecules in the food vibrate very rapidly. The heat is passed by conduction from the outside to the inside of the food and the food is cooked.

THE OUTPUT OF THE MICROWAVE

The output of the microwave oven is measured in watts.

MICROWAVE MAGIC

Microwave ovens are available for the domestic market with different maximum power ratings, i.e. 700w, 650w, and 500w. As the output controls the cooking time it must be noted that the 700w models will cook faster than the 500w models, e.g. a 3lb chicken will take roughly 21 minutes to cook in a 700w microwave and it will take 28 minutes to cook in a 500w microwave.

The microwave cooks by weight and time, not temperature, so the more you put in, the longer it will take to cook.

VERSATILITY

There is no wasted energy in a microwave. As there is no heat in the oven itself, there is no pre-heating time and no cooling down period. In the main, the containers do not become very hot, which is a boon for young children and elderly people. Remember, though, that some foods, such as casseroles, which are in the oven for a considerable time, will pass their intense heat back to the container and oven gloves will then be necessary.

Modern microwaves provide variable power, which enables the oven to be used for cooking a wide variety of foods and although not suitable for deep fat frying, the microwave oven may be used to shallow fat fry, braise, roast, poach, steam, boil and bake. It may also be used to blanch small amounts of fresh vegetables for the freezer and of course to reheat and defrost food.

STIRRING AND TURNING

The microwave cooks from the outside to the inside. It is therefore very important to stir those foods where stirring is possible, such as stews, casseroles, rice puddings, sauces etc., several times during the cooking process. This will simply ensure that the completed dish is thoroughly and evenly cooked.

Foods which cannot be stirred, such as cakes, lasagne, meat loaf, bread pudding etc., should be turned, a quarter turn 2 or 3 times during the cooking time to ensure even cooking.

STANDING OR EQUALISING TIME

This is simply time taken at the end of the microwave cooking time for the food to complete cooking. The standing time will vary according to the weight and density of the food. A few peas will need a standing time of only 1-2 minutes, whereas a 4lb sirloin of beef will need 20 minutes to equalise. Standing time may take place either inside the microwave with the oven switched off or on the kitchen work top. In almost all cases the food should be covered during the standing time to help to keep the heat in. Standing time is also very important after defrosting frozen foods.

BROWNING

Combination microwave ovens are available with a browning system. These are the more expensive models as they incorporate different cooking methods in the one unit, and the 'browning' is achieved by hot air or a grill. Some models brown and microwave at the same time while others microwave and then brown. Browning may be achieved in ordinary microwave ovens by using a browning agent in or on the food, such as adding Oxo, Bovril, or Bisto to a meat recipe or some brown sugar, brown colouring or liquid gravy browning to a cake recipe or dessert.

BROWNING DISH OR SKILLET

These are special dishes which are extremely useful as they may be pre-heated in the microwave to a temperature of up to 400°F. It is the base which becomes very hot and is used rather like a frying pan. The dish is used to cook such foods as chops, sausages, hamburgers, bacon and egg etc. The food is turned over during cooking to brown the other side. The dish, which comes with a lid, also doubles as a casserole.

Please note that these dishes may not be used in conventional ovens.

OTHER DISHES

Some plastics, pyrex, china and glass are all excellent. The dishes specially made for microwave cookery are particularly good as they are the correct shape and density to allow fast and even cooking. Round dishes should be used whenever possible or oval or oblong containers with round corners.

Cover with a lid or microwave cling film to keep the moisture in and help the food to cook quickly. Roasting bags are ideal for vegetables and roasting joints. Remember to pierce cling film and roasting bags so that the steam may escape.

CAN I MICROWAVE A COMPLETE MEAL?

A microwave is designed to be used in conjunction with other conventional cooking methods, although with practice and careful planning it is possible to cook an 'all in one' microwave meal, such as a casserole cooked with vegetables or a rice dish such as a paella. By employing 'stage cookery' and microwaving the longest cooking items first, i.e. the meat or root vegetables, a complete meal may be cooked as these denser items will continue to increase in temperature during their standing time, while the less dense items such as the peas and gravy are microwaved to complete the meal.

A quick sweet may be cooked whilst the first course is being eaten.

THE QUALITY AND STARTING TEMPERATURE OF THE FOOD

The microwave will quickly and efficiently cook good quality foods, but please don't look for miracles by expecting it to deal with tough meat or vegetables past their prime.

The starting temperature will obviously alter the cooking time as food will either be taken from a refrigerator or already be at a warm room temperature. Please note that the timings given in these recipes are calculated for food at average room temperature unless otherwise stated.

ALTERING TIMINGS

The recipes used in the series may be cooked in any model of variable power microwave oven available. Each recipe was tested in a microwave with an output of 700w. If the output of your oven differs, please convert as follows:–
If using an oven of 500w add 40 seconds for each minute given.
If using an oven of 600w add 20 seconds for each minute given.
If using an oven of 650w increase the overall time by about 1–2 minutes.

A FEW THINGS THAT CANNOT BE DONE

Do not try to use foil containers. As foil repels microwaves, the food in these dishes will not heat and foil in quantity may damage the magnetron. Tin foil should only be used if specifically recommended by the manufacturer.

Do not try to boil eggs – the pressure may build up under the shell and the egg could explode.

Do not attempt Yorkshire pudding or toad in the hole as there is no dry heat in the microwave to caramalise or brown the surface. These foods may, however, be cooked very successfully in the combination models.

Do not try to deep fat fry or cook crisp roast potatoes as neither is successful.

Do not attempt to toast bread.

Do not attempt to cook the top of a shortcrust pastry pie. Suet crust, baking blind and some puff pastry recipes are excellent. Cooked pies may be re-heated on power 4 or simmer.

74

SCRAMBLED EGGS

Scrambled eggs cook amazingly quickly in the microwave and there's no messy saucepan to deal with afterwards. Remember that the more you put into a microwave, the longer it will take to cook, so use this simple chart and scramble your eggs perfectly every time.

No. of eggs	Amount of milk and butter	Container	Time at High/100%
1 size 2	1 tbsp milk, ½oz butter	½ pint jug	45 secs– 1 min.
2 size 2	2 tbsps milk, 1oz butter	1 pint bowl	1½ mins – 2 mins.
4 size 2	3 tbsps milk, 1oz butter	2½ pint bowl	2½ mins – 3 mins.
6 size 2	4 tbsps milk, 1½oz butter	4 pint bowl	3½ mins – 4 mins.

Season to taste with salt and black pepper in all cases

1 Put the eggs, milk, seasoning, and butter into container.
2 Agitate with a wire balloon whisk or fork.
3 Microwave uncovered on High/100% for stipulated time, removing from microwave and beating with whisk or fork every minute and at the end. Allow a standing time of 30 seconds – 2 minutes depending on number of eggs. When scrambling one egg, beating once only after cooking time and before standing time will be adequate.

APPLE JELLY
4 servings

1 Bramley cooking apple – 8 oz unpeeled weight
1 tablet strawberry or lime jelly
1 level tbsp castor sugar

1 Peel, core and thinly slice apple.
2 Layer the apple slices into a 2½ pint casserole dish with the sugar.
3 Cover and microwave on High/100% for 5 minutes, stirring after 2 minutes. Stir and set aside, covered.
4 Break jelly into pieces and put into a litre jug with 3 tablespoons of cold water.
5 Microwave, uncovered on High/100% for 1 minute. Stir.
6 Microwave, uncovered on High/100% for 30 seconds. Stir.
7 Stir in cold water as directed on jelly packet.
8 Pour jelly over apple, stirring gently. Cool and then refrigerate to set.

LEMON STUFFED MACKEREL WITH SOURED CREAM SAUCE

4 servings

4 fresh mackerel, filleted with heads and fins removed, approx. 175g/6 oz per fish
100g/4 oz fresh breadcrumbs
50g/2 oz shredded suet
Grated rind of 1 lemon
2 tsp fresh lemon juice
10ml/2 tsp finely chopped fresh tarragon or 5ml/1 tsp dried tarragon
1 small onion, finely chopped
Seasoning
1 egg, size 2, beaten with 1 – 2 tbsp milk
30ml/2 tbsp pure orange juice

To garnish

Lemon butterflies and sprigs of fresh parsley

1 Put the breadcrumbs, suet, lemon rind and juice, tarragon and onion into a mixing bowl.
2 Mix well and season. Bind with the beaten egg and milk mixture.
3 Lay out the filleted fish cut side up and divide the stuffing between them, spreading the stuffing evenly onto one half of each fillet and then folding over the other half to close the fish.
4 Make two incisions in the thick side of each fish, using a sharp knife.
5 Arrange the fish, nose to tail in a shallow dish. Pour over the orange juice.

6 Cover tightly with cling film and pierce. Microwave on High/100% for 8 minutes. Allow to stand, covered while preparing the sauce.

SOURED CREAM SAUCE

4 servings

100g/4 oz curd cheese or cream cheese
4 tbsp soured cream
10ml/2 level tsp tomato pureé
5ml/1 level tsp french mustard
2 rounded tbsp creamed horseradish
Seasoning
1 level tsp dried oregano
3" piece of cucumber, diced

1 Put the curd or cream cheese into a 1.7 litre/3 pint mixing bowl. Cover and microwave on defrost for 2 minutes.
2 Beat with a wooden spoon, beating in the soured cream, tomato pureé, french mustard, seasoning and the oregano.
3 Fold in the cucumber just before serving.

To serve

Carefully lift the fish onto a serving dish. Garnish with the lemon butterflies and parsley and serve immediately with new potatoes and broccoli, handing the cold sauce round separately.

LEMON STUFFED MACKEREL WITH SOURED CREAM SAUCE

2 servings

2 fresh mackerel, filleted with heads and fins removed, approx 175g/6 oz per fish
50g/2oz fresh breadcrumbs
25g/1 oz shredded suet
Grated rind of ½ lemon
1 tsp lemon juice
5 ml/1 tsp finely chopped fresh tarragon or 2½ ml/½ tsp dried tarragon
½ small onion, finely chopped
Seasoning
½ an egg, size 2, beaten with 1 tbsp milk
15 ml/1 tbsp pure orange juice

To garnish As for 4

1 Proceed exactly as given for 4 servings through to point 6.
2 Cover tightly with cling film and pierce. Microwave on High/100% for 5 – 6 minutes. Allow to stand, covered whilst preparing the sauce.

SOURED CREAM SAUCE

2 servings

50g/2 oz curd cheese or cream cheese
2 tbsp soured cream
5 ml/1 level tsp french mustard
1 rounded tsp creamed horseradish
Seasoning
½ level tsp dried oregano
1 – 2 pieces of cucumber, diced

1 Put the curd or cream cheese into a 1.1 litre/2 pint mixing bowl. Cover and microwave on defrost for 1 minute.
2 Continue exactly as given for 4 servings.

To serve

Exactly as given for 4 servings.

RATATOUILLE

4 – 6 servings

This is colourful to make in the autumn when aubergines and courgettes are cheap and plentiful. Made the microwave way, the ratatouille doesn't absorb the calories which are present in the oil when it is cooked conventionally and an attractive low calorie dish results.

2 medium onions, peeled and chopped
3 medium sized courgettes

2 large aubergines (450g/1lb total weight)
Seasoning
½ green pepper, de-seeded and chopped
½ red pepper, de-seeded and chopped
1 level tsp dried basil
50g/2 oz butter
1 lb tomatoes peeled and chopped
1 Wash the courgettes and aubergines.
Cut off ends and discard.
2 Slice into ¼" slices and layer in a
colander, sprinkling each layer with salt.
Top with a plate and a heavy weight and
set aside for 30 minutes.
3 Rinse well under cold running water
and drain.
4 Put the butter into a 600ml/1 pint bowl
and microwave on High/100% for 1 – 2
minutes or until melted.
5 Stir in the onion. Cover and microwave
on High/100% for 2 minutes. Stir.
6 Layer the aubergines, courgettes and
peppers into a greased 2.3 litre/4 pint
round dish, with the tomatoes, onion
mixture and herbs. Season each layer
well.
7 Cover and microwave on High/100%
for 25 minutes. After 15 minutes,
carefully remove the lid and drain off
most of the liquid. Cover and return to
microwave for remainder of cooking
time.
8 Allow to stand, covered, for 8 minutes,
before serving with cold cooked meat
and garlic bread.

RATATOUILLE
2 – 3 servings
1 medium onion, peeled and chopped
2 small courgettes
1 large aubergine (225g/8 oz)
Seasoning
¼ green pepper, de-seeded and chopped
¼ red pepper, de-seeded and chopped
½ level tsp dried basil
25g/1 oz butter
8 oz peeled and chopped tomatoes
1 Proceed exactly as given for 4 – 6
servings but melt the butter for 1 minute

on High/100% and soften the chopped
onion for 1 minute only.
6 Layer the aubergines, courgettes and
peppers into a greased 1.4 litre/2½ pint
round dish with the tomatoes, onion
mixture and herbs. Season each layer
well.
7 Cover and microwave on High/100%
for 16 minutes. After 10 minutes carefully
remove the lid and drain off most of the
liquid. Cover and return to microwave
for remainder of cooking time.
8 Allow to stand, covered for 6 minutes,
before serving with cold cooked meat
and garlic bread.

CHEESY PORK BALLS
4 – 6 servings
350g/12 oz raw minced pork
225g/8 oz pork sausage meat
1 clove garlic, crushed
50g/2 oz fresh brown breadcrumbs
Seasoning
1 tbsp finely chopped fresh parsley
50g/2 oz red Leicester or coloured
Cheddar cheese, grated
2 tbsp milk to bind, if necessary
To garnish
Slices of fresh red and green skinned
eating apple, brushed on both sides with
fresh lemon juice.
1 Combine the minced pork, sausage
meat, garlic, breadcrumbs, parsley and
cheese. Mix well with the hands.
2 Add the seasoning and milk and mix to
bind.
3 Using damp hands, form into 15 meat
balls, each the size of a walnut.
4 Arrange in a ring on a large microwave
meat roasting rack or on 3 sheets of
absorbent kitchen paper on a dinner
plate.
5 Microwave, uncovered, on Power 7 or
roast for 14 minutes.
6 After 10 minutes, rearrange the meat
balls so that those towards the outer
edge of the dish and those towards the
centre are reversed. Continue to

microwave for remainder of the time.
7 Allow to stand for 6 minutes before
serving with the apple garnish and
tomato sauce.

CHEESY PORK BALLS
2 – 3 servings
175g/6 oz raw minced pork
100g/4 oz pork sausage meat
½ clove garlic, crushed
25g/1 oz fresh brown breadcrumbs
Seasoning
½ tbsp finely chopped fresh parsley
25g/1 oz red Leicester or coloured
Cheddar cheese, grated.
1 tbsp milk to bind, if necessary
To garnish
Exactly as for 4 – 6 servings
1 Make the recipe up exactly as given in
points 1 and 2 of the method for 4 – 6
servings.
3 Roll the mixture into 8 meat balls and
arrange in a ring on a microwave meat
roasting rack or on 3 sheets of absorbent
kitchen roll arranged on a dinner plate.
4 Microwave, uncovered, on Power 7 or
roast for 8 – 9 minutes. After 5 minutes,
rearrange the meat balls. Continue to
microwave for the remainder of the time.
Allow to stand for 5 minutes. Serve as for
4 – 6 servings. As an alternative, roughly
chop 25g/1 oz lightly salted roasted
peanuts and roll half the meat balls in
these nuts before cooking. Continue
exactly as directed.

INDIAN CHICKEN
4 servings
4 chicken breasts, skinned and boned
(total weight 450g/1 lb)
2 tbsp corn oil
For the marinade
125 ml/4 fl oz natural yoghurt
2 tbsp soya sauce
1 tbsp tomato purée
1 level tsp paprika
1 level tsp whole grain mustard
1 level tsp dried tarragon

Seasoning
2 cloves garlic, crushed
1 Put the chicken pieces into a suitable shallow container. Combine the ingredients for the marinade and pour over the chicken.
2 Cover and refrigerate for 2 hours, turning the chicken in the marinade occasionally.
3 Preheat a large browning dish without the lid for 6 minutes on High/100%.
4 Put the oil into the hot dish and microwave uncovered on High/100% for 1 minute.
5 Drain the chicken pieces, using a slotted spoon, and place in the hot oil. Do not cover. Microwave on High/100% for 6 minutes, turning the chicken over after the first 2 minutes.
6 Allow to stand for 5 minutes and then serve with rice and green salad.

INDIAN CHICKEN
2 servings
2 chicken breasts skinned and boned (total weight 225g/8 oz)
1 tbsp corn oil
For the marinade
50 ml/2 fl oz natural yoghurt
1 tbsp soya sauce
½ tbsp tomato purée
½ level tsp paprika
½ level tsp whole grain mustard
½ level tsp dried tarragon
Seasoning
1 glove garlic, crushed
1 Follow points 1 and 2, exactly as given for 4 servings.
3 Pre-heat the small browning dish, without the lid, on High/100% for 4 minutes.
4 Put the oil into the pre-heated dish and microwave uncovered on High/100% for 30 seconds.
5 Drain chicken pieces, using a slotted spoon and place in the hot oil. Do not cover. Microwave on High/100% for 4 minutes, turning over once after 2

minutes.
6 Allow to stand for 3 minutes and then serve with rice and green salad.

SAVOURY RICE AND VEGETABLES
4 servings
1 medium onion, chopped
225g/8 oz long grain rice
25g/1 oz butter
575 ml/1 pint boiling chicken stock
15 ml/1 tablespoon finely chopped fresh parsley
1 packet – 225g/6 oz frozen mixed vegetables
1 Put the onion and butter into a 2.5-2.8 litre (4-5 pint) bowl. Cover with a lid and microwave on High/100% for 3 minutes.
2 Stir in the rice and the boiling stock with the parsley.
3 Cover and microwave on High/100% for 12-13 minutes. Stir and set aside, covered, for 10-12 minutes.
4 Pierce the packet of vegetables once and put onto a dish. Microwave on High/100% for 4 minutes turning the packet over once after 2 minutes.
5 Allow to stand for 2 minutes and then drain the vegetables.
6 After the rice has completed its standing time, fork in the drained vegetables and serve immediately.
As an alternative
Instead of the mixed vegetables chop 125g/4 oz button mushrooms roughly, place in a bowl with 25g/1oz butter. Cover and microwave on High/100% for 1 minute. Stir. Cover and microwave on High/100% for 1 minute. Stir into the rice after the standing time.

SAVOURY RICE AND VEGETABLES
2 servings
1 small onion, chopped
100g/4 oz long grain rice
15g/½oz butter

275 ml/½ pint boiling chicken stock
8 ml/½ tbsp finely chopped parsley
125g/4 oz frozen mixed veg. (from a large packet)
1 Put the onion and butter into a 1.7 litre/3 pint mixing bowl. Cover with a lid and microwave on High/100% for 1½ minutes.
2 Stir in the rice and the boiling stock with the parsley.
3 Cover and microwave on High/100% for 9 minutes. Stir and set aside, covered for 6-7 minutes.
4 Put the vegetables into a small casserole. Cover and microwave on FULL power for 2-2½ minutes, stirring after 1 minute.
5 After the rice has completed its standing time, fork in the drained vegetables and serve immediately.

As an alternative
Instead of the mixed vegetables, chop 50g/2 oz button mushrooms roughly. Place in a bowl with 15g/½ oz butter. Cover and microwave on High/100% for 30 seconds. Stir. Cover and microwave on High/100% for 30-45 seconds. Stir into the rice after the standing time.

VEGETABLE MEDLEY

4 servings

225g/8 oz cauliflower florets
225g/8 oz carrots, peeled and cut into matchsticks
50g/2 oz celery, chopped
1 small red pepper, roughly chopped
45 ml/3 tbsps white wine
½ tsp dried mint
For the glaze
75g/3 oz butter
5 ml/1 tsp demerara sugar
1 clover garlic, crushed (optional)
Seasoning
To garnish
50g/2 oz toasted almonds (optional)

1 Put the prepared cauliflower, carrots, celery and red pepper into a roasting bag.
2 Dissolve the mint in the white wine and add to the bag.
3 Seal the bag loosely with an elastic band and stand in a large bowl or casserole.
4 Pierce the bag once, near the base, to allow the steam to escape.
5 Microwave on High/100% for 14-15 minutes, turning the bag over once after 6 minutes. Allow to stand for 5 mins while preparing the glaze.
For the glaze
Put the butter, sugar, crushed garlic and the seasoning into a 2.3 litre/4 pint bowl. Microwave, uncovered on Medium/50% for 2 minutes, stir after 1 minute.
To serve
Drain the vegetables after their standing time and toss into the buttery glaze. Serve in a warmed serving dish, sprinkled with the toasted almonds, if used.

VEGETABLE MEDLEY

2 servings

100g/4 oz cauliflower florets
100g/4 oz carrots, peeled and cut into matchsticks
25g/1 oz celery, chopped
½ small red pepper, roughly chopped
30ml/2 tbsp dry white wine
1·5 ml/¼ tsp dried mint
For the glaze
40g/1½ oz butter
½ clove garlic
Seasoning
To garnish
25g/1 oz toasted

almonds
(optional)

1 Proceed exactly as given for 4 servings from point 1-4 inclusive.

5 Microwave on High/100% for 6-7 mins turning the bag over, once after 3 mins. Allow to stand for 3 mins while preparing the glaze.

For the glaze
Put the butter, sugar, crushed garlic and the seasoning into a 1.1 litre/2 pint bowl. Microwave, uncovered on Medium/50% for 2 minutes. Stir after 1 minute.

To serve
Drain the vegetables after their standing time and toss in the buttery glaze. Serve in the warmed serving dish, sprinkled with the toasted almonds, if used.

MUSTARD GLAZED SIRLOIN
4 servings

3lb piece sirloin, boned and rolled
2 cloves garlic, cut into slivers
For the glaze
15 ml/1 tbsp whole grain mustard
15 ml/1 tbsp clear honey
10ml/2 tsp soya sauce
5ml/1 tsp tomato purée

1 Calculate the cooking time, allowing 11 minutes per lb which will result in sirloin, boned and rolled, cooked to a medium condition.
2 With a sharp vegetable knife, make small incisions all over the joint. Stud each incision with a sliver of garlic.
3 Mix all the ingredients for the glaze and brush all over the joint.
4 Stand the joint fat side down, on a microwave roasting rack or upturned tea plate, arranged in a suitable dish. Insert a microwave meat thermometer.
5 Cover joint and thermometer with a split roasting bag.
6 Microwave on High/100% for 5 minutes.
7 Microwave on Medium/50% for 25-30 minutes (carefully turning the joint over and re-covering after 15 minutes), or until the microwave meat thermometer registers 60°C or 140°F.
8 Cover with a tent of foil and set aside for 15 minutes before serving. Serve with a gravy made from the meat juices and a selection of fresh vegetables.

As an alternative
Omit the garlic and add 1 level teaspoon dried parsley or oregano to the glaze.

HONEY SUET PUD
4 servings

A little oil for greasing
45 ml/3 tbsps clear honey
175g/6 oz self raising flour
5 ml/1 tsp baking powder
2½ ml/½ tsp cinnamon
75g/3 oz shredded suet
2 size 2 eggs
45 ml/3 tbsp milk
75g/3 oz light soft brown sugar

1 Lightly grease a 1.1 litre/2 pint pudding basin with oil.
2 Spread the honey over the base and sides.
3 Sieve the flour, baking powder and cinnamon into a large mixing bowl. Mix in the sugar and suet.
4 Beat together the eggs and milk and stir into the dry ingredients. Pile into basin. Level top.
5 Microwave, covered on Medium/50% for 10-12 mins.
6 Allow to stand, covered, for 6 mins before turning out. Serve with extra honey and custard.

HONEY SUET PUD
2 servings

A little oil for greasing
30ml/2 tbsps clear honey
75g/3 oz self raising flour
2·5 ml/½ tsp baking powder
1·5 ml/¼ tsp cinnamon
40g/1½ oz shredded suet

1 size 2 egg
30-45 ml/2-3 tbsps milk
40g/1½ oz demerara sugar
1 Lightly grease a 0.8 litre/1½ pint pudding basin with oil.
2 Continue exactly as given for honey suet pud for 4 servings until point 5.
5 Microwave, covered, on Medium/50% for 6-8 minutes.
6 Allow to stand, covered, for 5 minutes before turning out. Serve with extra honey and custard.
As an alternative
Use apricot or strawberry jam instead of the honey and serve with a sweet white sauce.

PINEAPPLE UPSIDE DOWN PUDDING
6 servings

Oil and castor sugar
2 tbsp golden syrup
225g/8 oz can pineapple slices, drained
5 glacé cherries, halved
125g/4 oz soft margarine
125g/4 oz castor sugar
75g/3 oz self raising flour sieved
25g/1 oz cocoa   together
2 size 2 eggs
1 tbsp sherry or milk
½ level tsp cinnamon
1 Prepare a 19cm/7" soufflé dish. Lightly brush base and sides with oil. Sprinkle a little castor sugar on sides to coat lightly. Knock out any surplus.
2 Spoon the golden syrup over the base of the dish. Arrange the drained pineapple and cherries in an attractive pattern on the syrup.
3 In a large mixing bowl, put the margarine, castor sugar, flour and cocoa, cinnamon and the eggs.
4 Mix to combine. Add the sherry or milk and beat with a wooden spoon for 1 minute.
5 Turn the mixture onto the prepared decoration. Level the top.
6 Microwave, uncovered on High/100%

for 6 - 7 minutes. Turn the pudding ¼ turn, twice or three times during this time.
7 Allow to stand in the container for 10 minutes before turning out. Serve warm with cream or ice cream.

PINEAPPLE UPSIDE DOWN PUDDING
2 - 3 servings

Oil and castor sugar
30ml/1 tbsp golden syrup
2 slices from a 225g/8 oz can pineapple slices, drained
3 glacé cherries, halved
50g/2 oz soft margarine
50g/2 oz castor sugar
40g/1½ oz self raising flour
15g/½ oz cocoa
1 size 2 egg
1 tbsp sherry or milk
A pinch of cinnamon
1 Follow the recipe exactly as given for 6 servings but select a 5" round soufflé dish for the container and use the pineapple, syrup and cherries as directed in list of ingredients for 2 – 3. Make up sponge exactly as given for 6 servings but use quantities as specified for 2 – 3. Turn the mixture onto the decoration and level the top.
6 Microwave, uncovered on High/100% for 4 minutes. The pudding should be well risen and springy to the touch. Turn the pudding ¼ turn twice during cooking.
7 Allow to stand in container for 5 minutes before turning out. Serve warm with cream or ice cream.

ALMOND FAIRY CAKES
Makes about 15 cakes

100g/4 oz softened butter
100g/4 oz castor sugar
75g/3 oz self raising flour
25g/1 oz ground almonds
2 size 2 eggs

1 tbsp milk mixed with 2 drops of almond essence
30 paper cake cases
For the topping
150g/5 oz plain chocolate
A few toasted flaked almonds
1 Put all the ingredients for the cakes into a large mixing bowl. Combine with a wooden spoon and then beat the mixture for 1 minute.
2 Arrange double-paper cases in a microwave muffin pan or arrange 6 double-paper cake cases in a ring fashion on a dinner plate, if the muffin pan is not available.
3 Put a dessert spoon of mixture into each double -paper case.
4 Microwave on FULL power for 1 – 1½ minutes or until level with the top of the paper case and just set.
5 Allow to stand in the container for 2 – 3 minutes and then transfer to a cooling tray and allow to become quite cold.
6 Continue with this method until all the mixture has been used, remembering to reduce the microwave cooking time if reducing the number of cakes.
To Finish the Fairy Cakes
Break the chocolate into pieces and place in a 0.8 litre/1½ pint bowl. Microwave on Medium/50% for 2 minutes. Stir gently. Microwave Medium/50% for 1½ – 2 minutes, or until melted. Stir every minute and remove as soon as the chocolate has melted. Using a teaspoon, top the cakes with melted chocolate. Top with a few toasted nuts and allow chocolate to set before serving.

CHOCOLATE APRICOT PUD
4 servings

N.B. It is not possible to give accurate directions to serve 2 for this recipe.
Oil for greasing
1 commercially prepared packet of chocolate sponge mix
1 x 397g/14 oz can apricot pie filling
2 tbsp water

1 Prepare a 900 ml/1½ pint plastic pudding basin by greasing very lightly with a little oil.
2 Make up the packet mix exactly as directed on the packet, but add 2 extra tablespoons milk or water.
3 Transfer to pudding basin.
4 Microwave, uncovered, on High/100% for 4 minutes, or on 70%Roast for about 6-7 minutes until well risen and springy to the touch. Set aside.
5 Empty the contents of the can of pie filling into a bowl. Stir in water and microwave on High/100% for 3 minutes, stirring every minute.
6 Turn the pudding out onto a dinner plate and top with the heated fruit sauce. Serve immediately.
As an alternative
Use a plain packet sponge mix and a can of raspberry and apple or black cherry pie filling.

COUNTRY ROAST CHICKEN
4 servings

1 x 1.8 kg/4lb roasting chicken
40g/1½ oz butter
For the stuffing
100g/4 oz fresh brown breadcrumbs
125 ml/4 fl oz milk
50g/2 oz chicken liver (taken from the giblets)
1 tbsp freshly chopped parsley
Grated rind and juice of ½ lemon
1 small onion, finely chopped
50g/2 oz shredded suet
1 tbsp ground almonds
Seasoning
For the topping
2-3 tsps chicken seasoning
1 tsp mixed herbs
1 Prepare the stuffing in a 3pt bowl. Pour the milk onto the breadcrumbs and leave to soak for ½ hour.
2 Gradually mix in the chopped chicken liver, parsley, lemon rind and juice, suet and ground almonds. Season.
3 Spoon the stuffing into the neck end,

but do not pack too tightly. Secure with wooden cocktails sticks. Put remaining stuffing into cavity.
4 Put the butter into a small bowl and microwave on 70% or roast for 30 secs – 1 min to melt.
5 Using a pastry brush, brush the bird all over with the melted butter.
6 Combine the chicken seasoning and mixed herbs in a small bowl and sprinkle all over the chicken.
7 Weigh the prepared chicken and calculate the cooking time. Allow 7 mins per lb on High/100%.
8 Arrange the bird on a microwave meat roasting rack or an upturned tea plate in a suitable dish, breast side down.
9 Cover with a split roasting bag, keeping the bag inside the rim of the dish.
10 Microwave for calculated cooking time. Turn bird over and recover half way through cooking time.
11 Remove from microwave, cover with a tent of foil and allow to stand for 20 minutes before carving.
If your microwave manufacturer allows the use of foil in small quantities, the wings and the stuffed area may be protected with a small amount of foil before the bird is cooked in the microwave. This will prevent over-cooking. Please refer to the manual which came with your oven before you use foil.

COUNTRY ROAST CHICKEN
2 servings

1 x 2lb 8 oz/1.1kg roasting chicken
25g/1 oz butter
For the stuffing
50g/2 oz fresh brown breadcrumbs
50 ml/2 fl oz milk
25g/1 oz chicken liver (taken from the giblets)
½ tbsp freshly chopped parsley
½ tbsp grated lemon rind
½ small onion, finely chopped
25g/1oz shredded suet
½ tbsp ground almonds

Seasoning
Topping
2 tsps chicken seasoning
½ tsp mixed herbs
1 Proceed exactly as given for the country roast chicken for 4 servings, remembering that the butter will melt a little quicker.
11 The standing time may be shortened to 15 mins for the smaller bird.

MICROWAVE COOKING by Beverley Piper. Published by Colour Library Books for BHS Ltd. 99p.

COOKING IN COLOUR – MICROWAVE COOKING by Beverley Piper. Published by Octopus Books for Tescos. £1.99.

SIMPLY DIVINE

Recipes according to the Cooking Canon and Rabbi Blue

When the Reverend John Eley teamed up with Rabbi Lionel Blue as a one-off experiment in the Pebble Mill kitchen last year, it turned out to be a winning combination of faiths and tastes.

So we have invited them together again with some of their favourite recipes.

John, well known as TV's 'Cooking Canon', is the Vicar of Bromsgrove in Worcestershire. Lionel is Convenor of the Beth Din, or Rabbinic Court of the Reform Synagogue of Great Britain. He's well known for his regular broadcasts on 'Thought for the Day' and as a columnist and cookery writer.

REVEREND JOHN ELEY

I have always liked the Old Testament, because of the huge helpings of common sense in its pages, a commodity that is lacking in so much of what we aspire to today. That's probably why I am such a fan of the Radio Four 'Today' programme and the 'Thought for the Day' slot when Rabbi Lionel Blue is on. There is a sort of basic sense about the Old Testament that Lionel seems to bring to the fore; if you break the rules, you will burn your fingers, but God loves you and if you say you are sorry you'll get some help to get things right in the end. There is a similarity with cooking too. If you don't follow the recipe correctly then the chances are things will go wrong and then the result may be as tasty as a pillar of salt or something struck by lightning – a charred mess!

'Pebble Mill at One' viewers have kept me busy again this year presenting nationwide charity 'Cook-Ins'. Our common love of cooking means that we exchange recipes and I am thrilled to discover that people do actually try mine! Hospitality everywhere has been tremendous and it is such fun to sit at a new table with new friends and discuss life and food. One of the things we all agree is that it brings people together and breaks down barriers. There are far too many people who have to eat alone today because they no longer have a partner. I have started to suggest to some of the elder members of the Parish that once a week they get together with a few friends and each prepare part of the meal and eat at one home, a sort of mini-luncheon club. Some people have tried it and have had great fun occasionally inviting me along as a guest! Lionel and I are including some dishes for the lonely palate and some just to spoil yourself with!

Both Lionel and I have had adventures in the kitchen. Some of the less successful ones will probably need courage to relate, but with a helping hand from each other, we may just be able to manage it. We have both had to entertain unusual guests . . . What do you do if you have a Bishop and a Rabbi round to dinner?

RABBI LIONEL BLUE

Speaking professionally and ecclesiastically, both John and I know that perfection cannot be found in this world. It is reserved for the world to come when the most exquisite nectar (nicely chilled) will be served with quality ambrosia at room temperature for the select.

In this world, life never goes according to plan. Yes, you have made four lovely little soufflés (how nice they look in their individual pots!). But your spouse has brought five people to dinner, not four, and such high rise delights as soufflés cannot be reconstituted. (If you are imaginative though, you will serve the collapsed remnants as 'Oeufs à la Something' and you might get away with it, provided you are brazen enough). Or you have invited your new neighbours in for Sunday lunch and, as you slice away at the Roast Beef, they tell you shyly that for a variety of reasons involving their health or their belief, they never touch the stuff. They will make do with vegetables and nuts, if you have any. Or, and this is not so funny, a festival like Christmas has come and, while everybody is celebrating with everybody else, you have to comfort and cook for yourself alone.

The kitchen is the world in miniature, needing the resources of our body and soul. Even if you serve caviar (which is unlikely) it needs an accompaniment of kindness, and all food needs the seasoning of generosity.

Imagination is a very precious commodity in the kitchen. With imagination it is possible to make a main course without meat which satisfies both meat eaters and vegetarians. In John's recipe, for example, leeks can be luscious and his salmon creates no problems for many believers who have difficulties with meat.

Actually, difficulties make for interesting cooking. Mayonnaise, for example, was invented out of necessity, not out of luxury. There was a battlefield, and the only ingredients available were eggs and oil (and presumably vinegar or lemons). It was a stroke of genius to find a way of combining them.

I myself started to learn cooking as a child from my grandmother. She came from Eastern Europe and, God rest her soul, had to produce good things for a large family without a processor and in poverty. At an early age, I understood that even scraps of food are precious and a little has to go a long way. It is amazing how far you can stretch one avocado in the soup recipe and I think a paté of aubergine will present a pleasant surprise to those who have only tasted patés made out of liver and lights. Once you get the hang of it, aubergine is a good-tempered vegetable. Grandma would have approved of the soup and the paté.

Of course, in her day, nobody had ever bumped into a calorie, or would have recognised one if they had. So 'Janssen's Temptation' with potatoes cooking in a pint of cream was recommended for women and children, both of whom were preferred plump (How tastes change!).

Like hers, my cooking is limited by the Jewish food laws: I cannot, therefore, cook milk with meat or after it, and smoked meat substitutes for bacon rashers. But I do not think you will miss out, for the fruit salad is bathed in vodka, and the cream cheese is enriched with Irish coffee liqueur and walnuts. It's a fair swop!

AVOCADO SOUP (L.B.)

Salmon was once so cheap that it was written into servants' contracts that they should not have too much of it. Herrings, which in my childhood were almost give-away, are still inexpensive, but certainly not for the taking. On the other hand, trout is still a treat, but affordable if you have a job, and avocados, if you buy them when they are ripe and being sold off, are cheap. They are also nutritious and very versatile. It is simple to turn them into an hors d'oeuvres, a soup, a dip or a dessert. Here is a recipe for thick chilled avocado soup, filling enough to require only good bread and fruit for a summer lunch.

1 large ripe avocado
½ pint hot vegetable stock (it can be made with a cube)
¾ pint milk
4 oz single cream
2 tsp salt
12 grinds pepper
2 oz dried potato flakes or 4 oz left-over boiled potatoes
2 spring onions
1 tbsp lemon juice (or more to taste)
Chopped chives

Mix the hot stock with the potato flakes.

Chop the spring onions and scoop out the flesh of the avocado. In a blender or a food processor, mix all the ingredients except the cream and lemon juice. When the mixture is well blended stir in the cream and then the lemon juice. Chill thoroughly for 2 to 3 hours. Serve garnished with chopped chives.

EGG AND LEEK PIES (J.E.)

Savouries are always a welcome punctuation mark in any meal and this one fits well with many other dishes, or indeed as a main course dish for those who do not necessarily like meat for religious or other reasons.

Try these at a family party; they always tell the truth about food.

1lb leeks
2 oz butter
5 fl oz soured cream
4 large eggs
4 heaped tsp of Parmesan cheese
1lb packet of puff pastry
½ tsp of grated nutmeg

Roll out the puff pastry to make enough to fill four 4" flan or torte tins and lids.

In a thick saucepan, melt the butter gently and add the chopped leeks and season a little with salt and black pepper. Cover and allow to cook until they are absolutely soft. This will take ten to fifteen minutes.

Remove them from the heat and allow them to cool. Divide this mixture amongst the four flan cases. Make a little shallow in the middle of the leek mixture, just enough to hold an egg when broken into it. Then break an egg into each of the shallows.

Place a dessertspoonful of cream on the top of each egg with a little grated nutmeg and then a teaspoon of Parmesan cheese on top of the soured cream.

Seal on the lid of the puff pastry and brush well with a beaten egg.

Place in the middle of an oven Gas 7 – 425°F for about ten minutes and then turn down to Gas 5 – 375°F for about 20 or so minutes.

Remove from the tins and serve immediately.

A variation on this dish is to serve it with some crispy bacon mixed into the leeks.

In the past I have made them for buffets about the size of mince pies, having carefully scrambled the egg first and they have gone down well.

SABAYON STRAWBERRIES (L.B.)

I normally dislike the dishes which have to be cooked at the last moment. They make me edgy and I can't enjoy my own party. Sabayon Sauce is an exception because it is docile and if you make simple preparations there are no nasty surprises. It costs a lot in a restaurant, but very little if you make it yourself.

For 4 people you will need 1lb of strawberries
2 tbsp of icing sugar
4 egg yolks (use whites for meringues) from size 3 eggs or larger
4 tbsp of castor sugar
4 tbsp of sweet sherry or any other sweet fortified wine such as port or madeira
You will need the following implements;
An electric hand-held beater
A saucepan half full with simmering water
A china bowl which fits into the saucepan and sits on its rim
4 large wine glasses or tumblers

Hull the strawberries, cut them in half, and dust them with 2 tbsp of icing sugar. Divide them among the 4 glasses. Chill in the fridge.

When the main course is being served, put the saucepan on the stove to simmer.

It should start to simmer when you are collecting up the main course plates.

Now you have to work speedily but not recklessly.

In the bowl put the egg yolks, castor sugar, and fortified wine. Sit the bowl in the saucepan half filled with water, simmering on the stove. Beat the contents of the bowl immediately, without stopping the electric beater (if you only have a manual beater, make rice pudding or something else instead).

The egg/wine mixture will gradually increase in bulk and thickness (about 6 or 7 minutes). When it holds its shape like whipped cream, turn off the heat, lift the bowl out, and spoon the Sabayon into the 4 glasses over the strawberries. Serve immediately.

Two cautions; if you beat too long you will get scrambled eggs. If you don't serve it immediately and let the sauce cool, the egg and wine will separate. But don't be frightened; it is easy enough and one practice makes perfect.

It is really a very superior custard and much more interesting with strawberries than any cream, except perhaps clotted.

AUBERGINE PATÉ (L.B.)

Aubergines with their bulbous shape and shiny purple skin look exotic on the greengrocer's shelf. They have two drawbacks for the cook. They can absorb oil like blotting paper and some people don't like their bitter juice, so they cut them, salt them and drain them before cooking.

This recipe avoids both problems. The aubergines are baked, not fried, and I don't taste any bitterness, only a smokiness which is interesting and makes me want more. It is an hors d'oeuvres which goes well with sesame biscuits, or crackers, or Greek Pitta bread, or toast. It will remind you of romance, little mediterranean cafés and your last package holiday.

2 large aubergines (1¾ – 2 lbs)
1 large onion
2 cloves garlic
3 tbsp of olive oil
1 tbsp lemon juice
1 small onion
½ tsp sugar
1 tsp salt
12 grinds pepper
Tomatoes, olives and parsley for garnishing.

Prick the aubergines with a fork and bake them in a hot oven (400°F – Gas 6 200°C) until they are soft and wrinkled – for about an hour. Peel and chop the large onion and garlic and fry them in the olive oil until brown.

When the aubergines are cooked, skin them. Chop together (I use a food processor) the aubergine flesh and all the other ingredients, except the small raw onion and the garnish. Chop the small onion finely and mix into the chopped aubergine.

Cooked aubergine has a greyish look, so decorate with slices of red tomato, green and black olives and chopped parsley.

flying start! Commercially soured cream can be bought in most supermarkets, for ordinary pasteurized milk does not go sour; it just goes off.

The red fruit that I have suggested can be varied – so can the quantities – but make sure you include berries, for they give it the fragrance of the great forests. For 4 people I use 1½ lbs of fruit in all, using redcurrants and 2 or 3 of the following: strawberries, raspberries, cherries or red plums cut up.

Stem the currants, cut the strawberries in half, and stone the cherries or plums. Layer the fruit in the glass bowl, contrasting where possible the shades of red. Sugar each layer. For 1½ lbs fruit you will need about 5 ozs of castor sugar. Pour over 2 fluid ozs of vodka. Cover the bowl and put it in the refrigerator overnight or for 3 or 4 hours.

Serve with a jug of soured cream. If you can't get it, mix together 1 small pot of plain yoghurt and 1 small pot of single cream (about 4 fluid ozs of each).

be able to share the meal with a friend.

4 salmon steaks
2 oz butter
1 bay leaf
5 fl oz of fish stock
5 fl oz soured cream
2 tbsp of freshly chopped chives
1 oz plain flour
Black pepper

Place the salmon steaks in an oven-proof dish and dot with the 2 oz of butter. Grate on a little fresh black pepper; add the fish stock and the bay leaf together with the chopped chives. Cover with lid or foil and place in the centre of an oven set at Gas 5 – 375°F and cook for 25 minutes, or however long you like to have your salmon cooked.

After cooking, remove the salmon steaks from the dish and keep them warm. Blend the flour with a little water and add to the stock left over from cooking the salmon. It may be necessary to add a little water or milk, or reduce the quantity of flour, depending on how you like your sauces. Sometimes I leave the flour out altogether and simply add the cream; however, in this case, let's add the flour and let it cook on top of the stove for one minute at least, before removing from the heat and adding the soured cream. Another variation is to use a mixture of soured and double cream, depending upon your needs.

TO SERVE

Heat an oval serving dish gently. Remove the bone and the skin from the salmon steaks and place them to one side. Pour the sauce over the heated serving dish. Arrange the salmon steaks on the serving dish and garnish with the rest of the freshly chopped chives.

TIP: If you use dried chives, soak them in water, using equal quantities of chives and water.

PETER'S PEACHES (J.E.)

"Peter was a choirboy who used to come to tea;
Whilst wandering in the garden he found our small peach tree!
He looked upon the single fruit and thought it going to waste;
So he deftly picked it out and took it home to taste.
Now Peter was a thoughtful boy who felt treasures should be shared;
So he took it to the kitchen and this dish he carefully prepared.
He thought How awfully clever this dish

CANON SALMON (J.E.)

I make no excuse; this is a dish that is one of my favourites and is one that I sometimes treat myself to when I feel the need to spoil myself; but it is always better to share this with a friend as half the pleasure is seeing others enjoy and pass judgement on your labours in the kitchen.

Alas, no longer does the odd salmon mysteriously leap upon my doorstep as it did in the days when I lived in the Cathedral Close at Carlisle; I never did discover who my mysterious benefactor was there. However, thankfully, there is now a wide supply of British produced and farmed salmon which serve us well, although I still think the mystery of the 'real thing' adds an awful lot to the dish.

I do hope that you enjoy this and will

RUSSIAN FRUIT SALAD (L.B.)

I like recipes for food which look after themselves, such as fruit which makes its own syrup.

This is a colourful Russian fruit salad, which graces any dinner party and is as lovely to look at as it is easy to prepare. It does need a glass dish to show off all the glowing red fruits that make it up; and the vodka gets the company off to a

to make by me;
I'll make a lot to share it with my Mummy for her tea."

And that's just how Peter's Peaches were presented to me, although I suspect slightly adapted for the adult palate by Mummy, but a tasty dish for one or two or more.

4 fresh peaches
4 oz chopped gammon ham
4 tbsp of mayonnaise
1 large tbsp of fresh mustard
2 tbsp freshly chopped parsley

A delightfully simple starter or indeed a dish to be included in that special buffet lunch when you wish to give your guests a treat.

If you can manage fresh peaches, all the better; but, if not, then do what I do and use tinned ones!

However, if you are using fresh peaches, they will need some preparation. Bring a large pan of water to the boil and dump the peaches in. Leave to simmer for about a minute. Remove the peaches with a serrated spoon and they will be ready to peel with the minimum of effort. Cut the peaches in half around the middle, rather than from top to bottom, and remove the stone. Ripe peaches are really best for this operation as the stone tends to get irreparably stuck in under-ripe ones.

Now for the filling. Make sure that you chop the gammon ham into small cubes. To help you do this try and buy your meat in one thickish slice.

Blend together your mayonnaise, mustard and half the chopped parsley. Mix in with the meat and then place a spoonful of this mixture into each half of the peaches. Sprinkle over the rest of the parsley, chill and serve.

TIP: To vary this a little, sprinkle on a little cayenne pepper!

JANSSEN'S TEMPTATION (L.B.)

I was first offered 'Janssen's Temptation' in Sweden. It was the centrepiece of an elaborate buffet. Unfortunately, I thought it was the main course and ate too much, but it was only a starter. What a starter! You can't stop eating it and it contains more calories than I ever thought possible in a single dish. It is the antidote to any cuisine minceur.

For the cook, the ingredients are simple to prepare. It is a good tempered dish which you can keep warm on a hot tray. Even if your guests dislike anchovies, I doubt if they will detect them – they melt into the potatoes.

This quantity will serve 4 generously as a main course (serve with a green salad) or 8 as a starter.

1½ lbs old potatoes
1 large onion
1 clove garlic
2 oz tin of anchovies (drain and reserve the oil)
1 tsp salt
12 grinds black pepper (¼ teaspoon)
1 dessertspoon butter
1 pint single cream
2 tbsp tomato purée

Peel the potatoes and slice them thinly (on a slicer, mandolin or food processor).

Chop the onions and the garlic and fry them in butter until soft, but not brown. Grease a shallow baking dish. Mix the single cream with the tomato purée, salt and pepper. Take the anchovies from the tin and chop them roughly. In the dish spread first a layer of potatoes, then a layer of onions and anchovies. Repeat once more and put another layer of potato on top. Pour the cream over and shake the dish so that it goes down among the layers.

Bake for half an hour (375°F Gas 5 190°C) covered with foil or any cover that fits. Then remove the cover, pour over the oil from the anchovy tin and continue baking for another 45 minutes or until the potatoes are cooked and amalgamated with the cream and the top is brown.

ASCENSION SOUFFLÉ (J.E.)

At the beginning of the Eighties, when I first started cooking on television, I was asked to do some dishes for the festivals of the church. Christmas and Easter were relatively easy as there are a wealth of traditional treats for those occasions. Ascensiontide, as well as being rather difficult to spell, provided me with a modest challenge. We aren't really Ascension-minded in the Church of England – well, at least not in parts. In France there is a delightful butter cake which traditionally has a china model of Christ in it which the lucky one finds. The answer was of course obvious for me in the end, and so this soufflé appeared. The addition of lemon mint highlights the flavour and has gone down very well with all who have tried it.

8 large eggs
9 oz castor sugar
6 lemons
¾ pint double cream
¼ pint soured cream
1 dessertspoon of freshly chopped lemon mint or mint
1 heaped tbsp of gelatine
A little water, quite hot

Place the gelatine in a cup of hot water and allow to dissolve. I use the packet variety that comes in sachets and that way I have the instructions and follow the rules!

Chop the mint up finely and add to the soured cream and allow to stand.

Separate the eggs. Place the yolks in a large bowl together with the castor sugar, lemon juice and the grated rind of the lemons. Whisk this mixture thoroughly until it is light and creamy. It usually takes about five minutes whisking to satisfy me that it is light enough. Then place this bowl in a large pan of simmering water and allow to thicken stirring with a balloon whisk all the time. When the mixture has thickened quite well, remove from the heat and stir in the gelatine and stir very well with the balloon whisk.

Whisk the double cream until it is very thick and to this add the soured cream. Fold this into the lemon mixture and make sure it is well blended.

Now whisk the eggs until they really peak well and are very stiff. If you are in doubt, hold the bowl of beaten egg whites over your head and if they fall out then they are not beaten well enough! With a large metal spoon, fold the egg whites into the lemon mixture. Use a figure of 8 stirring action to fold the egg whites in well.

Now prepare your soufflé dish. I recommend a 1½ to 2 pint size dish to which has been added a white collar (naturally!), made out of grease-proof paper which extends about 3" above the edge of the dish. Pour in the mixture and allow to set for at least 3 hours. If you do decide to make this in a hurry and you have not left yourself enough setting time, pop it in the freezer for about an hour; this helps speed the process up.

Decorate with a sprig of fresh mint to serve.

TIP: If you do decide to let this set overnight in a fridge or indeed take the short cut of popping it in the refrigerator, cover the top of the collar with plastic film.

If you would like to make the mint sprig more interesting, crystallize it by dipping it in some boiling sugar.

If you do not like the idea of fresh mint use some crumbled Mint Cake from the Lake District. Ah, yes . . . . you could also use a little cream!

85

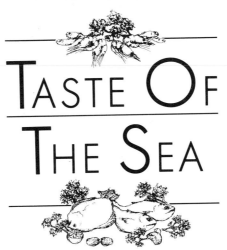

Taste Of The Sea

Sue Hicks has lived on the Isles of Scilly for many years and island resourcefulness and inventiveness have helped develop her great passion for fish dishes.

She brims with enthusiasm and with a determination to persuade viewers to cast aside their traditional attitude to fish and shellfish. And gradually the image is being changed. From the dreadful days of soggy fish and chips, boiled cod on Fridays and doubtful fillets cloaked in unimaginative sauces, we are now turning to fish for its health value, its subtlety and its freshness.

And so she makes the journey to Pebble Mill from the Scillies for another series armed with more exciting recipes.

From the Isles of Scilly to Pebble Mill – sounds exciting, doesn't it? Unfortunately, my style of travel rarely goes smoothly. Even though I can sport the jet-setting tan and dark glasses, I usually leave my home in oilskins and wellingtons and by means of wheelbarrow, tractor, open boat, pre-war bus and then bent double (and clutching my fish) in a small flying machine, I'm eventually airborne for the mainland. At Plymouth, I connect with a grown-up aeroplane. The baggage inspector pales as he solemnly draws out four very sharp twelve-inch knives from my briefcase; the queue behind me shrinks back a few yards. A sad shake of his head and a low whistle of breath as he opens a small plastic bag containing green grassy-looking leaves. "Tarragon," I explain. The

drug-taking terrorist continues the flight to Heathrow, where the knives are returned by a bemused stewardess. On the underground into London, my wellingtons and oilskins are curiously gazed upon by a glamourous family of Arabs. At Euston, I feel that perhaps the fish is beginning to smell – or why else in the huge milling crowd am I the only passenger with a clear space of twenty yards behind me? At Birmingham, I am relieved of the fish by a receptionist, who clearly thinks it might attack her, and it goes to some dark, cool, mysterious place in the bowels of the hotel: the tarragon goes in the toothmug and I go to bed, having first removed my wellingtons. When I arrive at the studio the following morning, the friendly but casual greetings imply that I have just stepped off my sun-kissed island and arrived by magic. Incidentally, I do not wear my wellingtons in the studio.

Another inconvenience for the tiny island cook is in the procuring of exotic ingredients. I mean, mainlanders might consider my consumption of oysters, lobster, crab and all manner of wonderful seafish as exotic – but the quest for two tomatoes, a pound of onions and three strands of saffron can often pose a major problem. So the island cook becomes

highly inventive and, happily, fish is one of the most delicious, versatile and nourishing foods on this planet. From my window, I can see the tell-tale ripples of shoals of grey mullet. And passing fishing boats have catches of monkfish and hake on their way to join the spectacular, gleaming displays on the slab of the fish markets.

I'm so glad to see the renewed interest in fish and the awareness of healthy eating reflected in the increased sales of fresh fish. I hope that my short series helps to demystify some of the techniques of cleaning, trimming, filleting and boning and that you will try some of the recipes. Be intrepid at the fishmongers: unbutton your imagination and have a go!

MARINATED PLAICE
Spicy and Hot

4 x 12oz plaice (or other suitable flat fish)
5 oz natural yoghurt
2 tbsp tomato purée
2 cloves garlic
Juice of ½ lemon
1 onion, chopped
½ tsp chilli powder, to taste
1 tsp coriander
½ tsp ground turmeric
Parsley
Sea salt and freshly ground black pepper
Butter (optional)

Clean the fish and cut slashes in a criss-cross pattern on both sides.

Make a paste with remaining ingredients, using a food processor or liquidiser. Smother the fish with this marinade, making sure it penetrates all the slashes and leave it in a cool place for 2 or 3 hours.

Then you can either gently fry the fish in butter, or grill them under a moderate heat, basting all the time with the remaining paste. As usual, plainly boiled potatoes and green salad with this dish.

GRAVAD LAX

Here's a wonderful and luxurious treat – Gravad Lax, or Gravlax, originally from Sweden. It is available in good food stores and is wildly expensive. But you can make it yourself quite easily and for no more than the cost of good fillet steak. I can rarely get hold of fresh dill just when I want it, but I've used fennel leaves with exquisite results. Mackerel and other fish can be given this treatment.

Middle cut of a salmon – about 1½ lbs
1 bunch of fresh dill or fennel leaves
½ tbsp crushed peppercorns
2 tbsp of sea salt } mixed
1 tbsp of castor sugar

First bone the descaled fish, fillet, leaving the skin on. Place one half of the fish skin down in a flat dish, scatter and rub half the mixture onto the flesh. Top with sprigs of dill or fennel, rub the other half with remaining mixture and place it skin side up on the first fillet, forming a sandwich. Cover with foil or cling film, then a weighted plate or basin on top. Refrigerate for at least 36 hours or so – turning every 12 hours.

The pale pink flesh of the salmon deepens to the colour of smoked salmon. To serve, scrape off the herbs and peppercorns, taken an extremely sharp knife and slice thinner than paper slices on the bias and hand round with the following sauce.

2 tbsp of Dijon or German Mustard
1 tbsp of castor sugar
1 yolk of a large egg
¼ pint olive oil
Chopped fennel or dill weed
Lemon juice or white wine vinegar

Mix the Dijon or German mustard

CHILLED MARINATED COD STEAKS

I've successfully used hake, pollack and grey mullet for this dish.
4 cod steaks
Vegetable oil
1 glass dry white wine
6 tbsp white wine vinegar
2-3 cloves garlic, crushed
Sea salt and good measure of freshly ground black pepper
1 dozen cloves
Juice and rind of 2 oranges and 2 lemons
Bouquet of parsley, tarragon, thyme and bayleaf

Fry the cod steaks gently in the oil for a few minutes each side and arrange them in the base of a dish suitable to hold marinade. Add all the other ingredients to the fish juices in the pan, bring to the boil and simmer for five minutes. Pour over the cod steaks to cover completely, cool, then refrigerate overnight. Lift the cod steaks onto a serving dish, pour over a little of the strained marinade and decorate with parsley or fresh tarragon.

with the sugar and beat in egg yolk. Proceed as for mayonnaise, finally seasoning to taste and adding chopped fennel or dill.

BOURRIDE
A Classic Soup

You can use your own choice of firm white fish for this dish – I recommend monkfish, or perhaps some fillets of turbot.

3lb firm white fish
2 leeks, finely sliced
1 onion, finely sliced
1lb sliced potatoes
2/3 crushed cloves garlic, to taste
<u>Aioli</u> **made with 2/3 egg yolks, ½ pint olive oil, lemon juice, seasoning, and 4 cloves of garlic.**
<u>Stock</u> **made with 8 oz fish trimmings, 2 onions, 2/3 sticks of celery, strips of orange and lemon peel, ¼ pint of dry cider or white wine and approx 1 pint water, sea salt and freshly ground black pepper.**

First make the stock in the normal way. Prepare your choice of fish, cut into largish pieces and arrange them in a large pan on top of the finely sliced leeks, onion, crushed garlic and sliced potatoes. Cover with the stock and poach for about ten minutes or until the fish is tender. Transfer the fish and potatoes to a heated serving dish and keep warm. Reduce the remaining stock to one third, then strain slowly and carefully into the aioli, beating all the time. Gently reheat, but do not allow to boil. Pour over the fish and potatoes and serve with croutons, or sliced French bread fried in olive oil.

<u>Aioli</u> – thoroughly pound 4 peeled cloves of garlic in a basin, then cream in the egg yolks. Add olive oil drop by drop, beating all the time and, as mixture thickens, increase oil to a slow stream until you have a nice thick consistency. Add a few squeezes of lemon juice and season to taste. All the ingredients for this mayonnaise should be at room temperature, the eggs more than four days old and the mixing basin perfectly dry inside.

GRILLED SOLE WITH SOUR CREAM AND GHERKIN SAUCE

4 fillets of sole (or plaice)
1 oz butter
Sea salt and freshly ground black pepper
½ pint fish stock
¼ pint sour cream
2 or 3 gherkins

Make stock with heads and trimmings of fish, a couple of roughly chopped carrots, one large onion, roughly chopped, a bayleaf and parsley, sea salt and freshly ground black pepper and about ⅓rd pint dry white wine or cider. Season the fillets and dot with butter. Then grill under a moderate heat for about five minutes or until the fish is tender. Transfer to heated serving dish and keep warm. Pour the sour cream into the fish stock and bring carefully to the boil – then add the sliced gherkins and cook gently for a minute. Pour the sauce over the fillets and serve immediately with plainly boiled potatoes or fresh brown bread and a simple crisp green salad.

FISH, FENNEL AND SPINACH TERRINE

8oz raw fillets of firm white fish – any kind
8oz double cream
3 eggs
Sea salt and fresh ground black pepper
1 tbsp of chopped fennel leaves
8oz crab meat
2oz pine nuts
Pinch cayenne
Sufficient large leaves of spinach (or cabbage) to line terrine and make layers.

Blanch the whole spinach leaves, drain, pat dry and set aside. If you have a food processor, put the chopped raw white fish, cream, eggs, seasoning and fennel into bowl and process until smooth. Alternatively, and for a pleasingly rougher texture, flake the fish, add the beaten eggs, cream, seasoning and fennel and combine with a fork. Season the crab, add cayenne to taste and add the pine nuts. Grease a loaf tin or terrine and carefully line with spinach leaves, leaving enough overlap to fold over top of the loaf. Then spoon in half of the white fish mixture and cover with a layer of spinach leaves. Add all the crab meat, lightly press down, follow with another layer of spinach leaves and complete the loaf with remaining white fish, folding the overlapping leaves to completely cover. Place a sheet of greased greaseproof paper on the top of the loaf and stand in a baking tin containing about 2 inches of boiling water. Bake in a moderate oven for approximately 45 minutes, or until loaf is nice and firm to the touch. Invert tin, turn out loaf, cool then chill in refrigerator for several hours. Carefully slice and serve this pretty dish with wedges of lemon and brown bread and butter.

STARGAZEY PIE

This is rather a production number – but highly recommended as a robust supper party dish, as well as being a fascinating conversation piece. How did this Cornish dish originate? There are many theories involving myths and a little fact.

1 dozen pilchards, sardines, or small herring (fresh or frozen – not canned)

Chopped parsley
1 tsp ground cloves
1 tsp allspice
1 small onion, finely chopped
5 hard boiled eggs
5oz pot double cream
Freshly ground black pepper
1lb approx shortcrust pastry
1 beaten egg

Carefully bone the pilchards, keeping their heads on and stuff their bellies with parsley, spices and finely chopped onion. Line a large flat pie dish with half of the rolled out pastry and arrange the fish in a wheel shape with their heads overlapping the edge of the pie dish.

Scatter the chopped hardboiled eggs all over, cover with spoonfuls of cream and a few shakes of black pepper. Moisten the edge of the pastry base, then place the pastry lid on top, allowing the fish heads to peep out through clefts in the rim of the pie. Brush with beaten egg (I like to decorate the pie with little shapes of pastry fishes). Bake in a hot oven for 10 to 15 minutes to brown and set the pastry, then for a further 15 minutes in a moderate oven (according to size of fish).

OYSTERS

The romantic and luxurious image of oysters wasn't always so – it was once the food of the poor. But with exciting developments in their production and distribution, they should soon be within the scope of the average household purse.

I love their sea-salty fresh taste as they slide off their shells and into your mouth – a wonderful sensation! All you need is a dash of fresh lemon juice, maybe some pepper, or perhaps a tiny drop of tabasco, and good brown bread. Preferably, you should stand on a balcony facing a magnificent sea view whilst eating them, and if champagne on ice is not at hand, then Guinness is highly recommended.

Alternatively, you may like to try this way of serving them hot.
6 oysters per person (for main course) or
3-4 oysters per person (for starter)
2 cloves garlic
Roughly chopped parsley
4oz butter
Wholemeal breadcrumbs
Freshly grated Parmesan cheese
(optional)

I'm not pretending that opening oysters is easy for the beginner. What you need is a steady hand, a clean tea towel, a knife with a short stout blade and probably a glass of the aforementioned champagne on the go!

Using the towel, grasp the oyster firmly in your left hand, making sure it lies flat side up in your palm – insert blade into the hinge and prise open. As you are separating the shells, slide in a sharp knife and cut the oyster free from top and bottom of the shells. Take care to keep the juice in and remove any flakes of shell that may have fallen on top of the oyster. Arrange the shells with their oysters in a baking dish. To keep them upright, stand them in thick slices of bread in which you have cut out round shapes to cradle the shells.

Cream the butter and crushed garlic and beat in roughly chopped parsley. Put a nut of this butter on each oyster, then a good sprinkling of breadcrumbs. For me, this is enough; but perhaps your palate might require the addition of some freshly grated Parmesan. No more than 10 minutes in a hot oven, or under a hot grill is needed to cook the oysters – brown bread will mop up the combined oyster juice and butter. You should eat them immediately, and that little mouthful from each shell is really quite rich and wicked.

LOBSTER OR CRAWFISH WITH TARRAGON SAUCE

1 small lobster, cooked
2 cucumbers
Small packet of frozen petit pois
½ tsp salt
1 tsp sugar
1 crisp lettuce
1-2 tbsp tarragon vinegar
7oz home-made mayonnaise
7oz natural yoghurt
4 tbsp lobster or fish stock

Lobster is a luxury, but you need only a small one for this exquisite dish. Alternatively, you can use monkfish; its lack of bones, firm texture and taste make it an ideal substitute. I have also used fresh salmon steaks, poached in a good stock, with wonderful results.

If you are using lobster, you can make stock by pounding the shell after removing the meat and boiling it in about a pint of water with seasalt, pepper and a handful of fresh herbs for about one hour. This stock will need straining before use, of course.

Meanwhile, cut the peeled deseeded cucumbers into large matchsticks and toss them in a basin of the marinade of sea salt, sugar and vinegar and leave them in a cool place for an hour. Cook the petit pois briefly, drain and leave to cool. Combine the mayonnaise, yoghurt and fresh chopped tarragon – then carefully stir in the 4 tablespoons of cooled lobster or fish stock. Cut the lobster (or monkfish) into nice chunks and pile onto a platter on which you have made a bed of shredded lettuce. Mix the petit pois with the drained cucumber and arrange around the edge of the dish. Pour over the sauce and garnish with sprigs of fresh tarragon or parsley.

More recipes by Sue Hicks are to be found in THE FISH COOKBOOK (Spring '86) Hamlyn £5.95

ODDIE
1,000 MILES FROM ANYWHERE

Bill Oddie in the Seychelles

The classic Seychelles beach – or is it the backdrop to a film set?

Over the years, 'Pebble Mill at One' has given viewers a glimpse of many of the exciting and exotic parts of the world. One recent expedition was to the Seychelles, the group of tropical paradise islands in the middle of the Indian Ocean. They are 1,000 miles from the east coast of Africa and a little more from the Indian continent; a 1,000 miles, in fact, from anywhere.

The Fairy Tern, a resident of Bird Island and without doubt the most endearing and photogenic of Seychelles birds.

Sooty Terns can be quite aggressive to human intruders. But they showed no fear when I got this picture.

The Seychelles have been described as a String of Pearls in the Indian Ocean and were claimed by General Gordon to be the original site of the Garden of Eden!

But, more than the palm trees and sun-drenched beaches, the islands are a naturalist's treasure house – especially for amateur birdwatchers like Bill Oddie. Bill has always wanted to visit Bird Island – a tiny coral reef populated by millions of unique birds – so he was happy to team up with Paul Coia for an 'island hop', taking in the Seychelles' spectacular beauty.

Here, Bill presents some favourite photographs and memories of his visit.

A scene from Hitchcock's 'Birds'? Bird Island has a colony of over a million birds, nesting in what appears to be exraordinary congestion. The noise is cacophonous.

This has to be the original Garden of Eden!

The limits we bird photographers go to get a magic picture for the album!

If Paul and I are looking quizzical it's because our guide Therese is telling us the legend of this giant nut, the famous Coco-de-mer, reputed to have aphrodisiac properties.

91

THE DONNY MACLEOD AWARD

Bob Langley writes:

The untimely death of our dear colleague Donny MacLeod in the late summer of 1984 came as a tremendous shock to everyone at Pebble Mill, for to us he had seemed almost indestructable. Large, inspiring, full of humour, integrity and compassion, he was universally liked and respected. Curiously, in many ways it seems to the people who knew him that he never died at all, for he was so much a part of the Pebble Mill scene that we tend to think of him as still being there. To nurture that feeling, we decided to create a Donny MacLeod Award to ensure that as long as the programme exists, Donny's name will be associated with it. Knowing of Donny's inherent wanderlust and his great affection for the written word, we invited viewers to submit short stories or articles of up to 1800 words which dealt with, or involved in some oblique way, the subject of travel.

To judge the entries, we chose bestselling authors Leslie Thomas and Lena Kennedy, and – on the strength of nine novels and two travel books – I was invited to complete the panel.

It proved a mind-boggling task. In the first place, we received nearly three thousand manuscripts, vivid proof of the inextinguishable human desire to communicate. In the second, it was virtually impossible to weigh one against the other, for some were funny, some sad, some daringly original, some unashamedly sentimental. In the end, bearing in mind Donny's incomparable talents for capturing the essence of a place with a few beautifully crafted phrases, we opted for a mood piece by Jim Mangnall of Liverpool. We were captivated by the simple rhythm of the sentences, the delicious Hemingwayesque sense of fatalism, and above all by the overwhelming feeling of atmosphere. More important still, we felt it was a story Donny himself would have approved of. Mr Mangnall receives £500 and a Royal Doulton crystal decanter. In the meantime, here in print is the first-ever winner of the Donny MacLeod Award.

It is night and I am at anchor. For the last hour I have been sitting in the lamplight of the small cabin looking at my last cigar lying on the table top. It is a long, slim tube of dark brown leaf. It rolls smoothly between my finger and thumb. It smells exquisite. It is the very last one. Months may pass before I see another and so, for an hour, I have been playing a silly game; finding reasons to light it and reasons to put it back in its place. Only smokers will appreciate this agony. Non-smokers will despise me or pity me. What do they know?

I have put a record on the old, wind-up machine, an ingenious instrument with a lid which serves as a sort of horn or amplifier. My choice of music is limited to eleven records, four of which are too worn to be listened to in comfort, and one which I can't bring myself to hear. In order to avoid playing the same favourites again and again, I have devised a method of random selection by rolling dice and so, with a glass of gin beside me and the river all about me, I am listening to a tenor, thinly singing Danny Boy. It's not too bad.

From the deck, the moon is as clear as the tenor's voice is faint. The smoke from the cigar (which I knew all along I would light) drifts over the rail and across the dark water.

I was quite old before I discovered that Danny Boy was not a heterosexual love song but a message from a father to a son. From that time the words made more sense but tonight I am not listening to the words. The siren voice has drawn from the forest a cloud of big, white, cartoon moths and caused them to hurl themselves at the caged light above the cabin door where they repeatedly bang their silly heads in unfathomable ecstasy. After the tenor stops there is no sound in the whole world but the fluttering tap of the frantic insects.

As far as it is possible for a man to do so, I have ended the restrictions of time. I go to sleep when I feel tired and rise when I feel refreshed. I make no ritual of eating, being guided only by hunger and so the days, sometimes short, sometimes long, tumble into each other with no consideration for the calendar. Even so, in the silence that comes with the ending of the record I am aware that this is the start of a new year.

I am astonished that this recognition of an artificial boundary should follow me so strongly, even to the innermost coils of this limitless river, but it does. The very stars, hung above the equator, speak of a new beginning and the ending of all things old. But they lie. There is no line to be crossed. The years, like the days, merely follow one another. Over and over. Changing things imperceptibly but never bringing an ending or a beginning.

Back in the cabin I switch off the door-light to give the moths a rest. Pinned to the wall is a calendar. It bears a painting of a barn owl alighting on the gnarled branch of an oak tree. The eyes of the owl stare straight out of its heart-shaped white mask. It has hung there, wings spread, since the boat was built and the dates underneath its talons have been crossed out so many times that it looks as though the owl is perched above a wide river of black asterisks. I pour another gin and, in spite of myself, raise my glass to the new year.

I was a young man when I first embarked from the landing at Macapá for what was to be a short trip up the Amazon. Some well-wishers waved me goodbye and the story even got into the local paper. Captain Lang the lone traveller. Captain Lang the solo adventurer. It was to be a game, a gesture. It would have been unreasonable to imagine that thirty years later I would still be cruising this colossal green highway.

Once I almost escaped. At Manáos, the port a thousand miles from nowhere, I nearly abandoned the aimless journey. It was a fine city. There was a fine house there, filled with good mahogany furniture. A cool house standing solidly with its back to the River Negro. And there was Caterina.

That there should be a city there at all was miraculous. Civilisation had pushed its hand into the interminable rain forest and, in the optimism of the rubber boom, had built a collection of majestic public buildings, a luxurious old-world city with gardens and an opera house, a metropolis that somehow survived, even flourished, in the heart of the inhospitable new world.

Manáos was a solitary oyster lying on the bed of a mighty green ocean and Caterina was the pearl within the oyster's shell. There were canoe paths everywhere, side channels spanned by bridges which divided the city into separate compartments in the way that we divide our lives into separate compartments.

But there was no escaping the big river. In the heavy summer evenings as the sun set, the ornate stone of the buildings took on a green cast and when the moon rose the green tinge was unmistakable. It was the river claiming its own. There were nights when even Caterina's coal-black hair was flecked with green.

I will never return to that city. Each year finds me further west, a little nearer the high Andes. The river gives and takes away and still there is enough of it to erase the past. I ask myself the impossible question. If I were standing now on the landing at Macapá, a confident innocent young man, would I begin the journey? I decide not to waste time looking for an answer. I am here. There are so many reasons to travel. To escape. To arrive. To encounter wonders along the way. Once, all these reasons meant something to me but not now. Now I have no excuses, no objectives. I have travelled beyond reason and simply exist like the forest and the river.

When it is quiet like this, the boat creaks. The timbers contract once the heat of the day is over. Above the hatch that leads to the galley the name of the boat is painted in fading blue. La Cuna – the cradle. It has certainly been my cradle, rocking me through the slow green years.

Tomorrow I will inch a little further into the curving liquid web. I will be looking for a village. I need fuel and tobacco. There must be a village soon, although it is weeks since I saw a canoe. Two nights ago I saw lights and heard what I took to be drums but it could have been thunder. Now that I am older I am no longer so sure of interpreting everything that I see and hear. Time and the river have stolen my self-confidence.

The days form slowly like droplets of water on the underside of big, fleshy leaves and then, when they become too heavy to be supported, they fall and shatter into night, spraying out the stars like a frightening jewelled shroud above my small boat. And yet the nights are the best. It is only at night that the cabin itself becomes a star, a pin-point of light rocking in the firmament.

There is still an inch of cigar left and I want to hear more music. The dice choose the disc that I don't want to hear. They persist in their selection even after a second and third throw, so, reluctantly, I take the record from its old cover and place it on the machine. While I am winding the handle I almost change my mind but I surrender to the inevitability of chance and set the little steel needle into the groove.

It is a strange, haunting song written by Weill and Brecht. It is sung in German, a language that I am not too familiar with, but I know that it concerns a drowned girl. As the voice begins I switch off the cabin light so that I can see out to where the ghostly tangle of trees merges with the water and I think again of Caterina. Why did she do it? How could she do it? To go alone at night to the river bank. To deliberately remove her clothes and lay them in a neat pile. To wade out into the black water and say goodbye to the stars and the years. Forever. She was twenty-three or twenty-four. Perhaps if she could have got this far, things would have looked different to her. The forest less threatening; the water less deep. But maybe she knew all along (and this is what frightens me),maybe, while I slept and dreamed of the lost city, of the fine house, of the green moon and of her long black hair, she was lying cruelly awake counting the dying stars.

The voice on the record is singing the strange foreign words that I know by heart. It is saying that God gradually forgot her. First her face. Then her hands. And at the very last, her hair.

It is now an hour since the song ended. The cigar is stubbed out and cold.

EVEREST
THE FINAL CHALLENGE

Everest – the name rings out as the ultimate challenge to high altitude climbers the world over.

For many, that fascination turns out to be fatal – one in two never returns from the Himalayas, so every professional climber can expect to lose at least one friend during an Everest expedition.

But such is the draw of the mountain that it is 'booked up' by expeditions until 1995.

One route to the summit still remains unclimbed, and when the Pilkington Expedition made its recent attempt to conquer this approach via the notorious North-East Ridge, a special film record was made for 'Pebble Mill at One'.

The film makers were a unique, award winning partnership, who have climbed together for ten years and have become known as 'The Highest Film Team in the World'.

The cameraman is 52 year-old Austrian Kurt Diemberger, internationally recognised as one of the greatest mountaineers of his generation, famed for being the only living climber to have made two first ascents on 8,000 metre peaks.

His sound recordist and assistant is Julie Tullis, Britain's highest climbing woman; indeed, the first British woman to attempt Everest. Julie, who has two grown-up children, celebrated her 46th birthday while filming on the way to the mountain. Kurt received the news that he had become a grandfather while the team was making a push for the summit.

Bob Langley now takes up the story of this latest assault on the North-East Ridge and recalls his own first sighting of this awesome peak.

Tracing the crest of a Himalayan ridge one winter morning in 1983, I paused for a moment near the summit to gaze out across the breathtaking rampart of snowcapped peaks and feather ice-canyons when I spotted, in the midst of this awesome array, a triangular hump soaring above its neighbours like the curving spine of a surfacing whale. The mountain was 'Chomolunga' – 'Goddess Mother of the Snows' – or, as we westerners prefer to call it, 'Everest', at 29,028 feet the highest point in the world.

It is impossible to describe the sense of elation you feel at your first glimpse of that remarkable mountain. It was first conquered via the traditional route on May 28th 1953.

But without a doubt, the unclimbed North-East Ridge is the most hazardous Everest route of all. The problem lies high up on the mountain's shoulder where, above 26,000 feet, a series of rocky pinnacles loom up like shark's teeth and stretch for half-a-mile or more, decisively blocking the climber's path. Now anyone who has experienced the effects of physical exertion at rare altitude will appreciate the dangers of tricky technical climbing at such a dizzy height. Every step the mountaineer takes makes him feel as if he is wading through an ocean of fudge. He is smitten by headaches, nausea, giddy spells and feelings of disorientation. In some extreme cases, these symptoms can actually kill, as his brain swells and crushes itself slowly against the inside of his skull. In 1982, two of Britain's finest high-altitude climbers, Joe Tasker and Pete Boardman, vanished in the pinnacle area never to be seen again.

On March 6th 1985, Kurt and Julie flew via Peking to the forbidden city of Lhasa, capital of Tibet. This in itself

CAMPS ON THE ROUTE

[1] 6850 metres. Snow cave.
[2] 7090 metres. Snow cave.
[3] 7400 metres. Tent.
[4] 7850 metres. Snow cave.
[▼] 8200 metres. High point reached by Rick Allen
[P] Pinnacles.
[S] Summit.

Inset photographs
1. The pinnacles
2. Base camp

THE TEAM
(Standing left to right) Chris Watts, Andy Greig, Alan Fyffe, Nick Kekus, Kurt Diemberger, Rick Allen, Sarah Squibb, Andy Nisbett.
(Kneeling left to right) David Bricknell, Liz Duff, Tony Brindle, Mal Duff (Leader), Julie Tullis.
Also in the team were Jon Tinker, Dr Urs Wigget, Bob Barton and Sandy Allan.

proved quite an experience, for until very recently few western eyes had ever seen Lhasa.

Today it is under Chinese rule, or at least under the authority of the TAR (the Tibetan Autonomous Region) which has its headquarters in Peking, but Kurt and Julie were delighted to discover that the Dalai Lama's palace, the Potala, had somehow managed to survive the infamous Cultural Revolution in which the Chinese Red Guards destroyed most of Tibet's major monasteries, and continues to dominate the city, rising in solitary splendour seven hundred feet above the surrounding streets.

It was at the Potala that Kurt and Julie got their first taste of what was waiting for them on Everest's joy slopes; Lhasa's altitude – 13,000 feet – made climbing the palace's hundreds of steps a lung-searing endurance test and they had to keep on stopping for breath amid the rancid odour of butter-lamps and the eerie echo of gongs, bells and chanting lamas.

From Lhasa they drove over four hundred miles to the Rongbuk Glacier, the climbers wrapped up like mummies against the icy cold as they lurched and bounced on the back of an open truck. Then, on the third day, as they topped a high mountain pass, they spotted the immense backcloth of the Himalayan range with Everest towering above them. It was an incredible sight.

Now the basic groundwork for the assault itself could begin at last. Base Camp was established on a desolate plateau of stone at 17,000 feet, just below the Rongbuk Glacier. For the climbers, it was to be the nearest thing to home for the next few weeks as they literally 'laid siege' to the mountain, 'caching' their supplies higher up and returning again and again to recoup their strength for the push to the summit.

It wasn't just tackle, tents and cooking equipment which had to be dragged upwards, foot by foot. The team had to

Climbing an ice tower.

The Potala in Lhasa.

East Rongbuk glacier.

have food stocks to last several weeks. These alone weighed four tons and the expedition's shopping list makes fascinating reading. It includes: 2,000 tins of meat, vegetables, milk and fruit; 1,200 packs of biscuits; cakes and puddings; 6,000 teabags; 6,600 chocolate bars; 250 litres of packet soups; 5 litres of sauce and ketchup; 80 litres of whisky – "to lessen the chance of frostbite"; and 1,200 sticks of rock with 'Everest – NE Ridge' printed all the way through – "good for high

altitude sore throats".

Eventually an Advance Base Camp was established another 3,000 feet up the mountain's flank and hairy-coated yaks carried the heavier equipment on a spectacular three-day journey along precipitous ridges and glistening ice towers.

To fill in their time, Kurt and Julie set off on an exploration of the Karma Valley, on the eastern side of the mountain. The humidity clothes this face with fantastic ice formations, reaching up almost to the crest of the Ridge itself. It looked as forbidding as ever and it was easy to see why, in 1921, Mallory decided not to attempt Everest from this side.

They also set up a film point on the North Col – which would be the descent route for the expedition. Here they joined a small expedition of four Basque climbers and it was whilst they were filming, on May 12th, that they got a chilling reminder of just how dangerous mountaineering can be, particularly in such isolated and far-flung areas.

A storm had broken as the Basques were heading for the summit. They had no presentiment of the disaster. Weather conditions were appalling, and afterwards Kurt could not say why the tragedy happened at that particular point. He had just emerged from his tent clutching a piece of camera equipment and was on the point of saying something to Julie when suddenly, in front of their horrified gaze, two of the Basques began to fall.

"A cry ran through my brain," Kurt declared later, "I had no voice, but my eyes saw it. We stood petrified. They went on falling, on and on."
One man was dead, the other, miraculously, had escaped unscathed except for shock and a broken wrist.

It was a sobering experience and one which, temporarily at least, cast a cloud over their own endeavour, but, despite the vagaries of the weather, the preparatory ascents went surprisingly well, the climbers establishing a line of supply bases along the crest of the Ridge ready for the final assault on the mountain's summit; and it was on the Ridge that they made a remarkable discovery, a chilling link with the ill-fated expedition of 1982. Incredibly in all that area of icy waste, Mal Duff and Chris Watts stumbled across a snow cave which the Bonington team had dug out as a shelter from the 100 mile-an-hour winds. It contained their pots and pans and even food, but, most amazing of all, at the foot of the pinnacles, Rick Allen found Joe Tasker's camera, still in working order after three years at sub-zero temperatures. It was an experience which moved them all very deeply – a reminder of the perils they faced.

By May 14th it looked as if they were in a position to attempt the treacherous rocky pinnacles. Two members of the team, Andy Nisbet and Urs Wigget, reached Camp Four on the Ridge's upper shoulder, but, tired from lack of sleep, disorientated by the thinness of the air, they decided to rest up and replenish their dwindling energy resources. As they approached the Camp, they realised at once they were in serious trouble. Wind-driven snow had filled the snow cave, leaving it barely the size of a rabbit-hole, and in desperation they were forced to set to with shovels, digging out a shelter in the teeth of the mountain gale. The job took them hours to complete and when at last, chilled and exhausted, they managed to crawl into their narrow lair, they found there was no food-brewing material for their stove. Smothered by the cramped atmosphere, Urs felt he could not bear the prospect of spending the night in such a desolate location and set off on a solitary descent to a lower altitude. It was a rash decision, perilous in the extreme. He picked his way gingerly down the edge of the 10,000 foot Kangshung Face, but he made it back to Camp Two in one piece, conscious that he was lucky to be alive. Andy, for his part, spent an agonising night, coughing and shivering in the cold and when at last morning broke, he too decided to withdraw, ending the first attempt to reach the pinnacles in dignified surrender.

For several days the weather remained atrocious and all thoughts of further ascents had to be temporarily abandoned, but on the 19th, despite continuing unsettled conditions, the expedition's leader, Mal Duff and his companion, Tony Brindle, set off on the long haul to Camp Four. Storm clouds cluttered the neighbouring peaks and the wind was like a living force intent on their destruction. Several times Tony was battered to his knees by the incredible power of the gale blasts. Mal was carrying oxygen, or 'English Air' as the Sherpas call it, when suddenly he felt his lungs beginning to contract and a permeating numbness spreading through his diaphragm. His entire ribcage seemed to buckle as he choked and spluttered, struggling desperately to breathe. It took several moments to discover that the tube of the oxygen-set had frozen solid and, gasping for air, the two men were obliged to begin a teetering retreat to the comparitive security of the Advanced Base Camp.

Undeterred, another expedition member, Rick Allen later set off alone and climbed nearly two-thirds of the way up the first pinnacle – a remarkable piece of mountaineering. But heavy, unremitting snow forced him to retire; and as he descended the ridge, the weather closed in fiercely behind him.

By now time was running out. The climbers were tired and some were ill. It was left to their leader, Mal Duff, to make the disappointing decision. They had to withdraw. The battle was over.

But even then Kurt and Julie were not prepared to give up. Their long experience in appalling conditions, and their incredible stamina they felt, would support them for one last attempt to film high up on the mountain – this time on the North Col route. So while the rest of the team withdrew, and eventually flew back to Britain, the film-makers sat tight, hoping for a weather window.

It is hard to imagine the nightmare that they lived through over the following days as the weather battered their tiny tent, now alone on the mountainside. More than once they gave up all hope of survival, desperately trying to hold onto their sanity as the wind screamed around them, deafening and pummelling, and threatening literally to blow them off the mountain.

It was unrelenting – the notorious mountain had won again and Kurt and Julie had finally to face it.

In one sense, the expedition had ended in defeat, but for Kurt and Julie it had been an unforgettable experience. They had visited one of the remotest and most fascinating places in the world. They had produced for 'Pebble Mill at One' viewers a riveting record of the trials and tribulations of a major mountaineering ascent. And, most intriguing of all, they had encountered in a land steeped in legend, mystery and mysticism, a new riddle. For while the storms were raging, a lone unidentified climber was spotted on the Ridge's crest. Where he was heading, or what he was doing there, no one had been able to explain. But like the mountain itself, sombre and eternal, the question will remain with Kurt and Julie for the rest of their lives.

Photographs copyright of Kurt Diemberger.

RENOVATING
OLD
FURNITURE

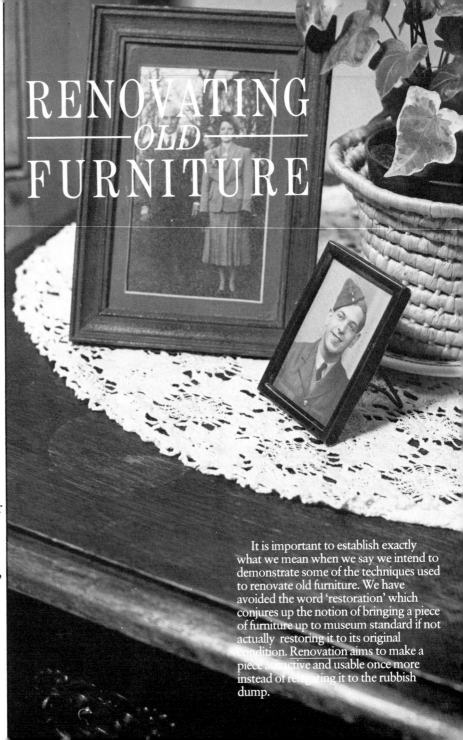

Got a tired old chair or sideboard which you just can't bring yourself to throw out?

Or maybe you've spotted a good, but damaged, table at your local junk shop – going cheap, but needing some restoration?

Well, that's where a new 'Pebble Mill at One' series on furniture renovation featuring Albert Jackson and David Day is really going to help you out. Albert and David have published many successful books and have become widely known since their series 'Better Than New' on BBC TV.

So here, for novices as well as the more experienced renovators, is their guide to the new series.

It is important to establish exactly what we mean when we say we intend to demonstrate some of the techniques used to renovate old furniture. We have avoided the word 'restoration' which conjures up the notion of bringing a piece of furniture up to museum standard if not actually restoring it to its original condition. Renovation aims to make a piece attractive and usable once more instead of relegating it to the rubbish dump.

To describe this type of furniture as 'antique' is equally misleading. If you can afford to buy genuine antiques you should have them restored professionally because it is too risky to practise on anything valuable. On the other hand, we are not talking about junk. It wouldn't be worth spending time and money on absolute rubbish.

Keep your eyes open for batch-produced furniture from the turn of the century onwards, aimed at a market that demanded attractive, functional furniture at a reasonable price. Furniture from that period was nearly always made by hand and from materials which would be considered quite exotic today. Mahogany, oak and satinwood were all commonplace, and even pine, which was thought to be suitable for veneered or painted carcasses only, was of a superior quality to anything you can buy today at your local timber store. Then there are the decorative veneers and inlays, carvings, solid-brass handles and castors, all supplied at what was even then, bargain-basement prices.

IS IT GENUINE?

A lot of people are reluctant to buy old furniture in case they are lumbered with a fake. A true fake, however, is made specifically to fool the purchaser but faking takes a great deal of time and effort and it just wouldn't be worth it for the kind of money we would be paying for furniture.

What we are really talking about is reproduction furniture, often skilfully made to look superficially like the genuine article but, because deception is not the point of the exercise, it is fairly easy to tell from the genuine article. Look at the overall colour and the condition of the surface. Most old furniture shows the ravages of time – dents, scratches, faded polish and so on. A lot of reproduction furniture looks unnaturally pristine and

the varnish is almost glassy in appearance.

However, appearance alone is not a reliable guide to the age of a piece because the more skilful manufacturers artificially age the finish so that the item of furniture will not stand out in a room

full of real antiques. On the other hand, if you notice chipped or blistered veneers you can be sure that the piece is not reproduction. Look at the back of the cabinet and at the drawer bottoms. These parts were made from thin strips of solid wood in the old days but now they are made from plywood. Check all the drawers in case a broken bottom has been replaced with a plywood substitute.

IS IT WORTH BUYING?

We are not particularly concerned with rarity when buying old furniture from the local junk shop. As renovators we are more concerned with the condition of the piece because we wouldn't expect to pay a high price for something that needs attention.

As we discuss specific items of furniture, we point out the type of damage you can expect to find, but there are problems common to all furniture. You will find many an old table or a cabinet stained with white rings or patches where water or alcohol has attacked the surface of the polish. With luck you can burnish out the stains with a liquid metal polish or even ordinary car

paint cleaner on a damp cloth. At worst, the finish can be stripped and replaced.

Woodworm damage is another common problem but it is not as devastating as many people seem to think. In fact, literally anyone can eradicate the pest using fluid available from any DIY outlet. Look for the small flightholes left by the adult beetle as it escapes from the wood and treat these first using a special applicator to inject fluid into a hole every 2″ or so across the surface, then paint unpolished surfaces with fluid or use an aerosol to spray it into all the crevices.

STRIPPING OLD FINISHES

We have become so used to the idea of stripping paint from old pine chests and the like, that all manner of finishes tend to be removed without a second thought; but before you strip the polish or varnish from a nice piece of furniture, make sure it is absolutely necessary. An old finish in good condition has a quality that is difficult to match. The patina, as it is called, adds considerably to the value of the piece. Unless a finish is obviously beyond redemption, try cleaning off the old wax dressing and surface dirt. The underlying polish could be in surprisingly good condition. Mix a 'reviver' from 4 parts white spirit to 1 part linseed oil, and use it to wash the surface with a pad of coarse sacking. If the surface is very grimy, use a ball of very fine, 000-grade wire wool to apply the reviver. Rub in the

99

direction of the grain but not too hard or you might damage the surface beneath. Wipe it over with a cloth dampened in reviver, dry it with a damp cloth, then apply a light coat of wax or French polish.

APPLYING COMMERCIAL STRIPPERS

If you want to remove an old damaged finish completely so that you can repolish or paint a piece of furniture, you can either do it yourself or take the piece to a professional.

INDUSTRIAL STRIPPING

To save time and effort, a lot of people prefer to have a piece stripped commercially by having it dipped in a tank of hot caustic soda. The process is fine for large, solid items like room doors but it can be too severe for furniture, especially if it is veneered. There are companies using a cold chemical dip who will guarantee that their process does not lift veneers and it is certainly kinder to solid timber. Before you submit any item to chemical dipping, always ask the company for advice and don't take a chance if it appears too risky.

CHEMICAL STRIPPERS

Using a DIY chemical stripper to remove an old finish is very easy but it is somewhat laborious and can be messy. Whatever type of stripper you use, always follow the manufacturer's recommendations to the letter and wear vinyl work -gloves at all times.

Apply liquid or gel stripper by painting it onto the surface with an old brush. Leave it for about 10 minutes, then scrape a small patch to see if it has stripped the finish right down to the wood. If not, stipple more stripper on top of the first application and leave it for another 5 minutes. Use a flat scraper to remove the softened paint or polish and deposit it onto old newspaper ready for disposal. Use a ball of wire wool to clean mouldings and carving. When you have removed the bulk of the finish, use balls of wire wool dipped in fresh stripper to clean the residue out of the pores of the timber, rubbing in the direction of the grain only, then wash the surface with white spirit.

Thick paste strippers are designed to remove old finishes from deep carvings and delicate mouldings. Spread a $3/8''$ thick layer onto the furniture with a trowel or scraper, then lay a polythene sheet on top of the paste to keep it moist. Eventually the paste dries to a leathery consistency when you can peel it off the wood along with the old finish. Wash the wood with water or white spirit and leave it to dry.

HOT AIR STRIPPER

Electrically-heated hot air strippers are marvellous tools for removing thick paint. They are similar in appearance to hair dryers, but are considerably more powerful.

Hold the nozzle of the stripper about $2''$ above the paint and move it slowly from side to side until the paint begins to blister and lift off the surface. Immediately remove the soft paint with a shavehook or scraper.

If you plan to repaint the piece of furniture, rub down the stripped surface with fine abrasive paper but, if you want to finish the wood with a clear polish or varnish, you will have to clean scraps of paint out of the grain with chemical stripper on balls of wire wool.

FINISHING WITH OIL

After stripping, the real pleasure comes with the application of a finish. We shall be discussing various wood finishes later but, as a taster, try using a teak oil on old pine. It is designed for finishing any of the oily hardwoods like afromosia or teak but it brings out the colour of pine beautifully and it is so easy to apply. Simply paint it on with a brush or spread it with a soft cloth. The first coat soaks in almost immediately but apply two or three coats and finally buff the surface to a subtle sheen with a clean cloth.

CLEAR FINISHES FOR WOOD

Everybody admires the incredibly varied grain patterns and colours of different woods and yet the wood itself is often remarkably featureless in its natural state. It is the finish applied to the piece of furniture that brings out its true beauty.

GRAIN FILLING

Sand the stripped wooden surface as smooth as possible with very fine abrasive paper. Don't be misled into thinking that a polish or varnish will hide small blemishes, they won't. In fact, any finish emphasises imperfections, which is why grain filler is often used. If you glance across the surface of a piece of wood towards the light you will see a mass of tiny holes – the pores of the timber. When you apply a coat of clear varnish, it sinks down into the holes, leaving a pitted surface which should be glossy and smooth. Grain filler, available from any DIY shop, is a paste which is colour-matched to various common timbers.

Spread it onto the wood with a piece of sacking using a circular motion to press it into the pores until you have covered the whole surface, then wipe out the excess filler with clean sacking in the direction of the grain. Leave the filler to harden overnight, then sand the surface smooth with fine abrasive paper.

VARNISH

When you suggest applying a modern varnish to old furniture, traditional restorers throw up their hands in horror. It's understandable, because it would be unthinkable to varnish a valuable or decorative antique designed more for its appearance than function. On the other hand, if you want to put an old pine chest or table to use, there is no point in applying a finish which is so delicate that it would be ruined in weeks. Even so, acknowledging that it makes perfect sense to use a modern varnish on working furniture, the finish does have a rather treacly appearance which is out of character with an old piece. The secret is to apply a varnish for protection but soften it visually with wax polish.

Paint two or three coats of polyurethane varnish onto the bare wood, rubbing down between coats with fine abrasive paper or wire wool. Apply a surface dressing of wax furniture polish with a ball of wire wool on top of the varnish and buff it vigorously with a soft cloth or duster.

FRENCH POLISH

The mirror-like surface of French polish is the finish most people associate with antique furniture. At one time, almost all furniture was French polished but its rather delicate nature has made it unsuitable as a protective coating on modern furniture for everyday use. Nevertheless, a great number of amateur renovators would love to acquire the skill of a professional French polisher. Fortunately, some manufacturers have risen to the occasion and have produced French polishing kits which have been designed to make the job as easy as possible. Each kit contains a bottle of

shellac polish and a burnishing liquid for putting on the final high-gloss finish.

Apply two coats of polish to the bare wood using a large paintbrush. Leave the first coat to harden for about half an hour and rub it down very lightly with fine silicon carbide paper – a pale grey abrasive paper dusted with a powdered lubricant. It is obtainable from good DIY stores and paint specialists if it is not supplied with the kit.

Build up the final layers of polish with a rubber. Soak a clean square of linen in methylated spirit and wrap it around a ball of cotton wool soaked in shellac polish. When you rub the pad across the furniture, the polish is squeezed out onto the wood. Cover the surface evenly by using a combination of circular and figure-of-eight strokes. After you have covered the area about 12 times, finish with straight strokes parallel to the grain and leave the polish to harden thoroughly. Sand down and repeat the process, then make one more application but with slightly less polish on the rubber. Leave the polish to harden overnight then wet a ball of cotton wool with the burnishing liquid and vigorously rub a small area of the polish to bring it up to full gloss. Cover the piece in small overlapping patches then put a final gloss on the whole surface with a soft duster.

PATCHING VENEERS

Veneered furniture has an undeserved reputation for being an inferior modern substitute for old solid timber construction. The truth is, the art of veneering has been popular for hundreds of years and is responsible for the high values placed on some of the more exclusive antiques.

A veneer is a very thin slice of wood glued onto a thick structural backing called the groundwork. Consequently,

you can use expensive, rare timbers which would be far too costly or difficult to work if thick sections were used. At one time, all veneers were glued to the groundwork with a water-soluble adhesive – animal glue. It was excellent for the task – in fact it is still used today – but if it gets damp the veneer becomes loose, forming a blister. It also chips easily. It is such a common problem that you would be hard-pressed to find an old piece of furniture without some kind of veneer damage.

CURING A BLISTER

Animal glue is heated to a liquid state and sets as it cools. Fortunately, it can be reactivated by applying heat again so it is possible to press a blistered veneer back into place merely by ironing it down. Slit the blister lengthwise with a sharp knife to release the air trapped beneath it, then apply a heated iron over a damp cloth. Allow the steam to soften the veneer before you apply too much pressure or you may crack the veneer. Repair the finish if necessary.

REPAIRING CHIPPED VENEERS

Most loose veneers are chipped around the edge of a table or cabinet where they have become caught in someone's sleeve. The first task is to match a modern veneer as closely as possible to the existing one. There are always veneer specialists in large towns and cities who will help you select a matching veneer from their stock. If you live in the country, send a piece of the chipped veneer to a company who dispatches veneer by mail order. The Art Veneer Company is one such supplier and is based on the Industrial Estate, Mildenhall, Suffolk, IP28 78Y.

Try to match the veneer grain pattern, colour and thickness. Grain pattern can only be matched approximately and if the veneer is too thin, glue two pieces back to back. Colour matching is a little trickier. No two pieces of veneer are

101

exactly the same shade, and you will more than likely have to modify the colour of the new veneer with washes of wood stain. There is a wide range of commercial stains to choose from and you can mix them to vary the colour. Allow for the effect of the polish by mixing a stain which is slightly lighter in tone than the finished surface of the furniture. Colour matching is not easy and requires practice and experimentation.

Tape your colour-matched patch over the damaged area and cut through both thicknesses of veneer right down to the groundwork. Peel off the patch and chip out the old veneer inside the cut lines with a sharp chisel.

Veneers can be applied with traditional adhesive but there is a glue film available from the Art Veneer Company, which makes the task extremely simple. Press the film on the back of the patch with a heated iron. Remove the backing paper from the film, position the patch on the furniture and protect it with a piece of the backing paper before you iron it flat. Hold it down with a block of wood until the glue cools, then let it set hard before sanding it flush with the surrounding veneer. Touch-in the patched area with polish or varnish.

REPLACING INLAYS

If you have to replace missing inlays, consult a veneer supplier's catalogue to find a similar pattern. There are literally hundreds of coloured bandings and decorative motifs to choose from. Scrape the groundwork clean in the vicinity of the missing inlay and apply using glue film as described above.

REPAIRING A DINING CHAIR

At some time, every one of us must have leant back in our chair after a satisfying meal unaware of how much

strain we were putting on the joints between the seat rails and back legs. If the

glue holding the joint together has failed, before long the whole back frame of the chair works loose. It's worth checking the condition of these joints before you buy an old dining chair. Rock it back onto its legs, then press down the front of the seat. If you detect slight movement only along the shoulder of the joints, the chances are you will be able to knock the frame apart and reglue it, but if the joints are very slack, there's a strong possibility that the wooden part of the joint is broken, so leave the chair for a more experienced restorer and look elsewhere for your dining suite.

DISMANTLING THE FRAME

You may be able to inject fresh glue into a loose joint without dismantling the chair, but you cannot be sure of a successful repair unless you remove the back frame and clean the old glue out of the joints. Make sure there are no dowels or nails through the legs pinning the joints together. If necessary, drill out the dowels or remove the nails before you attempt to dismantle the frame.

Cushion your workbench with a piece of old carpet and lay the chair on its back. Rest a softwood block on the back leg

next to the loose joint and try tapping it apart with a small mallet or hammer. Loosen both back joints simultaneously because if one of them springs apart suddenly you could break the tenon in the opposite joint.

If one of the joints is still glued together firmly, don't force it apart; it will only result in more damage. Soften the glue with steam using a home-made device. Buy a length of silicone or rubber tubing from a hardware store or a shop specializing in equipment for modelmaking. Plug a thin brass tube in each end and push one tube through a

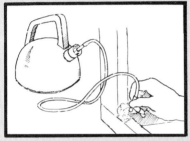

large cork that will be a tight fit in the spout of a whistling kettle. Half-fill the kettle with water and boil it to generate plenty of steam. Meanwhile drill a hole (slightly larger than the brass tube) into the joint through the underside of the seat rail where it will not show. Wear gloves to protect your hands from the heat and plug the steaming tube into the hole. After a couple of minutes pull the joint apart.

ASSEMBLING THE CHAIR

Scrape or wash the old glue from the tongues (tenons) on the ends of the seat rails and from the rectangular holes (mortices) in the legs.

Spread any woodworking adhesive onto both halves of each joint and plug the back frame onto the tenons. Clamp the frame in place using a sash cramp on each side of the chair, parallel with the seat rails, to protect the chair. Place a softening block under each end of the cramps before you tighten them. Use a damp cloth to wash off any glue squeezed from the joints.

Look across the seat frame to make sure the side rails are not twisted out of line and measure from corner to corner across the frame to ensure the 'diagonals' are equal.

USING A TOURNIQUET

If you don't have any sash cramps, rent them from a toolhire company or use strong twine to make a tourniquet. Wrap the corners of the frame in cardboard to protect the wood, then bind the twine around the frame. Tighten the tourniquet by winding a stick pushed through the lengths of twine.

FITTING CORNER BLOCKS

If you have an old upholstered chair with loose joints, either strip off the upholstery to reglue the frame as described above, or shape triangular wooden blocks to fit the angle between the seat rails, inside the frame. Screw through the block into the inner face of each rail.

PROBLEMS WITH MECHANICAL TABLES

Because a full-size dining table takes up so much room, there have been a number of developments in furniture design to provide tables which can be stowed away into a smaller space. Two typical examples are the draw-leaf table which is extended by withdrawing additional sections of tabletop, one from each end, and the gate-leg table which has folding flaps supported on pivoting underframes. Both mechanisms are ingeniously simple and efficient but, although wood is an incredibly versatile material, it does have its limitations when used to make moving or mechanical

components. Even hardwoods wear after years of friction so that components work loose; being natural material, wood is constantly moving as it takes up and gives off moisture, and will sometimes twist or warp until working components no longer operate smoothly.

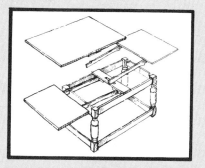

REPAIRING A DRAW-LEAF TABLE

There is rarely anything seriously wrong with a draw-leaf table, but when a number of otherwise insignificant faults occur together, it can be most frustrating. A leaf sticks every time you try to withdraw it and, when it finally gives way, it pulls right out of the underframe. When you manage to get it back in place it droops and refuses to align with the main tabletop. On top of all that, the finish on a lot of leaves is disfigured by a series of parallel scratches.

A STICKING LEAF

Each leaf is supported on two long wooden bearers which slide in notches in the underframe and between wooden guide blocks screwed to a piece of wood fixed across the underframe. Try lubricating the bearers by rubbing them with a piece of candle, and check the guide blocks are screwed into place. If they work loose they can twist sideways and jam the bearers.

If neither measure is successful, one of the bearers may be warped. Make a replacement by using the good bearer as

a pattern. Unscrew it from the leaf and clamp it to a piece of straight-grained hardwood. Mark and cut out the shape and screw the new bearer to the leaf.

MISSING LEAF STOPS

There should be small blocks of wood glued to the underside of each bearer which comes to rest against the underframe to prevent the leaf being extended any further than is necessary. If one or more stops are missing, pin and glue replacements to the bearers so that the leaf can be withdrawn just enough to allow the main top to drop into place.

A DROOPING LEAF

Make certain the bearers are screwed securely to the leaf then prop up the leaf until it aligns properly with the tabletop. Look under the top to see if the bearers are resting against the cross-piece to which the guide blocks are screwed. If there is a gap between the bearers and the cross-piece, glue small packing wedges to the top of each bearer to make up the difference.

A SCRATCHED LEAF

There should be a strip of felt glued under each end of the main tabletop to protect the finish of the leaves as they are withdrawn and replaced. If the felt is missing, hardened particles of glue score deep scratches along the leaf.

Turn the top upside down, scrape away the old adhesive with a chisel and glue new felt into its place. At the same time, scrape out any debris packed in the gaps between the panels making up the top, in case particles of grit are contributing to the damage.

REPAIRING A GATE-LEG TABLE

The moving gate that supports the hinged flap of the table pivots on wooden pins located in the underside of the rail in the main underframe and in the lower stretcher rail. Constant movement wears the pins and the bearing holes until the gate becomes floppy.

On some tables the upper peg fits into

a slot cut into the side of the rail and is held in place by a wooden block screwed over it. By removing the block you can

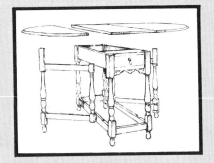

lift out the gate and replace the wooden pins with dowels before reassembling the mechanism.

When the gate is assembled along with the main underframe, remove it by sawing through both pins with a hacksaw blade. Extend the lower bearing hole by drilling right through the stretcher rail. To make a new bearing for the top pin, screw a metal plate over the original hole, having cut a shallow housing in the underside of the rail to make the plate flush with the wood. Drill a ¼" diameter hole through the plate directly over the original bearing.

Prepare the gate by planing flush the ends of the pivoting gatepost. At the bottom end drill a ¾" diameter hole in the centre of the post. Use epoxy adhesive to glue a ¼" diameter metal pin in the top end of the post. Cut a ¾" wooden dowel for the bottom bearing which will pass through the stretcher rail into the bottom of the post. Saw a slot across the bottom end of the dowel and file a chamfer around the top. Locate the metal pin in its bearing and slide the bottom of the gatepost over the new bearing hole in the stretcher rail. Lubricate the top of the prepared dowel with candle wax and drive it through the

stretcher rail into the gatepost. Make sure the gate pivots smoothly then tap a glued hardwood wedge into the slot in the dowel to lock it in place. When the glue has set, plane the end of the dowel flush with the rail.

CHECKING OUT THE FITTINGS

Considering how important fittings like knobs, handles and castors are to the overall appearance of an old piece of furniture, it is surprising how many times one comes across an item with the complete set of original handles replaced by cheap plastic substitutes. Our Victorian ancestors were just as guilty. They would discard the elegant swan-neck handles on an eighteenth-century cabinet in favour of the fashionable knobs of the day. Fortunately there are specialist ironmongers in every large town who sell high-quality reproduction fittings to fill any gaps but how do you know which to choose? An expert would know by the style of the furniture, and it would be worth doing a little research in the public library, but the piece itself will hold some clues to the identity of the original components.

If the present handles are masking large holes (they may be plugged) through a door or drawer front, then the piece was fitted with the commonplace, round wooden knobs You can turn replacements if you own a lathe, or buy plain wooden knobs and stain them to match the surrounding wood. Most knobs were fitted by means of a coarse-threaded dowel projecting from the back. If the thread in the original hole has been stripped, cut a slot across the dowel, position the knob and drive a glued hardwood wedge into the slot to spread the dowel.

Small holes drilled right through the

wood indicate some form of bolt fixing. A single hole would suggest a small drop handle, two holes, side by side, a hanging 'D' or swan-neck handle. A lot of handles have decorative backplates and you can often detect the outline of the original plate in the polish. Even if you cannot find an exact reproduction, it is an excellent guide to the style and pattern of the fitting.

FIXING FAULTY HINGES

Hinges on fine cabinets are sometimes delicately made in soft brass so it is hardly surprising that they become slack due to constant wear. Similarly, the tiny screws can be ripped out of the wooden frame all too easily.

WORN HINGES

Check the condition of hinges by opening the door and lifting it up and down to see if there is any movement at the knuckles of the hinges. You can extend the life of worn hinges by swapping them top to bottom so that different parts of the knuckle take the strain.

REPLACING SCREWS

When you cannot close a door without forcing it, check that the heads of all the screws holding the hinges are flush with their flaps. If a large screw has been used to replace one that has stripped its thread, the head will protrude and spring the hinge.

Remove the hinge and shape a thin wooden dowel to fit the stripped screw hole. When the glue has set, trim the dowel flush and replace the hinge with a new screw of the right size.

A SPLIT FRAME

A heavy door can put such a strain on its hinges that the wooden frame can split. When that occurs, the entire hinge falls out leaving the door hanging precariously from one hinge only.

Remove the door before any further damage occurs. Use a knife blade to introduce glue into the split, then clamp it closed with a G-cramp and softening blocks. Before the glue sets, clean out the screw holes with a damp paper tissue wrapped around a sharpened matchstick.

CLEANING BRASS

Polishing brass fittings is one of the pleasures of furniture renovation. Under normal circumstances, buffing with a standard metal polish is quite sufficient to restore a shine but occasionally the tarnishing is so severe that you find you are merely polishing the corrosion. Soften the corrosion with a level tablespoon of salt and a tablespoon of vinegar dissolved in half a pint of warm water. Use extremely fine wire wool dipped in the solution to wash the brass. Don't rub hard, let the solution do the work. Wash the cleaned brass in hot soapy water, then dry and polish it.

LACQUERING BRASS

Paint polished brass with a water-clear acrylic lacquer made especially to preserve the finish. With normal use, the metal should stay tarnish-free for years.

RECOVERING AN UPHOLSTERED CHAIR

The actual shaping of the upholstery of a fully-sprung dining chair is a complicated procedure to explain. Amateur renovators can learn the basic techniques in a relatively short time but it requires practice to become proficient. If you find a dining chair with sound upholstery apart from a rather shabby top covering, you can smarten it up very easily. Even if the springs have fallen out of the bottom of the seat, the repair is not too demanding as long as the stuffed seat pad is in good condition.

RENEWING THE WEBBING

The coil springs in a traditionally upholstered chair rest on a platform of tensioned cotton or jute webbing. If the webbing stretches or breaks, the platform no longer provides enough support to produce the required dome-shape seat.

Strip off the dust cover under the seat and remove the old webbing by driving out the tacks with the tip of an old screwdriver and a mallet. The webbing is sewn to the springs so cut the threads to release them.

Fit new lengths of webbing front to back. Fold over the end of the webbing and nail it to the frame with a staggered row of $\frac{5}{8}''$ improved tacks available from any hardware store. Hire a webbing stretcher to pull each length taut and nail

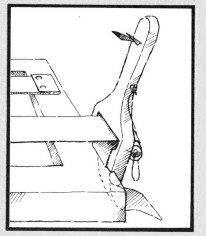

it with three tacks to the opposite side of the frame. Cut the webbing to length, fold over the cut end and secure it with two more tacks.

Adjust the coil springs inside the seat to rest on the new webbing, then fit the side-to-side webs in the same way, threading them under and over the front-to-back webs.

Use a curved needle to sew each spring to the webbing with three half-hitches using upholstery twine. You can buy a length of twine from a local upholsterer and some good DIY outlets.

Tack a new cotton or hessian dust cover to the underside of the frame.

COVERING THE SEAT

Cut an oversize piece of upholstery fabric and lay it squarely onto the seat with the warp and weft threads aligned with the main axes of the frame. Tack it temporarily in the centre of each rail. Cut a slit in the back corners to fit around the legs.

Temporarily tack each side of the seat working towards the corners from the central track. Smooth the domed seat with the flat of one handle while tensioning the edge with the other.

Cut away excess fabric at the front corners so that you can make two neat pleats. A rounded corner will require two pleats, but fold a single pleat on a square one. Fold under excess fabric to align with each side of the back legs when tacking the back corners.

When you are satisfied with the tension of the seat cover, drive home all the tacks and cut off the excess fabric along the edge of the rails with a sharp knife.

Cover the row of tacks with a length of braided ribbon. Fix it with a latex adhesive plus a small tack at each end.

For further information:
BETTER THAN NEW – a practical guide to renovating furniture. By Albert Jackson and David Day.
BBC Publications £4.75

Each year, thousands of people buy, or are given, a puppy or a dog and hope that, by some miracle, this new member of the family will become happy, well-adjusted and, at the very least, well trained.

But this doesn't happen automatically. So 'Pebble Mill at One' asked Sylvia Bishop to set out, step by step, the unique methods she has devised at her own Dog Training Centre.

The Importance of Play

It's surprising how many people don't know how to play and have fun with their dogs. Yet play is the essential foundation of my method of training. It not only makes learning pleasant for both of you, but the lessons learned are retained for longer. I don't exclude discipline, but I make sure it's always followed by plenty of fuss and games.

Determining the Pack Leader

Dogs living in the wild start learning about survival from about six weeks old. Whenever they play with their litter mates and parents they are also learning. At first they rough each other up fairly gently but as they grow older the games gradually escalate into fairly fierce ones. This does two things. It determines a pecking order in the litter and it is the basis for catching and killing prey. From about six weeks the parents also begin to discipline their young. Like play, this is gentle at first – perhaps only a slight growl – but it becomes more forceful as the puppies mature mentally and physically.

Since the domestic dog behaves in exactly the same way during the early months, when you take your puppy home, you must become a substitute parent and playmate. Instead of aimlessly playing with my puppies, I channel the play into teaching (without pressure) the response to various commands. The puppy also learns that I am the pack leader. A good relationship is formed during the first weeks that you and your puppy are together. SO DON'T WASTE THEM!

Very young puppies need long periods of sleep and short periods of 'play learning' together with food and warmth. When your puppy wakes, put him out to be clean and then play and train him before feeding him and letting him relax in his own way. Never ask him to 'play learn' when he wants to be quiet.

Getting to Know Your Puppy

Every day, time should be spent handling and talking to your puppy. Play with him, stroke him, love him. Get to know his personality and his temperament by watching his reactions to various types of play and various situations. Is he timid or bold? Is he a thinker or one who charges at new situations like a bull at a gate? Is he dominant? Does he growl when you touch

TAKING the LEAD

the food he is eating? Watch his habits. Does he readily sit or prefer to lie down? Does he bark? It is important for you to know your puppy so that you can train him accordingly, encouraging the good traits and discouraging the bad.

Whilst you are getting to know your puppy he is getting to know and respect you. He will learn that you provide food and that you can take food or anything else away from him. He will learn that you are his playmate but you are also the pack leader. He will learn to understand your different tones of voice and your different moods and react accordingly. If he has a dominant character, and growls if you take something away from him, you must show him that you are the boss, gently shake him and say "What are you doing?", take the food or article, fuss him and then give it back. Do this every day until the puppy accepts your dominance without demur because he will expect you to be in control and will only feel secure as long as you are.

The First Steps – collars and leads

Having given your puppy a day or two to settle in, put a collar on him and leave it on – no matter how he reacts to it. When he becomes indifferent to the collar, attach a light lead to it and let the puppy pull around on it for a few moments, then take it off and make a fuss of him. Gradually increase the time he spends on the lead until he continues to play in a relaxed way.

Later the collar and lead will become an extension of your arm for training, not just for taking your dog for a walk, so it is important that his early experiences on the lead are pleasant ones. I never use a metal choke chain on a dog as they not only tend to break the dog's fur, but they also make an unpleasant noise and they can bang around the dog's face.

Socialising

Ask your veterinary surgeon to give your puppy temporary vaccinations as soon as possible so that when he has adjusted to the collar and lead you can take him out.

Research on dog behaviour has shown that a puppy's earliest experiences leave the most lasting impression, so if he can have early <u>pleasant</u> experiences of as many situations as possible, your dog will be more likely to face strange situations with equanimity throughout his life.

Certainly I always suggest that, before he is three months old, you introduce the puppy to as many humans, dogs and other animals as possible. Take him to busy shopping centres and close to noisy traffic. But make sure these experiences aren't frightening.

Play Learning

Never expect a dog to come up to your level. Get down to his, both mentally and literally. Don't bend over your puppy as it will make him feel vulnerable. Instead, sit or lie on the floor and gently push and pull him around. Throw soft toys for him, play 'tug of war' with socks, push him away from you, clap your hands and call him back, grab at his legs and tail. In fact try to play with him as if you were another dog, but bear in mind that you are much bigger and stronger.

Incorporate the lead into the play. Roll the puppy away from you and gently pull him back using the word 'Come'. Let the puppy chew and bite the lead in the same way as he chews and bites your hands in play. This is how the puppy learns to enjoy the lead even though he's under your control. Choose a toy that will be suitable for training and get your puppy keen on it. I always use a small piece of carpet, but anything small and tough which the dog enjoys will do equally well.

Building a Vocabulary

Every dog owner uses the dog's name and he soon learns that it means "Pay Attention." In the same way he can learn the meaning of other words. From the outset, give a word of command to any natural action that you find clever or useful and always use the same word – for example, every time he lies down you should say a word such as "settle" or "bed" and in time you will be able to use this word to get him to lie down quietly. When the puppy sits say "sit". When you are putting him into the car say "in the car". Whatever you are doing with your dog give it a word or phrase.

Whenever I throw my puppy's toy for him to fetch, I always say "Kill It" and then have a tug of war. These then become my release words to let him know training is over. In this way, by constant repetition and without force or pressure, the dog slowly builds up a vocabulary.

The First Exercise (Teaching the Sit and Stand)

You can easily start teaching your first exercise during playtime with your puppy. Get down onto the floor with him or for the benefit of the elderly or the disabled, who might find this difficult or impractical, teach this first exercise on the table top. In fact, I did train my own Chihuahua by this method.

Play with your puppy, push him away from you and as he runs up to you, stop him in his tracks by cupping your hands around his chest, at the same time giving the command "Control." The puppy will probably sit but may just stand. If the puppy sits immediately say "Sit," if he remains standing give the command "Sit" and at the same time push him back into the sit position with your hand on top of his hindquarters. Gently stroke and praise. When he becomes restless, put one hand under his body and raise backwards and upwards into the stand position, giving the dog's name and the command "Back." Stroke and praise for a couple of seconds. Release by gently pushing him backwards, at the same time throwing his toy behind him and playing with him and his toy. INCORPORATE THIS INTO EVERY PLAY SESSION.

107

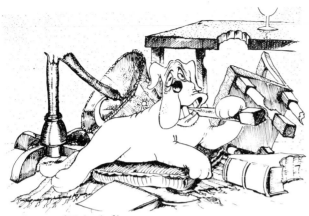

Praise and Discipline

The most important attribute you need is patience. Every good action carried out by your puppy – even everyday actions, must be followed immediately by praise. Go overboard with this, using phrases such as "What a super puppy," "Clever dog," and "Brilliant puppy" delivered in a really excited voice.

Every dog has to be disciplined, but until the puppy's understanding is such that it knows without a doubt what is wanted of him, no correction should be used. When it does become necessary, correction should at first be verbal – say in a gruff voice "What are you doing?" or "Think about it."

If it isn't enough, you can escalate to a shake by the scruff of the neck or a shake accompanied by an eye to eye stare and, on rare occasions, with a very difficult dog, perhaps a nip on the ear. All these simulate corrections which would be given by the pack leader. The degree of correction must be estimated correctly for each dog. Too little is ineffective – too much will cause the dog to cower and become worried.

COMMON PROBLEMS

Chewing

Probably the first problem you'll come across with your puppy is chewing – whether it be furniture, wallpaper or doors. There are a number of different things you can use, but one of the most effective products is simple household salt. Make it into a paste with water and apply it to wherever the dog chews. It is very easy to hoover up when dry and it doesn't stain. It can make the dog a bit sick, but with no harmful effects.

Always ask yourself why the dog is chewing. If it's through boredom, then try to make sure the dog isn't left alone for too long and give it plenty of toys and paper to play with. It's far better to have to sweep up bits of torn newspaper than to have to pay for a new three piece suite.

Barking

There's nothing more irritating for neighbours than to be disturbed by a dog barking all day in the garden or house next door. There are also dogs which bark every time the bell rings or at some other regular occurrence. It's important to know why a dog barks. If, for instance, it happens every time someone approaches you or your home then it is more than likely that he is merely being protective and it could be unwise to discourage him. Nevertheless, you do need to be able to control the dog so that he will stop when you tell him to.

The easiest way to ensure that your dog not only understands the command "Quiet," but also knows you mean it, is to use the front door. Ask a member of your household to walk up to the door and ring the bell. Have your dog on the lead and when he barks pick up the lead, open the door and hand the lead to the other person. They should then pull the dog through the door giving the command "Quiet," but without raising the voice. Repeat the exercise, but this time you walk up to the door and the other person hands the lead to you. It comes as quite a shock to the dog to be suddenly pulled through the door and it is a most effective way to get your dog to obey on the command "Quiet."

Jumping Up

Many dogs get into the habit of jumping up even if you've only been gone a few minutes. It's a problem which is tackled best at the puppy stage. Most people make the mistake of picking the puppy up when he tries to jump, but once he has outgrown the loveable baby image he becomes a nuisance to one and all. The answer is never to let the problem start. I always make sure I have something the dog likes such as a toy or tasty tit-bit, so that when I come in the door and the puppy rushes towards me, I say "Hello, what's this" and immediately throw the toy or tit-bit to the floor. This gives me time to collect myself ready to train the dog to keep all four feet on the floor. As the dog comes back towards you, kneel in front of him and slip one hand into his collar and stroke him with the other hand as you get up. Each time the dog tries to jump up give the command "Get off" and enforce this with a downward movement of the hand holding the collar. Immediately stroke him with the free hand.

Pulling on the Lead/Bolting through Doors

There is nothing worse when taking your dog for a walk than to have him pull you through the front door and continue to drag you along at breakneck speed. This should first be corrected in the home.

Put your dog on the lead and open the front door. As your dog charges through, close the door, leaving him on the outside and yourself indoors, still holding the end of the lead. Your dog will suddenly be feeling very much alone and will want to come back in. Open the door and bring him back, at the same time giving the command "Back." Bring your dog behind you and close the door. Each time you open the door to go out, give the command "Back," making sure the dog is behind you. Never repeat the command if he disobeys, but let him go through the door and close it on him as before. You will be amazed how soon the dog realises that if he goes in front of you he will be out on his own. The next step is to repeat this exercise coming back into the house.

You should soon have control of your dog going out of, or into, the house and he will understand that the command "Back" means not to go in front of you. You can now introduce this new word "Back" into your ordinary everyday walking to replace whatever word or phrase you have previously used which hasn't stopped your dog pulling.

Go outside with your dog on the lead and the lead in your left hand. Proceed to walk down the path and as he forges ahead of you to the end of the lead call his name for attention, smartly about turn, snapping the lead as you do so. As the dog comes up to your side again, snap the lead behind you and give the command "Back." Do not re-command. As he gets ahead of you repeat the exercise. Be prepared to about turn frequently to begin with, remembering to call his name for attention each time and to give the command "Back" whenever he comes in line with you. Quietly praise your dog if he stays in the correct position.

Runaways

The next problem is that of the dog who will not come back when called. Invariably I hear the same statement: "When I let my dog off the lead in the park he won't come to me when I call him." This can be an easy trap to fall into because, when the puppy is very young and you take him to the park, he will invariably stay close to you and not wander off. But as he gets older he will certainly get bolder and that is when the problems start. It is not the dog's fault. He does not understand. So the thing to remember is that you should not let your dog off the lead until he fully understands and you are 100% confident that he will come back when called. Once again we can prevent this problem ever starting.

I would recommend you to invest in a Flexi-Lead. These come in different sizes for different types of dogs. Take this with you, together with two ordinary leather leads. Have your dog on one of the leather leads keeping him under control and, as you get to your normal walking area, pretend to let your dog

off the lead by clipping at the clip on the lead. As the dog jumps away immediately call his name and, using the command "Come," bring the dog back to you using the lead to pull him in, and praise him. He is going to be quite surprised. At this stage you are enforcing the command "Come." You can then put on two leads so the dog can get a few more feet away. Once you have total control of the two leads and your dog immediately obeys the command "Come," you can progress to the Flexi-Lead which you can gradually let out further and further. Once you have your dog coming back to you from the end of the Flexi-Lead, you can then try putting the handle over a post or something similar and put the clip to free running. Walk away and let your dog have a few minutes free running on the Flexi-Lead, then call him by first using his name for attention. As the dog looks, give the command "Come." If he does not respond, pick up the lead, say something like "What are you doing?" or "Think about it," and snap back on the leads with the command "Come." Praise, but do not overdo it. I normally say "Now come when you're called. Good boy, off you go," and repeat the exercise. Once you feel confident you can try this with distractions. Go to a park where there are other dogs and use the same exercise following it through each time.

I have tried to give you an insight into some basic training and into some of the more common problems which people face with their puppies or dogs. At no time do I ever tell anyone that they should use my methods. They work for me and have worked for many other people also. But if you are following a training programme which is successful for you and your dog, then please stick to it. Only you know your dog and his capabilities, so you are the one to judge the progress you make. It is always helpful if you can join the local pet dog club because that way you meet other people with similar problems and also it helps your dog to socialise with other dogs and humans.

Good luck!

Further reference

"IT'S MAGIC" – TRAINING YOUR DOG WITH SYLVIA BISHOP. Available by mail order. Price: £14.45 including postage and packing from:–
The Office, 1–10 Arundel Mews,
Arundel Place, Brighton,
East Sussex
BN2 1GD

SEW
EASY

Hilary James first joined the lunchtime team to pass on her now famous 'Sew Easy' dressmaking tips.

For those who have missed them in the past, we include here full details of the five women's patterns (A – E) and the two children's patterns (I and O) which we've presented in previous series.

To bring the patterns to life and to illustrate how they can be mixed and matched, we photographed a selection of garments.

Cream dress with back buttons *Pattern C*
Top and khaki skirt *Pattern C*
Hilary's top *Pattern D* and skirt *Pattern A*

Blue tracksuit *Pattern D*
Cream tracksuit *Pattern D* and blue jacket *Pattern E*

SEW EASY PATTERN A

This pattern contains a loose-fitting dress, a mini dress or long shirt and a conventional length shirt. The skirts are in 2 lengths below knee and mid-calf and either can be made with waistline gathers or tucks. There's also a buttoning bib, plus 2 reversible waistcoats. (multi-sizes 8-10-12-14-16-18)

BEST SELLERS BY MAIL ORDER

These are Pebble Mill's multi-size paper patterns for a whole range of children's, girl's and women's clothes. Each envelope contains all the sizes quoted and instructions full of the helpful tips Hilary has demonstrated during the programmes. If you missed any of them and would like a copy you can still send for them. All the adult patterns complement one another and have been designed so that they can be mixed and matched.

Each multi-size pattern costs £1.75 including p&p and can be obtained by sending a cheque or postal order to: 'Sew Easy Patterns,' P.O. Box 50, Bradford, West Yorkshire BD1 5BZ. Please ensure you state clearly which one(s) you require and don't forget to include your name and address on a label.

SEW EASY PATTERN D

This pattern includes 3 pull-on dresses and 4 pull-on tops with a choice of 3 necklines and 3 different sleeves. There are also 2 trouser styles. They are designed to flatter both larger and small sizes and comfortable elasticated waists are used throughout. (multi-sizes 10-12 14-16-18-20)

SEW EASY PATTERN B

These simple pull-on dresses and tops have 3 sleeve variations and are ideal for jersey fabrics as well as wovens. The 2 trousers and the shorts are cut fashionably loose and have a very simple mock fly fastening. (multi-sizes 8-10-12-14-16-18)

SEW EASY PATTERN C

The 2 chemise dresses and both the slim and gathered skirts button (or fasten with snaps) at the back, though the gathered skirt can also be worn with buttons at the front. The 3 pull-on tops have a variety of sleeve, trim and length details. (multi-sizes 10-12-14-16-18)

SEW EASY PATTERN E

Designed to look good on both large and small sizes, the raglan-sleeved blouson jackets in this pattern have a varied choice of collars and trims. There's also a softly gathered pull-on skirt, stylish and practical elastic waisted culottes and a smart straight skirt. (multi-sizes 10-12-14-16-18-20)

111

Red top *Pattern D* with grey check skirt *Pattern E*
Red jacket and culottes *Pattern E* with black top (under jacket) *Pattern D*
Red/black print dress *Pattern D*

Black dress *Pattern D*
White blouse and skirt *Pattern A*
Black/white top and trousers *Pattern B*
Josephine's yellow jacket and culottes *Pattern E* with black top (under jacket) *Pattern D*

112

Hilary is back with us again in the spring for an eight-week series we've called 'The Sew Easy 1986 Collection.'

Tune in then for details of how to get hold of the four sensational new patterns with designs for adults and children.

SEW EASY PATTERN I – INDOOR

These children's unisex separates include baggy trousers, straight trousers, cuffed trousers and gathered skirts – all simply pull-on. There's also a skirt, a blouse and buttoning bib. Knitwear too – a polo or round neck sweater and knitted braces. (multi-sizes 2-3-4-5-6)

SEW EASY PATTERN O – OUTDOOR

This pattern features children's unisex outer-wear. There's a duffle coat and a smart 'Knightsbridge' coat – both in 2 lengths, together with a zip-fronted anorak. The knitted garments include an Aran sweater, Fair Isle Tam o' Shanter with matching mitts, plain mitts, gloves and a brimmed hat. (multi-sizes 2-3-4-5-6)

113

Blue coat, knitted tam o'shanter and mittens *Outdoor Pattern*
Aran sweater *Outdoor Pattern* with trousers *Indoor Pattern*
Yellow/grey jacket *Outdoor Pattern* with trousers *Indoor Pattern*

·THE· WILD LIFE GARDEN

Landscape Architect Chris Baines has presented several highly popular wildlife series on 'Pebble Mill at One'. Chris, in constant battle to preserve Britain's threatened wildlife, has recruited the help of viewers by encouraging them to set up their own mini nature reserves.

Here he describes how you can set up your own wildlife garden and outlines the extent of conservation work being tackled by ecology groups up and down the country.

British wildlife has suffered terribly in the past forty years. Since 1949 we have lost 97% of our wildflower meadows, half the ancient woodlands have been destroyed, and most of our wetlands have been drained or polluted with chemicals.

Most of the habitat destruction has been encouraged, to make way for greater agricultural production, for expanded towns and such major land users as motorways and airports. As habitats are destroyed, the wild plants and animals of Britain disappear. Species such as primroses, cowslips, dragonflies and butterflies, which were common forty years ago, have become threatened rarities and, in some cases, precious plants and animals have become extinct.

The British love nature. In the past two or three years, there has been growing anger at so much destruction and now people are eager to do something practical to repair at least some of the damage. It is time to begin putting something back. We have 1,000,000 acres of gardens in Britain, and my wildlife garden at Pebble Mill has been created to show you that even a patch as tiny as this (12 yds by 6 yds) can be full of life, can still look beautiful, and can help provide a really positive contribution to nature conservation.

GREEN PIECES

WHO'S DOING WHAT TO PROTECT OUR WILDLiFE

Suddenly, all sorts of people are beginning to worry about our environment.

Acid rain, river pollution, motorways through the countryside, pesticides and food additives, lead in petrol and threatened wildlife are just some of the issues that people care passionately about. There are over two million members of environmental organisations in Britain – that is far more members than any of the political parties can boast – and it is largely the work of these voluntary bodies which has persuaded politicians and other decision makers to take environmental issues much more seriously.

Of course, to the fifty odd million Britons who aren't members, the various lobby groups all share a foggy image of wholefood, long hair, sandals and badges. That may have been the case ten years ago, but it certainly is not a fair description now. Environmental pressure groups are highly professional and they employ enthusiastic staff; but the driving force is still the passionate commitment of their members.

On 'Pebble Mill at One,' I introduce you to some of the people and issues that are behind the initials; looking at pesticides and food additives with campaigners from FOE (Friends of the Earth) and seeing how the RSPB (Royal Society for the Protection of Birds) work round the clock to protect rare nesting birds. Staff from WWF (World Wildlife Fund) save animals and plants throughout the world. BTCV (British Trust for Conservation Volunteers) are a very practical bunch, and we see their members hard at work conserving the countryside.

RSNC (Royal Society for Nature Conservation) show us how their members in the County Naturalists Trusts go about saving and managing nature reserves. The UWG (Urban Wildlife Group) explain how they help local people unravel the local planning system and run campaigns to save wildlife; and Greenpeace (no mysterious initial) show us just how far they are prepared to go, and the risks they are prepared to take, to save the whale or stop nuclear waste being dumped at sea.

All these organisations, and many more besides, are battling away to make a better, safer, greener world for future generations to inherit. The stories and the people are exciting – I hope they excite you into doing something to help.

ENVIRONMENTAL ORGANISATIONS DIRECTORY

British Association of Nature Conservationists
c/o Rectory Farm
Stanton St. John
Oxford OX9 1HF

The British Butterfly Conservation Society
Tudor House
Quorn
Loughborough
Leicestershire
LE12 8AD

British Trust for Conservation Volunteers
36 St Mary's Street
Wallingford
Oxford OX10 0EU

British Trust for Ornithology
Beech Grove
Tring
Hertfordshire
HP23 5NR

Civic Trust
17 Carlton House Terrace, London
SW1Y 4AW

CLEAR
2 Northdown Street
London N1 9BG

The Commons Society
166 Shaftesbury Avenue
London WC2

Council for Environmental Education
School of Education
University of Reading
London Road, Reading

Council for the Protection of Rural England
4 Hobart Place
London SW1H 0HY

Ecological Parks Trust
c/o The Linnean Society
Burlington House
Piccadilly
London W1V 0LQ

Environmental Resource Centre
Old Broughton School
McDonald Road
Edinburgh EH7 4LD

Fauna and Flora Preservation Society
Zoological Gardens
Regent's Park
London NW1 4RY

Friends of the Earth
377 City Road
London EC1V 1NA

Green Alliance
60 Chandos Place
London WC2N 4HJ

Greenpeace
36 Graham Street
London W1 2JX

Landlife
The Old Police Station
Lark Lane
Liverpool 17

Nature Conservancy Council
19/20 Belgrave Square
London SW1X 8PY

National Council for the Conservation of Plants and Gardens
c/o RHS
Wisley, Woking
Surrey GU23 6QB

National Council for Voluntary Organisations
26 Bedford Square
London WC1B 3HU

Royal Society for Nature Conservation
The Green
Nettleham
Lincoln LN2 2NR

Royal Society for the Prevention of Cruelty to Animals
The Manor House
The Causeway,
Horsham,
Sussex RH12 1HG

Royal Society for the Protection of Birds
The Lodge
Sandy
Bedfordshire
SG19 2DL

Urban Wildlife Group
11 Albert Street
Birmingham
B4 7UA

Watch
22 The Green
Nettleham
Lincoln LN2 2NR

The Woodland Trust
Westgate
Grantham
Lincs NG31 6LL

World Wildlife Fund – UK
Panda House
11-13 Ockford Road
Godalming
Surrey GU7 1OU

Young Ornithologist's Club
The Lodge
Sandy
Bedfordshire
SG19 2DL

Helpful insects such as this ladybird need safe places to hide through the winter. Don't burn all your dead flower stems.

The Pebble Mill at One Wildlife Garden – just a patch of grass and a flower bed.

Buddleia is one of the best butterfly plants. Here is a late summer small tortoiseshell enjoying the nectar.

Foxglove

My little oasis at Pebble Mill is in a quiet corner of the grounds and was originally just a patch of lawn with an area of old tarmac in one corner. The site is windy, because it sits in the gap between a studio wall and a block of trees, but the trees themselves are an asset. I was also particularly pleased to be close to the little stream, the Bourne Brook, which flows through the grounds. Long thin leafy habitats like streams, railway embankments and hedgerows are especially important because they act as corridors for wildlife. The first aim in designing a wildlife garden should be to try to plug your plot into the nearest corridor and offer your garden as a wildlife service station.

I planted a hedge along one end of the Pebble Mill plot. This will shelter the rest of the garden as it grows up and it also provides a direct connection to the trees and the stream – an easy access route for hedgehogs, songbirds and a whole host of small creepy-crawlies. We have lost hundreds of thousands of miles of hedgerow from the farming countryside in the past few years, so it is a good idea to plant the kind of species that have disappeared. I chose a mixture of blocks of hawthorn and field maple – both very good for wildlife. If there had been more room I would probably have included other typical 'country hedgerow' shrubs such as holly, dog rose, oak, guelder rose and wild privet.

The most popular service stations are always the ones which offer a wide selection of appetising food and drink in comfortable surroundings. That is true whether you are a weary motorway driver or a hungry butterfly or bluetit. In the Pebble Mill Wildlife Garden I have planted a wide selection of wildlife food plants and put up a simple bird-table too. Bird-tables are marvellous things. Just put up a simple platform, preferably in a safe, open position in full view of a window, provide water for drinking (and bathing) and a regular supply of soft food such as fat, cheese and breadcrumbs and hard food such as corn and peanuts. Feed from late October till late March and you will soon be pulling in the birds from a wide area. Remember though, that these wild creatures do come to depend on you. Once you start feeding, you must not let them down.

Insects are the real key to a successful wildlife garden. They are fascinating in themselves, many of them are extremely valuable to the gardener and, of course, they provide essential food for many of the larger and more spectacular animals. At Pebble Mill I have included a nectar border, full of plants which will attract the insects. You will get the best results if you choose flowers which bloom very early or very late in the year – grape hyacinths for March butterflies, and Michaelmas Daisies for autumn stragglers. Flowers such as honesty and teasel have a second contribution to make, since they produce a useful seed crop for the birds in autumn. Goldfinches love teasel seed, and Bullfinches are crazy about honesty seed.

Some flowers are particularly good for certain types of insect. We have a buddleia bush for the late summer butterflies. Bumblebees love the foxgloves and snapdragons; and hoverflies – some of the most useful insects in any garden – seem to find yellow flowers irresistible. I've planted rudbeckia, Californian poppy and marigolds for them.

Pheasant's eye

Field poppy

A service station is all very well, but you have to borrow your butterflies and hedgehogs from somewhere else. If you have room, try and create real mini-habitats where wild plants and animals can live. At Pebble Mill we have four. The hedge itself is important. Lots of shelter; and as the hawthorn and field maple grow they will provide food for insects and a useful nesting site for such species as robins, dunnocks and blackbirds. As the dead leaves and twigs build up beneath the hedge, a wide range of small creatures will begin to benefit and we may well have the local hedgehog hibernating there next winter. I've speeded up the development of this habitat by bringing in a few old rotting logs and a sack full of autumn leaves. Already, the 'decay corner' is buzzing with fascinating insects and decorated with strange-looking toadstools.

There is a slight risk of bringing a disease called honey fungus into the garden if you put dead logs on the soil. If you are worried about this, place your log-pile on a paving slab. You won't attract quite so much wildlife, but it is a bit safer.

The other three habitats are a meadow, a marsh and a rubble patch. The mini-meadow is simply a piece of the original lawn, which now gets cut for hay in late July and again in September. I've planted meadow wildflowers such as cowslips, lady's smock and scabious in it – all grown by a specialist wildflower nursery. I make sure the edge is kept neatly mown, to make the longer grass of the meadow look respectable.

The mini-marsh is quite easy to make. My plot is too shady for a pond, so I dug a hole, lined it with waterproof butyl sheeting, and filled it in again. Obviously the marsh needs to be kept wet with an occasional hosepipe, but this artificial wetland makes it possible for me to grow such beautiful wildflowers as ragged robin, bugle, meadowsweet, marsh marigold and purple loosestrife.

The rubble habitat is perhaps the simplest to create and it certainly produces rapid results. I broke up the patch of old tarmac – no soil needed here – and then sowed down a seed mixture of all the colourful wildflowers that used to grow in our cornfields before the days of farm chemicals. Within six weeks of sowing, this patch was a riot of colour, with poppies, cornflower, pheasant-eye, mayweed and perhaps the most beautiful cornfield wildflower of all – corn-cockle.

Corn-cockle – now almost extinct in the wild.

Corn-cockle is truly spectacular – a wonderful shade of magenta – with flowers opening day after day for weeks. Fifty years ago it was a common weed of the countryside. In 1980 it was only found growing wild in six places in England and in the next few years it could well disappear completely from the wild. This and many other threatened species could well find a safe sanctuary in the wildlife gardens of Pebble Mill viewers. That will be marvellous for the wildlife, but it will be smashing for the gardeners too, because the nicest gardens are always the ones which are full of life. It is time to stop killing things, and provide a colourful, comfortable sanctuary for hedgehogs, butterflies, birds and wildflowers.

SUPPLIERS

WILDFLOWER NURSERIES SELLING POT GROWN PLANTS

G & J E Peacock
Kingsfield Tree Nursery
Broadenham Lane
Winsham
Chard
Somerset

Davison Hardy Plants
Magnolia Cottage
North Aston
Oxford
OX5 4HU

Rural Preservation
Association
Old Police Station
Lark Lane Liverpool 17
Merseyside

Ruth Thompson
Oak Cottage Herb Farm
Nesscliff
Shrewsbury
Shropshire
SY4 1DB

WATER PLANTS

Stapeley Water
Gardens Ltd
London Road
Stapeley
Nantwich
Cheshire
CW5 7JL

WILDFLOWER SEED

Naturescape
Little Orchard
Whalton in the Vale
Notts NG13 9EP

John Chambers
15 Westleigh Road
Barton Seagrave
Kettering
Northants
NN15 5AJ

Suffolk Herbs
Sawyers Farm
Little Cornard
Sudbury
Suffolk

Emorsgate Seeds
Middle Cottage
Emorsgate
Terrington St Clement
Kings Lynn
Norfolk

Helen McEwen
The Seed Exchange
44 Albion Road
Sutton
Surrey

MAKING · YOUR · WILDLIFE · GARDEN

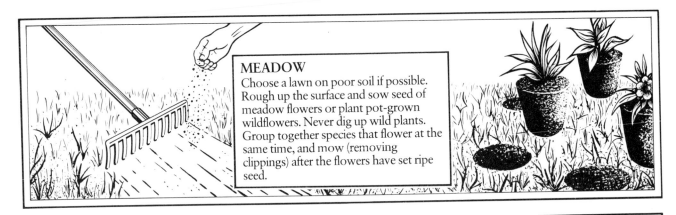

MEADOW

Choose a lawn on poor soil if possible. Rough up the surface and sow seed of meadow flowers or plant pot-grown wildflowers. Never dig up wild plants. Group together species that flower at the same time, and mow (removing clippings) after the flowers have set ripe seed.

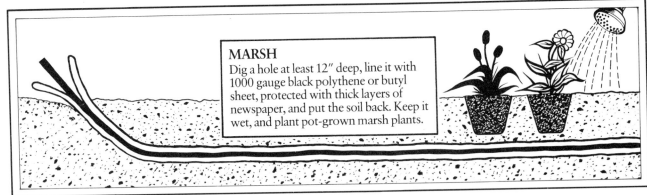

MARSH

Dig a hole at least 12″ deep, line it with 1000 gauge black polythene or butyl sheet, protected with thick layers of newspaper, and put the soil back. Keep it wet, and plant pot-grown marsh plants.

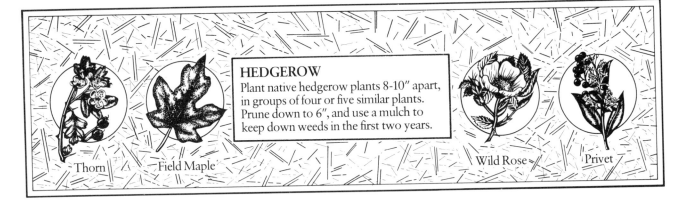

HEDGEROW

Plant native hedgerow plants 8-10″ apart, in groups of four or five similar plants. Prune down to 6″, and use a mulch to keep down weeds in the first two years.

Thorn   Field Maple   Wild Rose   Privet

Here are some suggestions for trees, shrubs and plants for the Wildlife Garden.

TREES
English Alder *Alnus glutinosa*
Silver Birch *Betula pendula*
Bird cherry *Prunus padus*

LARGE SHRUBS – native
Elder *Sambucus nigra*
Hazel *Coryllus avellana*
Dog Rose *Rosa canina*
Guelder rose *Viburnum opulus*

LARGE SHRUBS garden exotics
Cotoneaster watereri
Pyracantha coccinea
Buddleia davidii
Ribes sanguineum
Rosa Moyesii Nevada

CLIMBERS
Honeysuckle *Lonicera periclymenum*
Ivy *Hedera helix*
Jasmine *Jasminum officinale*

HERBACEOUS WILDFLOWERS

MEADOW
Vetch *Vicia species*
Oxeye daisy *Chrysanthemum leucathemum*
Cowslip *Primula veirs*
Yellow rattle *Rhinanthus minor*
Lady's bedstraw *Galium verum*
Greater Knapweed *Centaurea scabiosa*
Harebell *Campanula rotundifolia*
Self heal *Prunella vulgaris*
Bird's-foot trefoil *Lotus corniculatus*

MARSH
Ragged Robin *Lychnis flos-cuculi*
Bugle *Ajuga reptans*
Purple loose strife *Lythrum salicaria*
Meadowsweet *Filipendula ulmaria*
Hemp-agrimony *Eupatorium cannabinum*
Cuckooflower *Cardamine pratensis*

SHADE-LOVING
Foxglove *Digitalis purpurea*
Primrose *Primula vulgaris*
Common Dog Violet *Viola riviniana*
Lesser Celandine *Ranunculus ficaria*
Woodruff *Galium odoratum*
Red Campion *Silene dioica*
Wild Strawberry *Fragaria vesca*
Hedge Woundwort *Stachys sylvatica*
Bluebell *Endymion non-scriptus*

1 Oxeye daisy   2 Red campion
3 Self heal   4 Lesser celandine

HERBACEOUS PERENNIALS
(for nectar, pollen and seed)
White arabis *Arabis albida*
Aubretia *Aubretia deltoides*
Cranesbills *Geranium species*
Sweet bergamot *Monarda didyma*
Red Valerian *Centranthus ruber*
Lovage *Levesticum officinale*
Yarrow *Achillea filipendula*
Golden rod *Solidago canadensis*
Phlox *Phlox canadensis*
Mint *Mentha rotundifolia*
Globe thistle *Echinops ritro*
Michaelmas daisy *Aster species*
Ice plant *Sedum spectabile*

ANNUALS
Candytuft *Iberis amara* for butterflies
Californian poppy *Eschscholtzia californica* for hoverflies
English marigold *Calendula officinalis* for hoverflies
Night-scented stock *Matthiola bicornis* for moths
Broad beans *Vicia faba* for bumble bees
Corn-cockle *Agrostemma githago*
Pheasant's-eye *Adonis annua*
Mayweed *Tripleurospermum maritimum*
Common Poppy *Papaver rhoeas*
Cornflower *Centaurea cyanus*
Tobacco plants *Nicotiana alata* for moths
Snapdragon *Antirrhinum majus* for bees
Sweet Alison *Lobularia maritima* for bees
Borage *Borago officinalis* for bees
Poached egg plant *Limnanthes douglasii*

BIENNIALS
Honesty *Lunaria biennis* for butterflies
Sweet rocket *Hesperis matronalis*
Angelica *Angelica archangelica* for bees
Garden Common Evening primrose *Oenothera biennis* for moths
Foxglove *Digitalis purpurea* for bees
Teasel *Dipsacus fullonum* for bees and finches

The CHRIS BAINES' WILDLIFE GARDEN NOTEBOOK (Oxford Illustrated Press, £2.95) is a colourful little hardback with month-by-month notes and a section for keeping your own garden records.
HOW TO MAKE A WILDLIFE GARDEN (Elm Tree Books, £8.95) is a best-seller, beautifully illustrated with Chris's own photographs and filled with practical information about the flowers to grow and ideas for creating mini-habitats.

Wildflower photography by Andrew N. Gagg.

119

Endless energy and ageless ageing are the main goals of Leslie Kenton's enormously popular 'Positive Health from Pebble Mill'.

Her worldwide researches in the fields of fitness and diet are widely acclaimed and she has written several best-selling books which have pioneered a change of attitude towards the attainment of health and vitality.

Here Leslie summarises her current series, covering everything from organic farming to fasting as a means of growing healthier.

We also include her famous 'Spring Clean' diet and her 'Positive Health' directory.

Positive Health from Pebble Mill

This year, 'Positive Health from Pebble Mill' expands its horizons. We're looking at health in relation to how you eat, exercise and deal with stress, as well as at family health. In essence we're offering advice on ways and means of looking and feeling your very best, year after year. We also examine the relationship between the health of our land and the health of our families and even consider the health of the earth itself – something which I believe will come increasingly into the news in the near future. After all, we as human beings are completely dependent upon our Mother Earth for our well-being and even our survival. In our quest to explore the worrying issue of pesticides on our foods, we examine the rapidly growing alternative to high technology agriculture – organic foods grown on healthy soils. In our search for answers to the questions "What is it to be truly healthy?" and "How high can we set our sights?" we meet an extraordinary family of doctors, find out what they believe, look at how they live and what they eat and get them to share their secrets of long term glowing health with us.

Electromagnetic influences on mind and body are another fascinating realm which we explore. (Shh ... these are brand new findings since, so far, much of the research done in the West in this area has been classified.) Then we take to the hills for rock climbing, canoeing and sailing and we learn that outward bound skills can do a lot more for you than help you climb mountains – they can even help transform the way you think and feel about yourself. And we're also looking at the expanding range of growth and health holidays both here and abroad. And this is only just the beginning.

MYSTERIES OF YOUTH AND AGE

For me, personally, this season is a voyage of discovery. Several years ago, I became fascinated by the notion that age-related degeneration need not be inevitable. After all, certain long-lived cultures of the world – the Hunzas in Kashmir, the Georgians in Russia, the Vilcabambans in the Andes – all lived long and active lives without suffering the anguish of chronic illness and degeneration which until recently was considered a normal part of ageing in the Western world. Then, too, in my travels I have come across people who look and feel years younger than their contemporaries. I have been determined to find out why. After a lot of impassioned research on my part (after all I myself am coming to the age when unwelcome lines are beginning to appear on the face) and having interviewed many of the world's top scientists in the ageing field, I have come to believe that my hunch was right. The painful degeneration of health and vitality which we so often associate with growing old is <u>not</u> a normal part of ageing. A combination of well tried natural ways of eating, exercising and dealing with stress, used together with some exciting new scientific findings about how natural substances such as vitamins, minerals and metabolites, <u>can</u> help protect the body from degeneration. The scientific findings are there. It is time we began making practical use of them.

I realized that right now science is on the threshold of being able to extend life, prolong youth and prevent degeneration. And because I have always felt that so much of the precious wisdom and creativity of our old people tends now to be wasted in sickness and pain, I became very excited about exploring how the ageing process could be slowed down and how we could all potentially live longer, look younger and lead more vital and satisfying lives – in short, how we could make it possible for us to die young late in life. The results of all my research – and I hope some of my excitement about it as well – has gone into a book I've written called 'Ageless Ageing … The Natural Way To Stay Young.' Now I am busy trying to put into practice many of the valuable things I have learned.

THE WORLD HEALTH ISSUE

My fascination with learning what might help us in Britain to look and feel better far longer, seemed quite naturally to lead me on to investigate one of the most devastating health problems our world as a whole has ever faced – that of famine in the Third World countries. In the past year many of us have been moved to tears by the photographs of mothers and starving babies. We have dug deep into our pockets to help fund the rescue operations taking vital supplies to refugees in Ethiopia, the Sudan and Pakistan. Yet I, like many other ordinary people, have wanted so much to do more. But how? I began to read about the famine problem, and then I went to see for myself how the experts in the field believe it can be alleviated. I found that the problems of famine in Africa reach far beyond the drought. They are rooted in maldistribution of food crops, land and resources. I found that drought is a long-term problem which can only be alleviated by long-term responses to it. And while food aid is desperately needed in the short-term as well as feeding programmes for those most at risk only long-term investment in a better infrastructure – roads, improved agriculture, water supply and health services – can help prevent even more serious droughts from happening in the years to come.

Even more important, I discovered that there were things which we in Britain could do right now to help. We can learn not only how to deal with the immediate problem but also how to help build a future for Third World people. At the same time we can improve our own health, starting with eating less.

FAST AHEAD

It is well known that after the Second World War, the incidents of degenerative illness, like arthritis and heart disease dropped dramatically because people had been eating smaller quantities of simple foods. This supports my own research which proves that the best way of protecting your body from premature ageing is to eat good wholesome food, and less of it.

For some time now I have been fasting for one day a month and contributing the money I have saved to the Third World. This is how the idea for Pebble Mill's 'Fast for World Health' came about. A contribution of as little as £2.87 would buy a hoe for a young farmer in Tanzania and £9.00 would pay for training three village farmers in India.

If those Pebble Mill viewers who are adults, healthy and not pregnant contributed the proceeds of their 'fast day,' or even missed a meal, it would transform the lives of thousands of people in drought ridden countries and they would be much healthier in the process. For me it has been an enormously rewarding experience, and I have never felt fitter.

This year Leslie is taking film cameras out and about to better illustrate some of the health and fitness stories she is presenting for 'Pebble Mill at One'. And her journeys have taken her from the wild open sweep of the Brecon Beacons to a very special farm in Shropshire.

PESTICIDES AND ORGANIC FARMING

Last year, more than one billion gallons of chemicals were sprayed on Britain's crops. According to official Ministry of Agriculture statistics, between 97 and 99 per cent of all our fruits and grains and vegetables are sprayed with pesticides at least once. The chemicals designed to kill or control insects, weeds, plant diseases and other pests are now suspected of containing substances which can cause cancer and birth defects, allergies and other serious illnesses by ending up on the food we eat. We may be taking long-term risks with our health. Is there no alternative?

A growing number of doctors, farmers and scientists insist there is. The answer, as the saying goes, lies in the soil. There is a close relationship between the quality of the soils on which our foods are grown and the health of the people eating them. Organic foods are ecologically grown (eco foods) – with the aid of natural manures of either animal or vegetable origins. These foods are free of pesticide residues. Provided they are grown on healthy soil, eaten fresh and are little processed, they offer the highest complement to long-term, high-level well-being, as well as the highest protection from physical degeneration.

I decided to visit the large and flourishing organic farm of Richard Mayall, at Lea Hall in North Shropshire to learn about the organic method of growing crops and produce. After all, if Pat and Tony of the Archers – the bastion of Farm Life – can do it, then there's got to be something in it!

DRS GORDON AND BARBARA LATTO

Gordon and Barbara Latto are both medical doctors in their 70s. They are also a picture of glowing health, at an age when physical and mental degeneration are considered normal.
Both Gordon and Barbara have practised natural medicines professionally and in their personal lives.

Their philosophy is based on supporting and encouraging the body's own natural ability to heal itself and keep itself well.

Gordon was raised in a poor Dundee family where the only option for treating ill health was the natural way – folk remedies and 'Granny's Secrets'! These were so effective that even later in life when he qualified in medicine, he returned to their simple, successful solutions to health problems.

The Lattos' advice is straightforward – follow the example of a baby's needs for its well-being and use them as a basis to achieve healthiness at any age.

Good breathing for instance – so often neglected, and the cause of much ill-health – can be taught. The deep rhythmical, diaphragmatic breathing which can bring inner calm is something we can all learn to practise.

We also need movement and exercise – so natural to a baby in life, but again often neglected by us through daily pressures later in life. Barbara and Gordon regularly exercise by gardening in their totally organic plot at their home, by playing tennis and golf, bouncing on a permanent built-in trampoline in their garden and even ski-jumping.

They go on to list the many elements which contribute to a baby's healthy survival and which we should observe as a blueprint for all our lives: laughing, a very important healing force; crying – so helpful in learning how to deal with problems and finding the stepping stones to solutions; singing – therapeutic in breaking tension; good food – like a mother's milk, natural, low in protein and fat; and natural remedies to adjust ill health.

We dip into the lifestyle of this vibrant, energetic and peaceful couple to find out how their recipe for life can help us all.

GROWTH CENTRES or HEALTH COMMUNITIES

Growth Centres have been with us for some time – but the newer breed are a far cry from the spaced-out encounter groups of the Sixties.

These new centres have adjusted to the problems of our times and concentrate as much on the health and vitality of the physical body, as the personal, emotional and psychological development.

They are springing up in areas of natural beauty where the peace of the surroundings gives people the opportunity to relax in a friendly and caring community and where trained practitioners are on hand to aid personal changes in direction, or simply to help give a new look to an old problem.

The various centres, in Greece, Spain, France and this country offer slightly varying differences in emphasis, but most concentrate on encouraging the seed of change which will enable us to create a way of life which can help us renew our connections with other people, with our environment, with our bodies, with our sense of purpose and, ultimately, with our deepest selves.

CAER, the Centre for Alternative Education and Research, is one such centre in the starkly beautiful scenery of Lamorna near Lands End, where the courses on offer range from massage and tai chi to group workshops of a psychological nature. Threaded through the Centre's activities is the ever-present influence of its surroundings, rich in ancient history with its stone circles and prehistoric sites, its cliffs, harbours and spectacular coastline. We investigate claims that it is 'a place for change in changing times'.

OUTDOOR PURSUITS OR OUTWARD BOUND

It's not until you've successfully tackled the sheer mental and physical exhaustion of canoeing in wild water rapids or scrambling up a sheer rock face, that you come face to face with revelations about how to tackle more mundane problems in your life. At least, this is the message of the Outward Bound Trust whose philosophy of 'self discovery through learning certain physical skills' was developed to help soldiers in time of battle, but has been successfuly adopted by people from all walks of life. Orienteering courses are now believed not only to improve managerial abilities of businessmen, but also to better men's and women's views of themselves and their lives.

It is now possible for groups of women, from all walks of life, to take part in women-only outward-bound courses – or, if they prefer, to join in with mixed sex courses. The idea being that the change from domestic drudgery and everyday routine, coupled with the development of skills to meet new physical and mental challenges, can improve self confidence, heighten vitality and generate a whole new lease on life.

Some Outdoor Pursuits Centres now have crèche facilities – to encourage women to take part. Many of the courses are tailored to suit particular financial restraints.

Dolygaer Outdoor Education Centre, run by Mid-

Glamorgan Local Authority, offers a range of attractions. We follow the progress of a group of mums and single women whose aims range from personal discovery to simply experiencing the tough demands of the Brecon Beacons terrain.

THE BODY ELECTRIC

Life, we are taught, is simply a collection of biochemical processes. The human body is nothing more than a machine which runs on fuel from the food you eat and the air you breathe. Is it as simple as that though?

Some quite fascinating research into electrical and electromagnetic properties of living tissue is beginning to create new theories on basic life processes – theories which are so revolutionary that they threaten to shake traditional biochemistry to its foundations. It would appear that many of our normal biochemical functions, like burning glucose to make energy or making new tissue to repair wounds, are secondary not primary, processes and that such functions are being controlled by an electronic dimension which has been largely ignored by contemporary science. This new electronic view can embrace many of the body's mysteries and may have profound implications for healing, growth and consciousness.

Some 50 years ago, Nobel prize-wining scientist Albert Szent-Gyorgyi posed the question: "What is the difference between a living cat and a dead one?" His reply was simply: "Some kind of electricity". This notion that living things might have electrical or electromagnetic properties has been the subject of speculation by mystics and healers for centuries. Scientific research in the twentieth century, in Russia and America, has demonstrated that living cells have electro magnetic properties. These properties not only change as the health of the living organism changes, but they may help to direct and regulate growth and health.

Research suggests that, since electrical changes appear to take place in the cells prior to chemical or physical ones, it may be possible to detect the presence of illness long before the symptoms appear. The implications of such findings are obviously profound.

Outstanding American orthopaedic surgeon Robert O. Becker has taken the 'body electric' theories one step further by using minute electrical currents to repair damaged tissues – particularly broken bones – in the body. His further work has given credence to the theory of an 'electronic control system'

123

governing the body's healing mechanisms and has increased interest in the potential of electrical currents for healing and success in electro-acupuncture techniques.

In this country, unique research work is being carried out in Southampton at the Centre for the Study of Alternative Therapies. Doctors there are becoming extremely excited about their successful investigations in this field. We will be looking at the number of 'Bio-Electronic Techniques' used to detect all manner of diseases from food allergies and viral infections to more life-threatening disorders like cancer and also at the whole complex field of electromagnetic forces which govern our health.

Leslie's advice has been requested by over 100,000 viewers. So here is her most popular health diet of all – followed by a useful 'Positive Health' directory.

MY SPRING CLEAN DIET

If you want to get rid of post-holiday stodge, there is no better way than a week on a high-raw diet. Raw foods have remarkable properties. At famous biologically-oriented European clinics such as the Bircher-Benner in Zurich, high-raw diets are used to heal both chronic and acute illnesses. Research at University of Vienna has shown that uncooked foods improve cellular functioning leading to increased over-all energy and stamina. Raw foods form the basis of regenerative and rejuvenating diets at the world's most exclusive and expensive spas from the Golden Door in California to Switzerland's celebrated Bircher-Benner clinic. At such places people spend several hundreds of pounds in order to emerge at the end of a week or a fortnight looking (and _feeling_) years younger, lighter and more energetic.

This is because the diet of mostly raw fruits and vegetables has the ability to spring-clean your body from the inside out.

It helps to eliminate toxic materials and stored wastes which have formed in various parts of the body and which can make you feel fatigued and sluggish. It cleanses the digestive system, restores a good acid/alkaline balance to the cells and generally stimulates the proper functions of organs and tissues. In short, it puts you through a kind of transformation that leaves you sparkling with vitality.

Seldom is such sparkle and vitality more needed than in the post holiday weeks when exposure to air conditioning in offices and homes, too much (or too little) sunshine, and over indulgence in food and drink (which begets yet more

overindulgence) leaves you feeling that you need something to shake you out of your inertia. A week at a spa or health farm? Fine if you can afford it. But you can do it yourself a lot more easily (not to mention a lot more cheaply) at home. Here's the formula I use myself:

THE DIET
Breakfast
Live muesli or Yoghurt Energy Blend plus a piece of fresh fruit or a glass of fresh fruit juice if desired.
Elevenses
A cup of herb tea
Lunch
An appetiser-choose from: a slice of melon, half a grapefruit, or a bowl of clear consommé
Large salad
Fresh fruit if desired
Lunch is designed in such a way that you can eat your spring clean meal at a restaurant as easily as at home. If you take a packed lunch to work, here are some suggestions:
Packed Lunch
A large salad (undressed) in a plastic container, salad dressing separately (if you pre-dress your salad it will go soggy)
A hard boiled egg or some nuts/seeds (see recipes)
A slice of whole meal bread or 2 pieces of wholegrain crispbread
A piece of fresh fruit
Tea
A glass of vegetable or fruit juice or a piece of fresh fruit, or a cup of vegetable broth (Marigold do an excellent Swiss Vegetable Bouillon Powder – also from health food stores or direct from Marigold Foods, 2d Linfield Gardens, London NW3. Tel: 01-794 0114).
Dinner
A medium size salad of mixed vegetables
4 oz of grilled or poached fish cooked with no more than a teaspoon of oil
or 4 oz of chicken grilled or roasted with its skin removed
or 4 oz of lamb's liver grilled using no more than a teaspoon of oil
or 2 eggs scrambled in no more than a teaspoon of oil
or 6 ounces of cottage cheese
A baked potato with cottage cheese instead of butter on it or a small bowl of brown rice, or 1-2 slices of wholegrain bread/toast
A piece of fresh fruit

Drinks
On a high-raw diet your body needs very little to drink,

because the foods themselves have not been dehydrated by cooking and are therefore rich with organic fluids. The Spring-Clean Diet eliminates coffee, tea, soft drinks and alcohol. Instead, you drink fresh vegetable and fruit juices, Spring water (carbonated or plain), vegetable broth and herb teas.

THE RECIPES

NUT/SEED MIX

Chop equal quantities of three or more kinds of the following nuts and seeds (choose from hazel nuts, almonds, brazil nuts, walnuts, sunflower seeds, pumpkin seeds and sesame seeds) in a coffee grinder, blender or food processor. Keep the mixture in the fridge and use it for muesli or sprinkle it over salads.

LIVE MUESLI

1 heaped tbsp of oat flakes and 1 tbsp raisins soaked in ½ a cup of water for a couple of hours (or overnight)
1 tbsp of nut/seed mix
1 grated apple
½ a banana cut into small cubes
1 heaped tbsp of plain natural yoghurt
Squeeze of orange or lemon juice
1 tbsp of black molasses (Potters do the best tasting ones) or honey to sweeten (if desired)

Grate the apple and sprinkle with orange or lemon juice to prevent it from oxidising. Dice the banana and add to it. Stir in the soaked oat flakes and raisins. Top with yoghurt and sprinkle with nut/seed mix. Drizzle a little honey over the top and serve. You can create wonderful variations on the muesli theme so that it never becomes boring by replacing the apple with other fruit such as pear, banana, pineapple, berries, mango, or mixing more than one fruit together. You can even make it with dried fruit which has been soaked overnight in water to plump it up.

YOGHURT ENERGY BLEND

Soak a handful of dried fruit in a bowl with enough water to cover overnight. Choose sun-dried (not sulphur-dried) fruits such as: prunes, sultanas, raisins, peaches, pears, apricots and dates.

Blend the fruit with a cupful of plain yoghurt and a dash of real vanilla essence (if you can get it) in a blender and serve in a tall glass. Or if you don't have time to soak the dried fruit, blend a banana with the yoghurt instead, and add little honey and a pinch of nutmeg or cinnamon.

SALADS

When most people think of salads they groan with boredom at the thought of limp lettuce leaves, cucumber and tomato. That's not what we mean by a salad – which is nothing less than a symphony of colour and flavour which makes a meal in itself. Add together combinations of vegetables (chinese leaves, chicory, watercress, white and red cabbage, carrots, radishes, fennel, raddiccio, mushrooms, red and green peppers, Cos lettuce, endive, spring onions, cucumber, celery, Jerusalem artichokes, tomatoes, avocados, kohlrabi, etc.). Sprinkle with seeds, nuts, chopped egg or a little grated cheese and toss with a delicious dressing. It can be the beginning of a whole new way of eating. Here are a couple of suggestions to get you started.

APPLE SLAW

1 cup finely shredded white cabbage
1 apple diced
1 carrot diced
1-2 sticks of celery diced
A few raisins and a few pecans or walnuts

Combine all the ingredients and dress with an egg mayonnaise to which has been added a teaspoon of whole grain French mustard and a little water to thin.

COUNTRY SALAD

1 cup shredded chinese leaves or iceburg lettuce
½ red bell pepper
A little shredded red cabbage
1 or 2 tomatoes – diced
A few mushrooms – sliced
2 spring onions finely chopped

Combine the ingredients in a bowl and dress with a French dressing with plenty of basil and a little garlic.

SPECIAL SPINACH SALAD

A handful of spinach leaves (de-stalked) finely shredded
A few radishes
1 avocado – diced
2 tomatoes – chopped
1 small raw beetroot – grated (optional)
1 hard boiled egg – finely chopped

Toss all the ingredients together and dress with a tangy dressing. Try adding a teaspoon of curry powder to your ordinary French dressing and blending with a fresh tomato.

A week or two on such a spring cleaning regime should have you bounding with spring-time vitality long before spring arrives.

There are many more high-raw recipes in my book 'Raw Energy' published by Century.

NOTE: It is always wise to check with your doctor before beginning any new dietary regime.

'POSITIVE HEALTH' DIRECTORY

ALLERGIES
Action Against Allergy
Mrs Nathan Hill
43 The Downs
London SW20

Asthma and Allergy Treatment
Research
12 Vernon Street
Derby DE1 1FT
Tel: Derby 362 401

National Eczema Society
Tavistock House North
Tavistock Square
London WC1 9SR
Tel: 01-388 4097

McCarrison Society
5 Derby Road
Caversham
Reading RG4 0HF
Tel: Reading 473165
(Nutritional advice and help
concerning allergies)

Food Allergy Association
9 Mill Lane
Shoreham
Sussex

BODY ELECTRIC
(Research into bio-electrical
methods of diagnosis and
treatment)
The Centre for the Study of
Alternative Therapies
51 Bedford Place
Southampton
Hampshire SO1 2DG
Tel: Southampton 334752

BREASTFEEDING/
PREGNANCY/BIRTH/
CONCEPTION
La Lèche League BM3424
London WC1V 6XX
(Gives advice on every aspect of
breastfeeding to nursing mothers)

National Childbirth Trust
9 Queensborough Terrace
London W2 3TB
Tel: 01-221 3833

Foresight
The Old Vicarage
Church Lane
Witley
Nr Godalming
Surrey
Tel: Wormley 4500
(For help on pre-conceptual care
to avoid birth defects. Return
postage required)

Association for Improvement in
the Maternity Services
1 Styche Hall
Market Drayton
Shropshire TF9 3RB

The Birth Centre
c/o 16 Simpson Street
London SW11

Association of Radical Midwives
c/o 8a The Drive
Wimbledon
London SW20
Tel: 01-504 2010

HEALTH BOOKS
(Specialist suppliers)
AAA
43 The Downs
London SW20
Tel: 01-947 5082
(SAE for booklist)

Felmore Health Publications
Limited
PO Box 1
1 Lamberts Road
Tunbridge Wells TN2 3EQ
Tel: Tunbridge Wells 34574

The Whole Food Bookshop
24 Paddington Street
London W1M 4DR
Tel: 01-935 3924
(Mail order – send SAE for
proforma invoice on receipt of
cheque: the book is then sent to
you)

HEALTH COMMUNITIES
or GROWTH CENTRES
Community Health Foundation
188 Old Street
London EC1
Tel: 01-251 4076
(General advice on various centres)

The Atsitsa Club
1 Fawley Road
London NW6 1SL
Tel: 01-421 0867
(A holistic health and fitness
summer community on Greek
Island of Skyros)

CAER (Centre for Alternative
Education and Research)
Rosemerryn
Lamorna
Penzance
Cornwall TR19 6BN
Tel: Penzance 72530

HERBS AND HERBAL
TREATMENT
National Institute of Medicinal
Herbalists
148 Forest Road
Tunbridge Wells
Kent
(SAE for a list of practising
herbalists)

Herb Society
77 Gt Peter Street
London SW1P 2EZ
Tel: 01-222 3634
(SAE for list of herb growers and
suppliers)

HYPERACTIVE CHILDREN
(General Help)
Hyperactive Childrens Support
Group
59 Meadowside
Angmering
Sussex BN16 4BW
Tel: Worthing 725182
(30p in stamps required)

Young Family Life
Pre-School Playgroups
Association
Alford House
Aveline Street
London SE11 5OH
Tel: 01-582 8871

MENTAL DISORDERS
(Help for)
Sanity
Robina
The Chase
Ashley
Nr Ringwood
Dorset BH24 2AN
(Consumer organisation which
helps put people in touch with
physicians and other

professionals involved in
treatment of mental illness by
nutritional means)

Schrizophrenia Association of
Great Britain
Bryn Hyfryd
The Crescent
Bangor
Gwynedd LL57 2AG
Tel: Bangor 354048

The Dr Edward Bach Healing
Centre
Mount Vernon
Sotwell
Wallingford
Oxon
Tel: Wallingford 39489
(Natural remedies for treatment of
emotional/psychological
disorders)

NUTRITION
(Supplier of High Quality
Nutritional Supplements)
Nature's Best
PO Box 1
1 Lamberts Road
Tunbridge Wells
TN2 3EQ
Tel: Tunbridge Wells 34574

G & G Nutritional Supplies
51 Railway Approach
East Grinstead
West Sussex
Tel: East Grinstead 23016

McCarrison Society
(See under ALLERGIES)

ORGANIC FOOD
Henry Doubleday Research
Association
Convent Lane
Bocking
Braintree
Essex CM7 6RW
Tel: Braintree 24083
(Produce the excellent 'Organic
Food Guide' £2.50 – lists organic
food suppliers throughout Britain
and tells you where you can get
organic grains, fruit and vegetables
and organically raised meat. Also
at bookshops)

The Bio Dynamic Agriculture
Association
Woodman Lane
Clent
Stourbridge
West Midlands
Tel: Hagley 884933
(SAE for list of bio-dynamically
grown foods which can be
purchased)

The Soil Association
Walnut Tree Manor
Haughley
Stowmarket
Suffolk
Tel: Stowmarket 67235
(Produce a quarterly review)

Friends of the Earth
377 City Road
London EC1V 1NA
Tel: 01-837 0731

OUTDOOR PURSUITS or
OUTWARD BOUND
COURSES
The National Centre for Mountain
Activities
Plas-y-Brenin
Capel Curig
Betws-y-Coed
Gwynedd
Tel: Capel Curig 214

The National Outdoor Training
Centre
Glenmore
Aviemore
Invernesshire
Tel: Aviemore 86256

The Outward Bound Trust
12 Upper Belgrave Street
London SW1
Tel: 01-245 9933

Dolygaer Outdoor Education
Centre
Pontfticill
Merthyr Tydfil
Wales
Tel: Merthyr Tydfil 5305

Association of British Mountain
Guides
Orchard House
Laithes
Penrith
Cumbria
(courses for women)

STRESS
Relaxation for Living
Dunesk
29 Burwood Park Road
Walton-on-Thames
Surrey
Tel: Walton-on-Thames 227826
(They offer classes in relaxation
throughout Britain)

WHOLEFOODS
Food Watch
Butts Pond Industrial Estate
Sturminster Newton
Dorset DT10 1AZ
Tel: East Stour 261
(Specialist wholefood emporium.
SAE required for list and prices)

CHINA crisis

Marianne Morrish is an artist – hardly surprising, when you consider she is a direct descendant of the great painter Turner. Marianne's art, however, isn't expressed in oils or watercolours, but in restoring china. Her love for porcelain and pottery began when she had a stall on the Portobello Road in London and was saddened at how many cracked and chipped pieces she had to sell. So she decided to learn how to restore professionally and, in 1978, opened her own studio in Purley near Pangbourne and started to teach.

Here, then, is Marianne Morrish's special 'Pebble Mill at One' advice on how to restore that much-loved family treasure, be it aunty's Coronation mug or a fine piece of Staffordshire pottery.

I take eight students at a time. They come from all over the world. I call my studio the 'china surgery' because students and I have to wear medical-looking white gowns to keep the china free from any dust. In fact, broken china is laid out on the table just like a hospital operation! After intensive study, some of my pupils set up their own studios and each year I hold a 'Resoration Reunion' where I can find out how everyone is getting on.

Students often bring their own, historically rare, pieces along to a course

– one Greek Cypriot walked into the studio with a carrier-bag full of Greek pottery dating back to 4,000 years B.C.! Another time, I had great trouble with a camel-shaped piece of pottery which kept vibrating mysteriously as I worked on it. It eventually transpired that the piece had been dug up from an Egyptian tomb. A priest had to exorcise it before work could begin again.

If you're collecting china, it's worth remembering that the most sought-after items come from the eighteenth century – German Meissen, for example, which is rare because many of its pieces were made from unique moulds, destroyed by bombing during the last war. In Britain, the main china industry is in Staffordshire around Stoke-on-Trent: famous names such as Wedgwood, Minton and Doulton all come from that area. Design has had to be simplified over the years because of labour costs. In the

eighteenth and nineteenth centuries, china was handpainted to order. Today, a transfer method is used with a team of painters applying different colours on an assembly-line system. Some original designs are copied, but only figurines or limited editions still get the old treatment. Pottery, however, is often handpainted by local craftsmen.

To help you, here is a simple guide to restoration work. And take heart: you don't need art training. All you do need is patience, good eyesight and a love of china.

HOW TO REPAIR A BROKEN HANDLE

If the handle of the cup has been badly stuck, apply paint stripper and leave for 30 minutes. Immerse in very hot water with washing up liquid. Wear rubber gloves and scrub the china clean. Dry and repeat if necessary. When satisfied it is clean, leave to dry for 1-2 hours before applying Araldite and placing handle back on. Tape with damp brown paper straps. When doing this, it is helpful to place the cup on plasticine to steady it, or push it into a gravel box (if there is gold leaf on the cup, make sure you place some tissue paper on the gravel before pushing the cup in. Otherwise, it will scratch the gold leaf off – in the same way as if using sellotape to stick a handle on, removing the sellotape will pull off the gold leaf). Having taped the handle, leave for 24 hours before removing tapes. Tidy

127

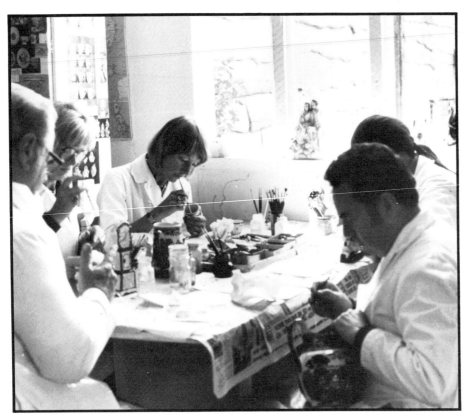

up excess Araldite and fire in domestic oven for 30 minutes at 110°F or 60°C.

Materials for Cleaning
Polystripper
Rubber gloves
Small paint brush
Plastic bowl
Washing up liquid
Boiling water
Nail brush or washing up brush
Materials for sticking handle
Araldite – slow setting or rapid
Brown butterfly tapes, or Sellotape
Water
Oven – gas or electric – fire to strengthen for 30 minutes 110°F or 60°C

SPLIT IN A CUP

Hard paste china cup or dish. If the split is badly stained, first clean with hydrogen peroxide 30 vol., 3 caps to 1 cap Scrubbs Ammonia. Brush over the stain with an old toothbrush or leave to soak with soaked tissue paper, until the split is clean. Throw away any unused mixture – do not keep it in a screwtop jar as it will explode! When mixing the peroxide and Scrubbs Ammonia, the measures must be accurate.
If the cup or dish is soft paste china, the stain will have penetrated too much into the split to get thoroughly clean. In both cases, leave to dry for 2 to 3 hours.

Then, heat the china up in the oven 200°F or 100°C for 20 minutes. The china should be too hot to handle. Mix Araldite (slow setting) with titanium dioxide and push a razor blade into the top of the split to hold it open as much as you can. In some cases this is not possible. Run the Araldite down until it melts through and pull tightly together with Sellotape. Leave until next day, remove Sellotape, clean off excess glue. Fire to strengthen at 110°F or 60°C.

Material Required
Araldite – slow setting
Titanium dioxide
Sellotape
Surgical spirits for cleaning
Kitchen towel
Cocktail sticks – for mixing Araldite
Gas or electric oven

REPLACING HANDLES WITH NEW MOULDED HANDLES
VINAMOULD

This is a newer mould-making material which can be re-used indefinitely. Cut it into small pieces and melt over low heat in saucepan, stirring all the time. If heated rapidly it will burn. Open all windows, as fumes are a problem.

Build a box of plasticine around the article you wish to mould, leave at least ½″ space all round, unless a plate or similar article when the plasticine can be brought up the back. Leave ½″ around edge and build up ½″ wall to contain Vinamould.

When the Vinamould has reached a syrup-like consistency, it is ready for pouring. Always pour in one continuous movement onto plasticine and let it creep over the china. Most moulds can be made with one pouring, but handles should be made in two halves. Pour first lot to middle of handle and leave 15 minutes.

With heated metal skewer, make holes in Vinamould around handle to act as keys for next pouring, which can be poured to the top of the plasticine box.

Leave for a further 30 minutes before removing Vinamould.

Fill both halves of mould with modelling mix and bring both halves together, locating by means of the keyways. Strap together with gum paper or Sellotape. A handle made this way can be attached immediately in its final position, but remember to use cement, or it can be attached separately as a china handle after it has been tidied up.

It is important to remember that the mould you are taking is of a finished article, whereas you still have to paint and glaze your model, so always rub your model down slightly.

Although Vinamould can be re-used indefinitely, there are occasions when you will want to save a useful mould, particularly a common flower, teapot knob, etc. Always keep Vinamould in the greaseproof paper in which it is sent from Tiranti Ltd and if you have an accident and burn Vinamould, throw it away, NEVER mix with new Vinamould.

Vinamould is obtainable from: Alec Tiranti Ltd, 21 Goodge Place, London W1 or 70 High Street, Theale, Berks. For filling moulds I recommend: Liquid Araldite from local suppliers, Resin AY103, Hardener AY956.

Measure 5 parts resin to 1 part Hardener. Mix equal parts titanium dioxide, whitening agent only and French chalk, industry (grey), used as a binding agent. Add to Araldite and mix. Bubble will rise, and over the next 20 minutes, scrape the bubbles off with the back of a spoon. When free of bubbles, pour into mould. Leave to set until the next day, remove from mould trim. Fire at 110°F or 60°C for 30 minutes. Attach with neat Araldite glue from tubes, not liquid. Leave until next day and fire at low temperature.

THE FINAL STAGE – PREPARATION FOR PAINTING

Preparation for painting is most important. If you have made a mistake or haven't sanded a piece down enough, don't imagine that your paint will cover it. It will not; it will only emphasize it. Many restorers make the mistake of applying thick paint to cover up the joins straight away. By doing this, the piece then looks too opaque. If one applies the coats of paint thinly and fires in between each coat, the look becomes more translucent.

Materials for Sanding
China mending sander
Transformer plus attachments from:
Expo Drills Ltd., Clock Tower Works, Warsash, Hampshire SO3 6FH.

The best paints to use are Windsor and Newton's Best Artists Oils, mix with glaze.
Glaze and thinners from:
Chintex, Wraxall, Bristol (by post only: you cannot phone or call).
Recommended Brushes
Sable hair – (not nylon)
Middle of road. Series 16 nos. 5, 3, 2, 1, 0, 00.
Fan brush no. 4 or no. 6

Further reference:
'HOW TO MEND YOUR OWN CHINA AND GLASS' by Susan Wells. Publishers: Bell Hyman, 37/39 Denmark House, Queen Elizabeth Street, London SE1.

For details of courses write to:
Marianne Morrish, The Studio Westbury, Westbury Farm, Purley, Berkshire.

YOUTH CARING AWARDS

Now firmly established as a major national community project, our Youth Caring Awards have become a highlight of the Pebble Mill year.

And the final has become a traditionally 'Royal' day at Pebble Mill with H.R.H. The Princess Anne taking a special personal interest in the scheme. She has presented the trophy for two years running.

The competition, run in association with Dettol, aims to give nationwide recognition to young people who are voluntarily helping the less fortunate in their home communities.

And the 1985 competition, like the others before it, attracted thousands of entries, emphasizing the huge range of community work being carried out in cities, towns and villages.

This particular group of finalists each receiving a £1,000 prize included, from Merseyside, young people who arrange holidays for mentally handicapped children, a sea search and rescue team from Hampshire and a youth enquiry service in Kilmarnock where unemployed youngsters provide advice on consumer rights, welfare benefits, education, housing and law.

But the group which received the £5,000 first prize from Princess Anne was the Music Collective from Gateshead, Tyne-and-Wear. They provide rehearsal facilities, musical equipment and tuition for hundreds of unemployed youngsters who would otherwise be hanging around the streets, and have given them a place to meet and an interest in life.

If you know of a young people's voluntary scheme which deserves recognition, why not enter them for our next competition?

Send your nomination to Youth Caring Awards, 57 South Street, Epsom, Surrey KT18 7PX.

1. H.R.H. The Princess Anne is shown the Pebble Mill Heritage Tapestry by Pebble Mill Editor Peter Hercombe as she arrives for the 1985 Youth Caring Awards.

2. Carl Sherwin and Alan Allman of the Music Collective, winners of the 1985 Trophy.

3. Princess Anne meets some of the presenters of the Awards programme: Josephine Buchan, Paul Coia, Sarah Greene and Peter Powell.

Christmas at Pebble Mill is a time when the foyer is filled with bright-eyed children competing in our national schools Carol Competition, when Hilary James unveils more original ideas for presents in her 'Sew Easy Gifts for Christmas' series and the Pebble Mill kitchen bustles and bubbles away as Michael Smith adds his own special magic to our Christmas Fare.

CHRISTMAS at PEBBLE·MILL

TEDDY BEAR

Teddy Bear Toy, Appliqué for Child's Sweatshirt, Scarves

Irresistible for children of any age, my teddy bear is made in the traditional way with jointed arms and legs –and a growl! For real togetherness I've also included details for making the sweatshirt appliqué and the matching scarves.

Last Christmas the Pebble Mill office was buried in an avalanche of over 100,000 requests for the details of Hilary James's series on Christmas gifts.

So to avoid disappointment for this festive season, Hilary has given us all the details of her 'Sew Easy Gifts for Christmas' series on the following pages. As usual,

SEW EASY
GIFTS·FOR ▪
CHRISTMAS

she has come up with a marvellous assortment of items – woodwork, knitting, toymaking and paper craft to name just a few. There's something for everyone.

131

TEDDY BEAR

SIZE
Approx 37cm (14½") tall.

MATERIALS
25cm (¼ yd) of 140cm (54") wide fur fabric in main shade, oddment in contrast, 500 gm bag polyester stuffing, strong polyester or poly/cotton thread such as Coats Duet, pair 16mm (⅝") safety eyes, 23mm (⅞") safety nose, four 35mm (1⅜") safety joints, growler.

STOCKISTS
Fur fabric, stuffing and thread are readily available nationwide. Should you have any difficulty, the following items can be obtained by post from John Lewis, Oxford St. London W1., adding 75p for p & p. Eyes (no. 68401) in brown, amber or blue 11p per pair, nose (no. 69202) 6p each, joints (no. 67002) 15p each, growler (no. 6630) £1.45.

CUTTING OUT
*Draw the pattern shapes onto paper, taking care to transfer all the markings and wording. Pin the pattern to the wrong side of the fabric so that the arrows on the pattern correspond to the downward pile of the fabric. Using the pattern as a template, mark the cutting line onto the wrong side of the fabric using a felt pen. Mark the notches, dots, joint positions and all construction and placement lines. Leave the pattern pinned to the fabric for easy identification.

TO MAKE
All seams are stitched with right sides together, taking 5mm (¼") turnings and matching circles and notches as appropriate.

ARMS
Join the arms together in pairs, leaving an opening between the notches for stuffing. Turn right side out and stuff up to the opening. Snip through just one thread of fabric at the joint position on one arm. Insert a joint (see diagram), stuff the top of the arm very firmly and catch stitch the opening. Complete the second arm in the same manner but take care when inserting the joint to make a pair.

LEGS
Stitch the leg sections together in pairs, leaving an opening at the lower edge for inserting the sole and another between the notches for stuffing. Matching the centre front and centre back dots, stitch the sole to the lower edge. Turn right side out and stuff up to the opening. Complete the legs in exactly the same way as the arms.

BODY
Stitch the body sections together leaving the neck edge open. Snip through just one thread of fabric at the four joint positions then turn the body right side out. Push the limb joint through the corresponding hole in the body, slide on the plastic washer, then push the metal safety washer firmly in place (see diagram).

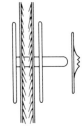

Stuff the body very firmly, placing the growler in the tummy area with the perforated end fairly close to the fur at the centre front and only lightly protecting it with stuffing. If it's buried too deep, it won't work properly. Run a gathering thread around the neck opening edge and draw it up to form a rounded 'shoulder' shape, adding stuffing behind the gathering thread. Fasten off the thread end securely.

EARS
With right sides uppermost and following the position indicated on the pattern, pin a contrast inner ear onto an ear section. Stitch the outer edge of the inner ear to the ear using a close machine zig-zag stitch. Tack the loose raw edges together. Stitch this prepared ear section to one of the remaining three ear sections. Tack the loose raw edges together. Make the second ear in the same manner.

HEAD
Stitch the centre front seam of the side head from the dot downwards. Stitch the head front to the side head, pivoting at the centre front dot.

Using a contrast coloured thread, transfer the muzzle placement line markings to the right side of the fabric with tacking stitches. Tack the ears to the front and side head between the notches, taking care that the inner ears face forward. Stitch the centre back seam of the head back. Stitch the head front to the head back, sandwiching the ears. Turn right side out.

MUZZLE
Fold the muzzle in half along the centre front line and stitch the notched edges together. Fold the muzzle along the fold lines and stitch across the stitching line, then trim back the turnings of the pointed end of the muzzle to about 6mm (¼") from the stitching (see diagram).

Turn the muzzle right side out. Insert the safety nose just below the crosswise seam, forcing it between the seam's stitches. Push the safety washer firmly in place. Pin the muzzle to the head along the line of tacking stitches, matching the

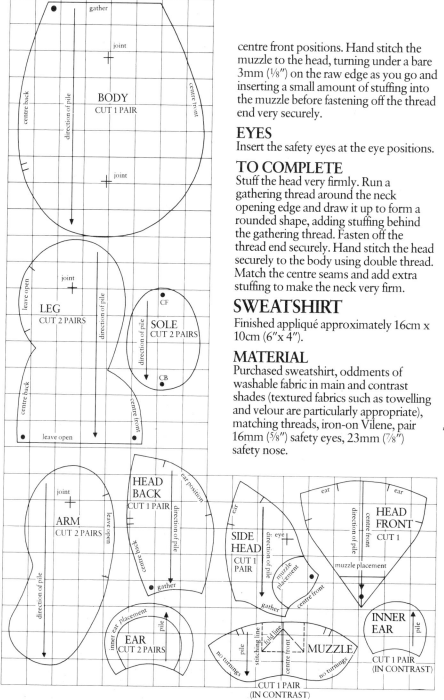

centre front positions. Hand stitch the muzzle to the head, turning under a bare 3mm (⅛″) on the raw edge as you go and inserting a small amount of stuffing into the muzzle before fastening off the thread end very securely.

EYES
Insert the safety eyes at the eye positions.

TO COMPLETE
Stuff the head very firmly. Run a gathering thread around the neck opening edge and draw it up to form a rounded shape, adding stuffing behind the gathering thread. Fasten off the thread end securely. Hand stitch the head securely to the body using double thread. Match the centre seams and add extra stuffing to make the neck very firm.

SWEATSHIRT
Finished appliqué approximately 16cm x 10cm (6″x 4″).

MATERIAL
Purchased sweatshirt, oddments of washable fabric in main and contrast shades (textured fabrics such as towelling and velour are particularly appropriate), matching threads, iron-on Vilene, pair 16mm (⅝″) safety eyes, 23mm (⅞″) safety nose.

CUTTING OUT
N.B. The entire head is cut from the main fabric and the contrast inner ears and muzzle are added on top.

Pre-shrink the fabrics first by washing them.*Draw the appliqué design onto paper to form patterns.

To prevent excessive fraying and distortion, apply iron-on Vilene to the wrong side of the appliqué fabrics prior to cutting out.

Cut out the entire shape from the main fabric and the inner ears and muzzle from contrast.

TO MAKE
Neaten the outer edge of the head using a close machine zig-zag stitch. If necessary, stitch around the edge again to obtain a firm crisp finish. Trim away any stray wisps. Stitch the inner ears and the muzzle to the head using a close machine zig-zag. File away or cut the stalk of the safety nose and eyes leaving just enough to prevent the washer falling off. Attach them to correspond with the pattern. Force the washers on very tightly. Stitch the appliqué to the sweatshirt by machine or by hand.

*Actual size Teddy Bear patterns can be obtained free (+ sae) from: "Teddy Bear Patterns", Pebble Mill at One, BBC TV, Birmingham B5 7QQ.

SWEATSHIRT APPLIQUE PATTERN

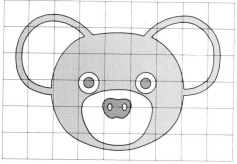

5mm turnings are included on all pattern pieces, unless otherwise indicated.

Square width = 2cm

133

SCARVES AND SHAWLS

Simple as ABC is how I'd describe these last minute 'Sew Easy' ideas. You can literally save pounds on the cost of a ready-made equivalent, with the added bonus of an almost infinite variety of fabrics to choose from. Something for the whole family was the goal, so I've given a selection of various shapes and sizes.

MATERIALS

Choose woven fabrics not knits. Traditional Viyella is ideal for scarves and comes in a wonderful array of plains, prints, checks and tartans. Liberty print wools are perfect for scarves or shawls, as is Viyella's new challis fabric. For cosy long scarves, heavier woollen types are best – something with a touch of cashmere is extra special, but anything warm to handle can be used.

TO MAKE

All the edges need to be finished exactly on the grain. A fabric such as Viyella can be torn very successfully across the grain. The selvedges can also be removed by tearing.

Heavier woollens almost invariably need to be cut, but their more obvious weave makes it fairly easy to cut along the grain – especially if you choose a check.

Once all the edges are squared off, they can be fringed to a depth of about 6mm (¼"). At the ends of long woolly scarves, a fringe of about 2.5cm (1") looks nice.

With very loosely woven fabrics a machine zig-zag can be worked to prevent further, unwanted fraying.

CHILD'S LONG SCARF

A finished length of approx 110cm (43") and a width of 23cm (9") is appropriate for a small child. Over about 8 years, make the length approx 120cm (47") and the width 25-30cm (10-12"). Teddy's scarf approximately 65cm x 10cm (25½" x 4").

LADIES' SQUARE SCARF

Make a square using the full width of 90cm (36") wide fabric. A square from a full width of 115cm (45") fabric gives a really generous scarf which can almost be termed a small shawl.

LADIES' SHAWL

Make a square using the full width of 140cm (54") or 150cm (60") fabric.

LADIES' AND GENTS' LONG SCARF

Use the full width of a 140cm (54") fabric cut about 35-40cm (14-16") deep. This allows plenty of length for tying into a knot.

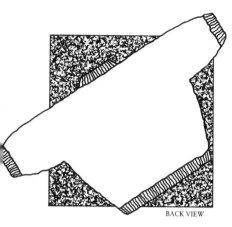
BACK VIEW

MOHAIR AND KNITTING RIBBON SWEATERS

Quick and easy to make – even for beginners – these luxurious sweaters combine the very newest knitting ribbon with fashion's favourite mohair yarn.

The red version teams a plain mohair with a lurex-trimmed ribbon. For the lilac version, the theme is reversed. This time it's the mohair which is glittery and the ribbon which is plain. Either way – a fashion success story.

SIZE

One size, fits bust 86-97cm (34-38″).
Actual measurement approx 107cm (42″).
Finished length approx 56cm (22″).

MATERIALS

8x25g balls of Emu Filigree Supreme mohair yarn – shades Poppy or Blue Diamond.
6x50m spools of Offray polyester Knitting Ribbon – shades Red Lurex (5) or Iris (447).
1 pair each of long 3¼mm (No. 10) and 5mm (No. 6) Knitting Needles.

STOCKISTS

Emu Filigree Supreme costs £1.59 per ball for plain colours, £1.65 per ball for glittery colours. Offray Knitting Ribbon costs £3.99 per 50m spool for plain colours, £4.45 per spool for lurex-trimmed colours. Both are available nationwide, or by post from Ries Wools, 242 High Holborn, London WC1V 7DZ –post free.

TENSION

16 sts and 24 rows to 10cm (4″) over pattern using 5mm (No. 6) needles. Check your tension by working a tension square. If the knitting is loose and there are LESS stitches to 10cm (4″), use a thinner needle; if there are MORE stitches to 10cm (4″), use a thicker needle.

ABBREVIATIONS

K = knit, P = purl, M = mohair yarn, R = ribbon, sts(s) = stitch(es), cm = centimetres, ″ = inches, yfd = yarn forward (bring the yarn forward under the right hand needle, taking it over the needle before knitting the next stitch), yrn = yarn round needle (take the yarn over and under the right hand needle, then proceed as pattern), alt = alternate, rep = repeat, patt = pattern, cont = continue, beg = beginning.

BACK

Using 3¼mm (No. 10) needles and M, cast on 86 sts and work 6cm (2¼″) in K1, P1 rib.
Change to 5mm (No. 6) needles and K 4 rows.
Proceed in patt as follows:—
1st Row: (right side) Using R, K3, * K10, (K1, yfd) 10 times, rep from * to last 3 sts, K3.
2nd Row: Using R, P3, * (drop yfd loop, P1, yrn) 10 times, P10, rep from * to last 3 sts, P3.
3rd Row: Using M, K all sts, dropping the yrn loops.

4th, 5th, 6th Rows: Using M, K. (Weave R LOOSELY up side edge.)
7th Row: Using R, K3, * (K1, yfd) 10 times, K10, rep from * to last 3 sts, K3.
8th Row: Using R, P3, * P10 (drop yfd loop, P1, yrn) 10 times, rep from * to last 3 sts, P3.
9th Row: Using M, K all sts, dropping the yrn loops.
10th, 11th, 12th Rows: using M, K. (Weave R LOOSELY up side edge.)
These 12 rows form patt.
Cont in patt until work measures 34cm (13½″) from cast on edge, ending with a 2nd Row of patt.

Shape Sleeves

Next Row: Cast on 30 sts at beg of row then work as 3rd Row of patt. (116 sts)
Next Row: Cast on 30 sts at beg of row then work as 4th Row of patt. (146 sts)
Cont in patt, commencing with 11th Row•, until work measures 56cm (22″) from cast on edge, ending with a 10th Row of patt.
•This jump in row sequence is required to keep the pattern repeat correct after the sleeve stitches have been added.
Cut off yarn and slip first 61 sts onto a holder for right shoulder, slip next 24 sts onto a holder for back neck and remaining 61 sts onto a holder for left shoulder.

FRONT

Work exactly as given for Back until Front measures 51cm (20in) from cast on edge, ending with a 10th Row of patt.

Shape Neck

Next Row: Patt across 68 sts, turn and leave remaining sts on a spare needle. Work on first set of sts as follows:–
Cast off 3 sts at beg of next row and 2 sts at beg of following two alt rows (61 sts). Work straight until Front measures same as Back ending with a 10th Row of patt.
Cut off yarn and leave these sts on a holder for left shoulder.

135

With right side facing, return to sts on spare needle and slip first 10 sts onto a holder.
Join M to next st, cast off 3 sts and patt to end. (65 sts)
Complete to match first side of neck, reversing shapings, but leave sts on needle and DO NOT cut off yarn once this side is completed.

RIGHT SHOULDER SEAM
With right sides together, join right shoulder seam by casting off 61 sts on holder for right shoulder of Back, in one operation with 61 sts still on needle for right shoulder of Front (see diagram).

NECKBAND
With right side facing, join M to neck at left front shoulder and using a 3¼mm (No. 10) needle pick up and K 23 sts down left side of neck, K 10 sts from holder, pick up and K 23 sts up right side of neck, then K 24 sts from back neck holder. (80 sts)
Work 3cm (1¼") in K1, P1 rib.
Cast off loosely in rib.

LEFT SHOULDER SEAM
Join left shoulder seam edges by casting off together, as for right shoulder seam. Join neckband seam.

CUFFS
Using 3¼mm (No. 10) needles and M, and with right side facing, pick up and K 68 sts evenly along sleeve edge.
Work 3cm (1¼") in K1, P1 rib.
Cast off in rib.

TO MAKE UP
Join side, sleeve and cuff seams.

If you experience any difficulty with the pattern, please write to Customer Services Dept., Emu Wools Ltd., Leeds Road, Greengates, Bradford BD10 9TE.

CHRISTMAS DECOR

A colour theme running through Christmas decorations always makes far more impact than a haphazard mixture of colours. I've homed in on blue and silver, as a change from conventional red, green and gold – in everything from the tree itself to prettily wrapped 'parcel' tree decorations. I've used the same tiny parcels again to make an eye-catching table centre, larger mock presents around the base of the tree and pretty wall or window hangings.

TREE TRIMMING PARCELS
MATERIALS
Foil gift wrap, self-adhesive gift ribbon, narrow crinkled gift ribbon, beads, glue, double-sided tape, small empty boxes or expanded polystyrene cut to size – my parcels are 9cm x 6cm x 2.5cm (3½" x 2⅜" x 1").

TO MAKE
Cover the parcels with gift wrap, neatly folding in the ends and securing them in place with double-sided tape. Decorate with ribbons and beads, making full use of the curling properties of the ribbons. To curl the ribbon, pull it fairly forcefully over the back of a pair of scissors. Curled ribbon looks particularly effective if the ends are cut into strips which then form a tassel effect (cut the strips before curling the ribbon). Tie the parcels to the tree using silver thread or yarn which will merge into the foliage and remain invisible.

TABLE CENTRE
Using exactly the same idea, make more tiny parcels and pile them decoratively into a silver or blue bowl, or even a clear glass mixing bowl. Add a chunky non-drip candle for extra effect.

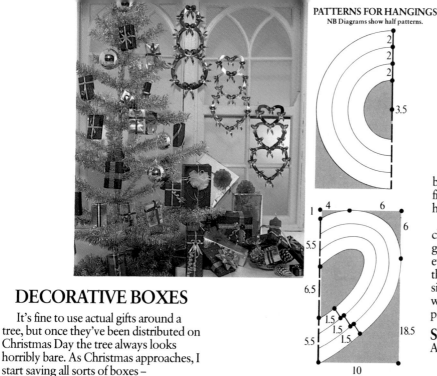

PATTERNS FOR HANGINGS
NB Diagrams show half patterns.

2
2
2
3.5

1 4   6
6
5.5
6.5
1.5
1.5
1.5 18.5
5.5   1.5
10

ALL MEASUREMENTS IN CENTIMETRES

DECORATIVE BOXES

It's fine to use actual gifts around a tree, but once they've been distributed on Christmas Day the tree always looks horribly bare. As Christmas approaches, I start saving all sorts of boxes – toothpaste, make-up, car spares, etc. I don't discard anything at this time of the year. Everything gets transformed into a mock present. Use the same gift wrap, curled ribbons and bead theme as on the tree. Because the parcels are larger, bigger bows can be used. Perfect for this is Berisford's 10 second bow – a ribbon with its own drawstring which becomes a bow with tie ends. Costing about 40p per metre, it's available from major department stores and specialist shops nationwide.

WALL OR WINDOW HANGINGS

These look most effective when identical shapes of differing sizes are joined together. The diagrams are for triple-decker circular and heart-shaped hangings. Hangings with more than 3 motifs could easily be made by adding further, larger outlines using the same principle.

MATERIALS
Glossy card, gift ribbon, beads, sharp pencil, craft knife, glue.

TO MAKE
Using the diagrams as a guide, make complete pattern templates from scrap paper (if you have a compass, the circles could be drawn straight on the card).

Place the pattern onto the right side of the card and transfer the lines onto the card by drawing along the lines with a sharp pencil which will leave a clear indentation. Cut along the lines very carefully till the segments are separated. Discard the centres (use them as gift tags).

Glue the segments together with the smallest at the top. Decorate with ribbons and beads. Either suspend the hanging with toning thread so it hangs freely, or use double-sided tape to attach to a flat surface.

LAST MINUTE GIFTS AND WRAPPING
WOODEN SOLITAIRE

Having left my home-made solitaire board out on display for decoration, I find that visiting friends and their children have become intrigued by it.

Adults and older children feel challenged to find the solution to the game (and make repeated attempts on every visit). The young are fascinated by the beautiful marbles I've used and simply love to play with them. Either way, a really successful 'conversation piece' to have around.

SIZE
At least 22cm (8⅝″) diameter.

MATERIALS
Unvarnished, completely flat, circular bread board at least 22cm (8⅝″) in diameter (a larger one with a channelled edge is even better), 32 standard size marbles, drill with 13mm (½″) countersink bit, soft pencil, ruler, fine glass paper, polyurethane wood varnish, wood dye (optional), brush.

137

TO MAKE

Divide the board into 4 equal segments with 2 lines drawn at right angles to each other. Draw lines 3cm ($1^3/_{16}$") apart to achieve the pattern of 33 intersections as shown in the diagram.

Centering the drill bit on each intersection, drill 33 'holes' just deep enough to seat the marbles. Rub down the surface using glass paper, removing the pencil lines and sharp edges. Remove all traces of dust with a damp cloth. Allow to dry thoroughly. Dye and/or varnish the board following the manufacturer's directions.

TO PLAY SOLITAIRE

Place all the marbles on the board, leaving the centre hole empty. The object of the game is to finish with one marble left in the centre hole. To do this, jump one marble over its immediate neighbour into the empty centre hole. Remove the 'jumped over' marble and place it in the channel. Continue like this working only in straight lines, NOT diagonals.

LACE-TRIMMED LINEN

If you're like me and you drool over luxurious lace-trimmed bedlinen in the shops, but can't bring yourself to lash out on the absurd prices being asked – here's a 'Sew Easy' solution. Simply add some pretty lace edging to inexpensive plain linen – better still if you can buy the linen in the sales.

MATERIALS

Pre-gathered lace with a finished inner edge, thread, narrow washable ribbon for decorative bows.

STOCKIST

I used Berisfords pre-gathered white cotton Broderie Anglaise with a bound edge, design 14849 (as illustrated) approx 6.5cm ($2^1/_2$") wide. It is available by mail order at £2.40 per metre from Gordon Thoday Fabrics, 60 St. Andrews Street, Cambridge CB2 3DN. Please add 50p for P&P.

QUANTITIES

I haven't given metreage details for individual projects. I'm leaving the measuring up to you because the sizes of the items you may want to trim will vary so much. With a pre-gathered, bound edged trim, just remember to allow for 2 things:
1 – sufficient for turning under and neatening the ends on sheets.
2 – a little extra for turning the corners on a pillowcase.

TO MAKE

On SHEETS, pin and stitch the bound edge of the lace in place to the top of the sheet, stitching under the raw ends of the lace to finish them off. Trim with one or two decorative bows if you like.

On PILLOWCASES, start about halfway along one long edge, pinning the bound edge of the lace in place on the upper side of the pillowcase so the edges just overlap. To turn the corners, make a neat double pleat in the lace (as shown in the diagram), so that it lies flat. Pin right the way around till the raw ends meet and overlap. These ends are seamed and neatened before the lace is finally stitched to the pillowcase.

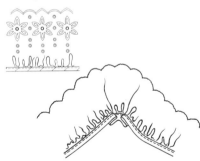

Make a neat seam in the lace by matching up the design detail. If necessary, ease the lace a little to fit, but don't stretch it. Stitch the seam, trim back the turnings to about 6mm ($1/4$") and machine-neaten them together for durability. Now stitch the lace to the pillowcase. Make 4 ribbon bows and stitch one to each corner.

BOXES AND CARRIERS

Doesn't it make you furious when you buy an awkwardly shaped gift that proves impossible to wrap neatly? Then you have to fork out more money for an expensive decorative box or carrier bag. You can end up paying more for the wrapping than the gift inside!

Spend a little time and a lot less money by making your own – you can even choose a colour to complement the gift inside.

BOXES

MATERIALS

Lightweight card, strong paper glue or double-sided tape, scissors, craft knife, ruler.

TO MAKE

Rather than marking the shapes directly onto the card, draw them onto scrap paper first. You can then use this paper pattern over and over again.

DIAGRAM MARKINGS

Solid lines indicate cutting lines. Dashed lines indicate scoring lines. Dotted lines are for drafting the pattern.

Measurements are in centimetres.

BOX 1

SIZE

10cm (4") square – height is adjustable.

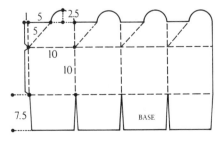

TO MAKE

Make the pattern following the diagram and selecting a height to suit the gift. Using the pattern, transfer all the outlines and scoring lines onto the wrong side of the card. Cut out along the cutting lines. Score lightly along the scoring lines on the wrong side of the card. Fold the sides to form a square. Fold up the base sections. Stick the lip in position. For the base stick 2 opposite sections together, then stick the 2 remaining sections in place one at a time. Fold the top to produce the interlocking design.

BOX 2

SIZE

Approx 25cm x 12cm (10″ x 5½″) when folded. Both these measurements are adjustable.

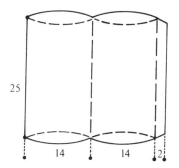

25

14   14   2

TO MAKE

Make the pattern following the diagram and adjusting any measurements as required. To obtain the curved cutting and scoring lines use a large plate. The deeper you make the curve, the deeper the finished box will be.

Using the pattern, transfer all the outlines and scoring lines onto the wrong side of the card. Cut out along the cutting line. Score lightly along the scoring lines on the wrong side of the card. Fold in the sides and stick the lip in position. When perfectly dry, fold in the ends.

CARRIERS

MATERIALS

Very firm paper, strong paper glue or double-sided tape, scissors, ruler, hole punch, ribbon or cord for handles.

TO MAKE

Make a re-usable pattern from scrap paper.

DIAGRAM MARKINGS

Solid lines indicate cutting lines. Dashed lines indicate fold lines. Dotted lines are for drafting the pattern. Measurements are in centimetres.

SIZE

Approx 16cm (6¼″) wide x 20cm (8″) high x 7cm (2¾″) deep. All measurements are adjustable.

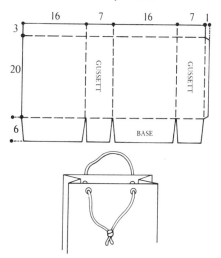

TO MAKE

Make the pattern following the diagram and adjusting any measurements as required (only one thing to bear in mind – always make the base sections 1cm (³⁄₈″) shallower than the gusset). Using the pattern, transfer all the outlines and fold lines onto the wrong side of the

paper. Cut out along the cutting lines. Fold in the sides. Fold up the base sections. Fold down the top edge. Stick the lip in position. For the base, fold in the short sections, fold in and stick one long section to the ends. Fold in the remaining long section and stick. Fold in the top edge. Form a pleat at the top edge of the gusset by bringing the corners together and making a neat crease. Punch holes and thread through the ribbon or cord (see diagram).

EARRINGS

There are certainly some pretty and unusual earrings sold nowadays, but they've usually got pretty and unusual prices to go with them.

Have fun rummaging around unusual places to find some inexpensive substitutes.

The component parts used in jewellery making are called 'findings.'

For pierced ears use: a ball hook (JF11) or kidney wire (JF12). For non-pierced ears use a flat clip (JF9) or screw (JF10). Together with: a 2″ headpin (JF18) or 1″ eyepin (JF20). Jump rings: large (JF14) or small (JF16).

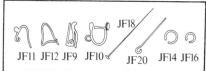

You may be lucky and be able to get findings locally. If not, they can be obtained by post from Creative Beadcraft Ltd., Unit 26, Chiltern Trading Estate, Earl Howe Road, Holmer Green, High Wycombe, Bucks.

139

Naturally, these can be made to any size you wish to suit your table; but since I made a fairly conventional size of placemat and a tablemat to take 2 serving dishes, the following measurements may prove useful as a guide.

Be adventurous and think about staining the wood and using coloured rope as an alternative, either for indoor use or alfresco dining.

SIZE

Placemat approx 175mm x 185mm (6⅞" x 7¼"), tablemat approx 220mm x 370mm (8¾" x 14½"). Both sets of measurements exclude the handle and rope ends.

MATERIALS

Wood – use 25mm (1") square prepared softwood. Each placemat takes 1.10m (1¼yd), the tablemat takes 2.50m (2¾yd). Rope – use synthetic rope approx 10mm (⅜") in diameter. Each placemat takes 61cm (24"), the tablemat takes 100cm (39½"). Drill with wood bit to make hole large enough for rope to fit through. 13mm (½") panel pins – 12 for each placemat, 22 for tablemat, polyurethane wood varnish, wood dye (optional), brush, sharp knife.

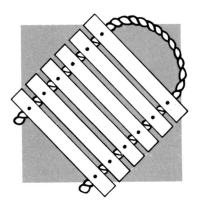

TO MAKE PLACEMAT

Cut 6 lengths of wood, each 175mm (6⅞") long. Mark a point on the centre line of one face of each piece of wood exactly 30mm (1³⁄₁₆") from each end. Drill at these 12 points, making a hole right through the wood. Rub down the surfaces using glass paper, removing any sharp edges. Remove all traces of dust with a damp cloth. Allow to dry thoroughly. Dye and/or varnish the wood following the manufacturer's directions. Cut a 61cm (24") length of rope and carefully seal the ends with a soft flame. Thread the rope through the holes, leaving about 13mm (½") between each slat (see diagram) and forming a handle at one end.

Secure the rope and slats in place with panel pins, as shown, using a nail punch, if you have one, to sink the heads and prevent them scratching a polished surface.

TO MAKE TABLEMAT

Cut 11 lengths of wood each 220mm (8¾") long. Cut a 100cm (39½") length of rope and make exactly as for placemat.

A Christmas Carol

3

1

2

One of the happiest 'Pebble Mill' events is our Christmas Carol Competition. Tens of thousands of children take part, making it one of the biggest music projects of the year for schools all over Britain.

Last year, the winning carol in the senior section was written by Katy Topping and Cathryn Ramsden of St. Augustine's R.C. High School, Billington, Blackburn; the junior winners were Alison West and Rebecca Smith of Tower Lodge School, Rugby. They won Casio electronic equipment for their schools' music departments.

We're all looking forward to this year's competition – and, for anyone thinking of taking part, the rules and details of entry are available from the 'Pebble Mill at One' office.

1. All six school choirs competing in the 1984 finals.

2. The senior winners – St. Augustine's R.C. High School, Billington, Blackburn.

3. The junior winners – Tower Lodge School, Rugby.

Christmas Fare

Even when the Pebble Mill office has closed down for Christmas, the switchboard is still besieged by viewers – only now their queries take on a distinctly festive note.

Problems have begun in the kitchen as people try to remember the detail of Michael Smith's sumptuous Christmas recipes. "Did he say one tablespoonful or two?" "Do you set the oven at 350° or 450°?" "What can we do that's different?"

Well, here are some recipes from Michael based on his 'New English Cookery', which will certainly brighten up your Christmas dinner.

CHRISTMAS (OR POMPION) SOUP
Serves 4

Pompion was the eighteenth-century word for a pumpkin. This is a rich warm-toned soup which combines all the autumn flavours and may be served hot or chilled.

4 oz (110g) onion, skinned and chopped
1 oz (25g) butter or olive oil
1 small clove garlic, crushed
12 oz (350g) cubed pumpkin (or melon), weighed after peeling and deseeding
6 oz (175g) freshly boiled and skinned chestnuts, or chestnuts in brine, strained
1 stock cube, crumbled
2 x 2 inch (5cm) slivers orange rind
1 tsp ground ginger
1 tsp mild sweet paprika
1 level tsp milled white or black pepper
1 tsp salt (or to taste)
1 'envelope' saffron powder (optional)
1 pint (570ml) fresh or carton of orange juice
½ pint (275ml) single cream (optional)

Optional Garnishes
½ a cooked chestnut per helping
1 or 2 orange segments per helping

Melt the butter and fry the onion over a low heat till transparent. Add the garlic and pumpkin or melon. Stir round, cooking gently until the juices 'draw.' Now add all the remaining ingredients and simmer, covered, until the pumpkin is tender. Pass through a mouli or blender, and then rub through a fine sieve. Cool, chill. Just before serving, mix in the chilled cream and garnish to taste. To serve hot, bring the soup to boiling point, stir in the cream, then bring back to just under boiling point. If the cream is omitted, thin the soup down to a light consistency by adding chicken stock, chilled or hot as the case may be.

SPECIAL STUFFING FOR TURKEY '1985'

6 oz bulgar wheat (cracked wheat)
1 pint plus chicken stock to cover (use stock cube)
1 tbsp olive oil or soy oil, plus 1 oz butter
6 oz onion, finely chopped (1 large)
6 oz celery, finely chopped (approx. 8 – 10 stalks)
6 oz lean unsmoked bacon, rinded and finely chopped
6 oz Californian raisins, plumped up in hot chicken stock overnight
2 tbsp finely chopped parsley
2 tsp ground mace
1 large clove of garlic, crushed (optional)
1 large egg beaten to bind
1 tsp salt and plenty of milled pepper
Grated zest only 1 lemon and 1 orange
Juice of half the lemon

Put the wheat in a bowl, pour over enough hot chicken stock to cover. Leave to swell for 2 – 3 hours. Squeeze out excess moisture with the hand.

In a heavy-bottomed pan heat the oil and butter together, swirling the pan around to ensure even melting. Do not allow to colour. Soften the onion and celery together without colouring, stirring from time to time and putting a lid over the pan. Remove to a bowl.

Fry the bacon until crisp. Drain off the fat and keep this for another use.

Mix all the ingredients together, binding with the egg and seasoning well. The mixture should be loose, but not sloppy. Fill into either the neck or the cavity of the turkey, depending whether you are making one or two stuffings.

Makes enough (approx. 2 pounds) for one 12 – 14 pound turkey.

I suggest you use a self-basting turkey for a trouble-free Christmas. The stuffing can be made one or two days in advance. Keep refrigerated and stuff the turkey just before roasting.

In place of the usual gravy – which seems to cause more hassle than anything else at Christmastime – try a rich tomato-sherry sauce for a change. This can be made two or three days in advance and is ready just to re-heat before serving.

RICH TOMATO SHERRY SAUCE
Serves 8 – 10

1 oz butter
2 oz onion, finely chopped
2 sticks celery, finely chopped
1 clove garlic, crushed (optional)
Half tsp flour

1 tsp Muscovado sugar, or other brown sugar, OR tip of a pointed knife of mild curry powder (¼tsp)
1 chicken stock cube, crumbled
1 fluid oz Amontillado type sherry
½ pint water
Milled pepper only

Melt the butter in a 3 pint heavy-bottomed pan. Add the onion and celery, and over a low heat allow to cook to a good golden brown. Sprinkle over the modicum of flour and stir well in.

Add the remaining ingredients, plus ½ pint cold water (The stock cube will be salty enough, so just add pepper).

Simmer for ½ hour. Strain and bubble down to 1¼ pint approximately. Cool. strain again. Store, covered, in the refrigerator.

'CHRISTMAS SALAD' OR ENGLISH WINTER SALAD WITH RED WINDSOR DRESSING
Serves 10 – 12

Radicchio (or finely shredded red cabbage)
Peeled, cooked beetroot (not in vinegar), cut into sticks or discs
Skinned and seeded tomatoes
Carrot sticks, cooked for 2 minutes only in chicken stock
Red peppers, deseeded, cut into sticks
Radishes, cleaned and cut into discs
Strawberries
For The Dressing
4 oz (110g) Red Windsor cheese, crumbled

¼ pint (150ml) olive oil
1 tbsp red wine vinegar
1 tbsp tomato pureé
¼ pint (150ml) orange juice
1 tsp grated orange rind
2 oz (50g) tin filleted anchovies
1 clove garlic (optional)
No salt
1 level tsp milled pepper

Make a pureé of all the dressing ingredients in a blender. This dressing is not dissimilar in idea, strength and texture to a blue cheese dressing. Don't miss out on the anchovies: they're the element of surprise and don't taste fishy. It can be made beforehand and stored in the refrigerator. Toss in the salad just before serving. The strawberries are a luxury touch if imported ones are available – if not, use frozen raspberries.

PLUM PUDDINGS
Serves 8

Who would have thought that almost the same ingredients that we use in what is perhaps our oldest – and virtually our national – pudding could become the confection I give you here!
16 ripe plums: 8 split and pitted, 8 left whole for baking
Up to 4 oz (110g) almond paste or commercial marzipan
Pastry
8 oz (225g) soft white cake flour

2 oz (50g) icing sugar
3 oz (75g) unsalted butter, cubed and chilled
1 large whole egg, beaten
Sugar syrup (optional)
For The Sugar Glaze
2 tbsp castor sugar
1 tbsp water
Cream Sauce
½ pint (275ml) single cream
4 egg yolks
1 oz (25g) castor sugar
2 tbsp Kirsch or gin

Preheat the oven to gas mark 7, 425°F (220°C). Make the pastry in a food processor, or in the usual way. It is a soft mixture, tricky to handle, but worth the hassle.

Divide the almond paste into 8 pieces. Roll and shape each one between your hands to the size and shape of a plumstone. Press the two halves of the split plums round these.

Roll out the pastry separately to enwrap each plum – you'll need approximately an 8 inch (20.5 cm) circle. Envelop the plum in this. Stand each one on a lightly buttered baking tray. Bake in the preheated oven for 25 – 30 minutes, or until crisp and golden-brown. Brush with sugar glaze, prepared by boiling the sugar with the water until it reaches the 'hard ball' stage. Serve hot, warm or cold, with the cream sauce. Make this by creaming the egg yolks and sugar together until light and fluffy. Bring the cream to the boil in a non-stick pan, and pour over the egg mixture, whisking briskly. Return the pan to minimal heat, stirring all the time until the sauce has thickened. Remove from the heat and strain into a pyrex bowl and add the liqueur. If served warm, keep over a pan of hot, not boiling water. Otherwise, cool, then chill, covered with plastic film.

Bake the remaining 8 plums, without water, separately until just soft. Serve a baked plum with a pastry plum on a pool of sauce.

ACKNOWLEDGEMENTS
Special thanks to Paul Howell, Liz Edwards, Christopher Pearson and Christopher Wedgbury for their huge commitment to this book; to Sandra Fraser and Eileen Bayliss for all the typing; to Stephanie Silk and David Lancaster for their editorial skills; and to the 'Pebble Mill' presenters, contributors and production team for pulling out all the stops.

Thanks also to Denby Fine Stoneware; Jack Evans Photography, Birmingham; John Hubbard Antiques, Birmingham; John Llewelyn; Poachers Cookshop, Birmingham; Statastone, Wolverhampton; Technique Typesetting, Birmingham; Tony Wass; 'Positive Health' photos courtesy of 'Ultrahealth', published by the Ebury Press.

Printed by James Upton Limited, Birmingham.

ISBN 0 9510065 1 7